David Gur

BROTHERS

FOR RESISTANCE AND RESCUE

The Underground Zionist Youth Movement
in Hungary during World War II

Edited by Eli Netzer

Translated by Pamela Segev & Avri Fischer

Enlarged and Revised Edition

The Society for the Research of the History
of the Zionist Youth Movement in Hungary

gefen
publishing house
JERUSALEM ◆ NEW YORK

This publication has been supported by a grant from the
Conference on Jewish Material Claims Against Germany.

The spelling of geographic terms is based on the
Vocabulary of Names of Localities beyond Hungarian Borders, by Sebők László, 1997 (in Hungarian).

Hebrew edition printed in Israel, by *Ma'arechet*, Kibbutz Dalia, 2004

Layout: Tony Negal
Cover Design: David Meir

ISBN 965-229-386-5

2 4 6 8 9 7 5 3

Gefen Publishing House, Ltd
6 Hatzvi St. Jerusalem 94386, Israel
972-2-538-0247
orders@gefenpublishing.com

Gefen Books
600 Broadway, Lynbrook, NY 11563, USA
516-593-1234
orders@gefenpublishing.com

www.gefenpublishing.com

Printed in Israel

Send for our free catalogue

CONTENTS

INTRODUCTION

It is one of the ironies of history that Zionism never struck deep roots in Hungary, the birthplace of Theodor Herzl and Max Nordau. Since their emancipation in 1867, the majority of Hungarian Jewry, especially those living in the Trianon parts of the country, followed the path of assimilation. Identifying themselves as "Magyars of the Israelite faith," they firmly believed that their destiny was firmly intertwined with that of the Magyars. The attitudes and perceptions of most of the Jewish leaders were forged during the so-called "Golden Era" (1867-1918) of Hungarian Jewry. Assimilated and largely acculturated, many of these Jewish leaders had come to convince themselves that the conservative-aristocratic leadership of Hungary would never forget the political, economic, and cultural services the Jews had rendered to the Hungarian nation since the Revolution of 1848-49. Patriotic and often jingoistic, they tended to perceive the idea of Zionism to be "alien" and counterproductive to the best interests of Jewry. Herzl, the founder of modern Zionism, had been apprehensive about the position of these leaders. He confided his foreboding in a 1903 letter addressed to Ernö Mezei, a Jewish member of the Hungarian Parliament. He presciently foretold: "The hand of fate shall also seize Hungarian Jewry. And the later this occurs, and the stronger this Jewry becomes, the more cruel and hard shall be the blow, which will be delivered with greater savagery. There is no escape."

The official leaders of Hungarian Jewry failed to heed Herzl's warning at their own peril. They continued their obsequiously patriotic stance even after the collapse of the Hungarian Kingdom in 1918, when a basically anti-Semitic counterrevolutionary regime had come to power in the country. Their cowardly reaction to the anti-Semitic measures adopted by this regime, including the enactment of the *Numerus Clausus* law (1920) - the first anti-Jewish legislation in post-World War I Europe - evoked the ire of the international Jewish organizations. In their eyes Hungarian Jewry had become a dried-out branch of World Jewry.

The basically anti-Zionist patriotic stance of the official leadership of Hungarian Jewry remained unchanged even after the Hungarian government, in emulation of Nazi Germany, adopted a series of increasingly harsher anti-Jewish laws starting in 1938. And, tragically, they continued to remain steadfast in their pro-Magyar stance even after the Nazis launched their Final Solution program in German-dominated Europe. They appeared almost oblivious to the tragedy that affected the neighboring Jewish communities, falsely convincing themselves that what happened in Poland and elsewhere could not possibly happen in what they believed was a civilized and chivalrous country like Hungary.

The relatively weak Zionist movement received a boost following the territorial acquisitions by Hungary in 1938-1941. The movement was energized by refugees from Nazi-dominated Europe, especially Poland and Slovakia, and by Zionist leaders who flocked to Budapest from the newly-acquired territories, especially Northern Transylvania. On the initiative of these leaders, a Budapest-based Relief and Rescue Committee (*Vaadah*) was formed early in 1943, which helped rescue and provide assistance to Jewish refugees fleeing the Nazis from the neighboring countries. Through their contacts with their *Vaadah* counterparts in Palestine, Slovakia, and several neutral countries, especially Switzerland and Turkey, these leaders soon became acquainted with the details of the Final Solution program. In retrospect, it appears that these Zionist leaders shared the perceptions and optimism of the national leaders of Hungarian Jewry, who later constituted the Central Jewish Council, about the safety of the Jews. They, too, assumed that Hungary, a member of the Axis Alliance that resisted German pressures to implement the Final Solution in 1942, would for a variety of political and international considerations safeguard the lives, if not the property, of its Jewish citizens.

The events following the German occupation of Hungary on March 19, 1944, proved both the official and Zionist leaders' assumptions wrong. The one group that was more prescient about the dangers confronting the Jews of Hungary was that of the *Hehalutz* youth. In contrast to the official and Zionist leaders, and often in opposition to them, these young Zionist pioneers engaged in illegal activities in rescuing Jews. Before the occupation, these pioneers -- numbering only a few hundred activists -- were primarily engaged in the "legalization" of refugees by providing them with the necessary (mostly Aryan) identification papers. Acting in conjunction with the *Vaadah*, they were also involved in the rescue of Jews from ghettos and concentration camps.

But it was during the Arrow Cross (*Nyilas*) era - the period following Hungary's ill-fated attempt to extricate itself from the war on October 15, 1944 - that the Zionist resistance groups provided some of the shiniest pages in the history of rescue in Nazi-dominated Hungary. They played a pivotal role in rescuing Jews from imminent danger and in protecting and feeding thousands of children.

Among the leaders of the pioneers were both Polish and Slovak refugees as well as native Hungarian Zionists. One of the most courageous of these leaders was David Gur (Formerly Gross), the author of this volume. While involved in many "illegal" rescue-related activities, he is credited with the skilful reproduction of a large number of "official" documents - German, Hungarian, Swiss, and Swedish - that helped the survival of many thousands of Jews. He was truly one of the authentic heroes of the Holocaust era in Hungary.

David Gur, to his credit, continued his commitment to the remembrance of the Holocaust in general, and of the *Halutz* resistance in particular, even after he settled in Israel soon after the Second World War. His commitment is reflected in many of the books and articles he published under the auspices of the Society for the Research of the History of the Zionist Youth Movement in Hungary, a Ramat-Gan based non-profit organization. His newest book - *Brothers for Resistance and Rescue* - is a monument to his comrades-in-arms. It includes the biographies of 420 men and women who, by virtue of their heroic activities during the Holocaust, wrote the finest chapter in the history of Hungarian Jewry. It is an invaluable sourcebook for anybody interested in the history of the Jews in general and of the Hungarian chapter of the Holocaust in particular.

Randolph L. Braham
Distinguished Professor Emeritus

FOREWORD

Collecting the materials for this book took almost two decades and the motivation behind the work was the wish to rescue underground activists from all streams from anonymity and to reveal their actions.

Collecting these materials was a complex and difficult task. There were no testimonies at all about many of the activists and their actions and some of them had already passed away. The process entailed the search for the people, their relatives or friends, personal interviews, finding written testimonies in archives in several languages, newspaper articles etc.

Listening to forgotten stories, meeting colorful personalities and wonderful events was a moving and interesting experience. At times it happened that, through the exposure of the materials, the children or spouses of the activists discovered a chapter in their loved ones' life. On occasion I was thrilled by the initiative, wisdom, courage and solidarity that came to light in the life stories of these comrades.

In this book there are only a few lines about each one of the activists and mainly facts about their underground activities. I am convinced that, due to various limitations, we did not reach many good comrades and that their biographies were not included in this book, for which I apologize. The biographies in the book are in a summarized form. There are detailed materials which over time we shall send to eight central archives in Israel and abroad. I think it is important to mention that there might be some inaccuracies in the book and will be thankful to anyone who can enlighten me.

The 20th century saw many territorial changes, and the borders within Hungary before WW I changed every few years and certain regions switched their political definition more than once. As a result, when mentioning geographical locations, we decided to give the name of the place in the original Hungarian and then the name of the place nowadays (in Slovakian, Ukrainian, Romanian or Serbian). The transcription of the names from Cyrillic letters to Latin ones was taken from the Dictionary of Geographical Names Beyond the 1997 Borders by Sebők László (Határontúli magyar helységnévszótár, 1997).

I wish to thank the many friends who helped me meet the people and find the materials, especially Yeshayahu Rosenblum, Peretz Révész, Baruh Tzahor and Professor Menahem Tzvi Kadari.

I wish to express my special thanks to Ze'ev Eisikovics, who supported the idea of publishing this book with the biographies of the underground activists from all movements, and my gratitude for his generous help in financing the Hebrew publication.

I wish to thank all those who have generously assisted with the publication of the English edition.

I am grateful to Eli Netzer for his editing of the biographies and writing the chapters that precede them. About the book Eli Netzer said: "We think it is of great importance to write a book that is both a personal and collective memory of the actions of individuals as well as groups in those terrible times. The book is an expression of respect for the underground activists and the members of the *halutz* youth movements who, thanks to the values they imparted to their comrades, consecrated the epos of rebellion and rescue that during WW II had no prior example or model in range and success. The book is first of all a commemoration of those who gave their lives to the rescue of the lives of others."

David Gur

ZIONISM IN RED-WHITE-GREEN

'Zion': the biblical name of Jerusalem. It originates in the name of the stronghold that King David captured from the Jebusites (II Samuel, V, 7). After the destruction of the temple the mourners were called 'mourners of Zion'.

The emissaries to the Diaspora were called 'Zion emissaries'.

The Middle-Age poets, with Yehuda Halevy at their head, called the Jewish people by the name of 'Zion'.

In modern times the Zionist movement adopted the name of 'Zion'.

The activists of the first *Aliya* called themselves 'lovers of Zion'.

The concept of 'Zionism' was coined for the first time by Natan Birnbaum in 1890.

The Zionist movement that was founded by Benjamin Ze'ev Herzl, who was born in Budapest, was established by the name of the 'World Zionist Organization'.

* * *

In Hungary Zionism faced many difficulties mainly because of the assimilation of Hungarian Jewry. Hungarian Jews saw themselves as Hungarians or wanted to consider themselves as such and were encouraged by the liberal ideas in Hungarian society at the end of the 19th century.

The Jews proved their loyalty to the Hungarian government many times. In the Hungarian War of Independence from the Habsburgs (1848) and during WW I (1914-1918), many Jews fought in the Hungarian army and thousands fell in battle. Hungarian Jews excelled in the fields of economics, art and culture and had a unique influence on life in Hungary in the last two hundred years.

This was changed in 1919 when there were violent events that were called the 'white terror' or the oppression of communists and their supporters among whom there were many Jews. The 'white terror' caused a series of pogroms against Jews and resulted in the legislation of the "Numerus Clausus" laws that limited the number of Jews in institutes of higher education. Hungary was the first country in 20th century Europe whose parliament passed anti-Jewish laws already in 1920.

Nonetheless it has to be mentioned that Jews, especially in the larger towns and in the capital city, Budapest, lived a prosperous life in relative safety.

Benjamin Ze'ev Herzl, who knew the Jewish reality in Hungary very well wrote in 1903 to Ernő Mezei, the representative of the Budapest Jews in the Hungarian parliament, the following words: 'Zionism in Hungary can only be in red-white and green...' (the colors of the Hungarian flag).

The first branch of the Zionist movement in Hungary was established in 1897 in Nagyszeben.

nowadays Sibiu. Romania. by János Rónai. who took part in the first Zionist Congress in Basel in 1897. The first Zionist organization in Hungary was called 'Zion Organization' (Czion Egylet) and according to its basic regulations it was intended for 'Jews without a homeland' who wanted to emigrate to Palestine.

Herzl himself visited Hungary a few times in order to convince Jewish personalities to join the Zionist movement but without much success.

The first Zionist Congress of Hungarian Jews was held in Pozsony. nowadays Bratislava. in Slovakia. János Rónai was elected president. In 1904 the first world convention of "Mizrahi" was also held in Pozsony (Bratislava).

In 1903 the 'Maccabea' association. which included young Jews who were sportsmen and studied at institutions of higher education was established in Budapest. Following the example of the 'Maccabea'. another association similar to the first one. by the name of 'Bar Kohba'. was established.

In 1909 Hungarian Zionists composed a declaration. which was presented to the government and the members of parliament. where they defined the goals of Zionism in their country. In that declaration it was emphasized that the goal of the Zionists in Hungary was mainly social. economic and ethical and definitely not national. One can also see this declaration as a tactical move to avoid causing damage to the status of the Zionists in the eyes of the assimilated Jews and the Hungarian government.

The First World War (1914-1918) and the defeat of Hungary caused many changes for the Jews as Jewish communities were separated from Hungary when regions were transferred to Czechoslovakia. Romania and Yugoslavia. These events also had a great influence on the Zionist movement. The center of activities moved to the big cities: Budapest. Miskolc. Debrecen. Nyiregyháza. Szeged. Székesfehérvár and others.

In 1927. after many experiments. the Hungarian Zionist Association (Magyar Cionista Szövetség) was established and recognized by the authorities.

The relations between the new organization and the Jewish community were quite strained. The leaders of the community resented that the Zionist center was beyond the Hungarian borders and that the funds for financing the activities as well as the instructions for operations came from there.

Hungarian Zionists tried very hard to win the sympathy and support of the Jews all over Hungary and especially in Budapest. but without success.

The Hungarian Zionists also did not derive any satisfaction from the World Zionist Movement that did not accept their offer to hold the Zionist Congress in Budapest in 1933. In their opinion the Hungarian Zionist Movement probably was not considered to be a 'worthwhile investment'.

In the meantime there was a slow process of Jewish *Aliya* to Palestine: the number of olim was between 200 and 300 per year and most of them left Hungary legally.

The number of members of the Zionist movement in Hungary never rose above 4,000-5,000 members.

The late 1920's and early 1930's were characterized by the establishment of Zionist movements and organizations in Hungary. In 1927 the "Hashomer Hatzair" movement was founded by Dr. Havas, an emissary who arrived from Transylvania to Budapest. In 1930 the first six Zionists made aliya.

In 1931, in the elections for the Zionist Congress, there were four lists:
"Aviv-Barissia" ("Hatzionim Haclali'im")
"Eretz-Israel Haovedet"
The Revisionists
"Mizrahi"

From that period of time onwards Zionist movements and organizations were founded, with thousands of members. It is worth mentioning that the Zionist movement in Hungary never had widespread support but despite that, it won the hearts of the youngsters who realized the Zionist goal, aliya.

THE UNDERGROUND ZIONIST YOUTH MOVEMENT
IN HUNGARY DURING WW II

Hungary was the first European country that, already in 1920, passed an anti-Jewish law, known as "Numerus clausus" (restricted number), in Parliament. This law limited the number of Jews who could be admitted to institutes of higher education in Hungary. The Regent, Miklós Horthy, was a moderate anti-Semite but the Hungarian Jews, about 450,000 people (about 6% of the population) felt safe under his rule in spite of the discriminating laws against them that were passed from 1938. Until 1941, when South Slovakia, Carpatho-Ruthenia, North Transylvania and a region from Yugoslavia were annexed to Hungary, there were about 900,000 Jews in Hungary.

The Second World War broke out in 1939 and from June 1941 Hungary fought with the Germans against the Soviet Union on the east front. At the end of the same year Hungary declared war to the Allied Forces: Great Britain, France and other countries.
In Europe, occupied by the Germans, the extermination of Jews had started, but until 1944 the Jews of Hungary were spared. Although some local events occurred in various areas of the country during which Jews were murdered and thousands of Jewish men were enlisted in forced labor units, there were no deportations to extermination camps.

The activities of the Zionist youth movements were forbidden in the early 1940's. In 1941 the first refugees started arriving from Poland and in 1942 from Slovakia. Most of them were young people, members of the Zionist youth movements in their country who found refuge with comrades of their movement in Budapest. The refugees needed accommodation, documents, food, clothes and either jobs or hiding places. These needs were fulfilled by the members of the Hungarian movements.

The dramatic change in the fate of Hungarian Jews took place in 1944. The defeat of the Germans and its allies was certain and the Red Army had already arrived at the Hungarian border. The Hungarian Regent, Horthy, intended to split from the alliance with Germany. The Germans, whose agents could be found in all the Hungarian governmental institutions, knew in time about this intention and in order to avoid it they invaded Hungary on 19.3.1944. Following the German army, Adolf Eichman and his staff also arrived in order to organize the extermination of the Jews. One after the other rules were published according to which the possessions and freedom of the Jews were taken away. The deportations to the extermination camps from country towns and villages took place between 15.5.1944 and 28.6.1944.

The Zionist youth movements got organized and soon started their rescue activities. In Hungary the conditions were not right for armed resistance: there were no important Hungarian anti-Nazi resistance groups whom to cooperate with; Jewish men were enlisted in forced labor units; the population was not supportive; there were no forests and mountains that could be hiding places and, most significantly, the end of the war seemed imminent. The members of the Zionist youth groups set themselves a goal: **to save as many Jews as possible**.

Missions to the country towns

Over one hundred emissaries, members of the youth movements, were sent to two hundred Jewish destinations and mainly to the ghettos outside Budapest where the Jews were to be deported from. The emissaries warned the local Jews of what lay in store for them and equipped them with forged documents and money to enable them to escape. There was a weak response to the warnings because the Jews believed that they were being taken to labor camps or being "resettled" and would be able to return to their houses later on. Continuing their activities the emissaries rescued many youngsters from the forced labor units before they were sent westwards to the German Reich.

The production of forged documents

An intensive operation started which was to obtain Aryan documents from the offices of the Population Registry and to produce tens of thousands of forged documents in improvised laboratories that were set up by the members of some of the youth movements. The documents were given for free members of the Zionist Youth Movement and to all who needed them. These documents included, among others, birth certificates, marriage certificates, identity cards, Police Residential cards and later Protection Documents from the neutral countries' embassies. Many Jews managed to survive thanks to these documents, especially in the capital, Budapest. The main workshop for forged documentation as far as the scope, variety and the intended recipients (youth, old people, non-Jewish resistance groups) was unique in all of German occupied Europe. According to a careful estimate, at the time of the liberation of Budapest by the Red Army, every other Jew was in possession of some kind of document produced in the workshop of the Zionist youth movements.

The "tiyul"

The "tiyul" was a nickname for an extensive operation that organized the smuggling of Jews across the Hungarian border mainly into Romania and from there, via the Black Sea ports, to Eretz Israel (Palestine). The Romanian Government was quite flexible and it was therefore possible to carry out this operation. Attempts on a smaller scale to smuggle Jews to the partisans in Yugoslavia were also made. The "tiyul" started after the German invasion of Hungary on 19.3.1944, was expanded and became more efficient during the summer months. The candidates for smuggling across the border were equipped with forged documents, money and relevant instructions. They arrived by train in the border towns where they met local smugglers who crossed the border with them. It is estimated that about 15,000 Jews crossed the border and that most of them reached Eretz Israel (Palestine) already in 1944. This operation was in fact discontinued at the end of August with the change of regime in Romania. In the same way about 400 members of the youth movements were smuggled into Slovakia where, in August 1944, they joined the Slovak uprising. Most of them fell in battle.

The bunkers

Most bunkers were set up in Budapest and the environments after the end of the "tiyul" operation. The bunkers were established in apartments, caves and cellars that were made fit for this purpose by the movements' members. The idea of establishing bunkers was born as a result of the experience of the Zionist movements in Poland which was transferred to Hungary by their members who arrived as refugees. They were meant to be used as hiding places and storage places for equipment, food and even weapons. However, very soon it became clear that most of the bunkers were traps for their occupants and, therefore, these preparations were stopped. One of the bunkers on Hungary Boulevard in Budapest was discovered and attacked by the fascists. The guard who stood outside was shot dead and the other members were caught.

The children's houses under the protection of the International Red Cross

Fifty children's houses were established in Budapest, most of them after 15.10.1944 when the fascist Arrow Cross Party rose to power. In those houses abandoned Jewish children, children without a father or mother and orphaned of both parents, who had been either murdered or deported to the camps, found a refuge. Friedrich Born, the representative of the International Red Cross in Hungary, put the offices of his organization in the center of Budapest at the disposal of "Department A" headed by Ottó Komoly, the president of the Hungarian Zionist Association. Komoly was the founder of the department. The Zionist youth movements located apartments and houses where the children they collected could live. The people in charge of the children's houses were members of the movements aged around twenty whereas the caregivers were seventeen-eighteen years old. There were some incidents with the fascists and even casualties but most of the children's houses managed to function until the liberation of the city in the middle of January 1945. Almost 6,000 children and also adults who joined them were saved in the children's houses. The children continued to be taken care of even after the war and many of them made aliya.

The smuggling and liberation from forced labor units and prisons

Many of the underground activists from the Zionist youth movements were caught by the Germans and the Hungarian fascists and efforts were continuously made to liberate them. Daring operations were undertaken with success. In some of these operations the underground members wore the fascist uniform and even used weapons. A group of 120 members of the Zionist underground, who were going to be executed, were liberated at the end of December 1944 from the central Hungarian military prison on Margit Boulevard. Members of the movements and other people were rescued from the forced labor units, reached Budapest and joined the underground activities.

The "Epic of the Beans" - the supply of food to the ghetto and the children's houses
Towards the end of 1944 seventy thousand Jews from Budapest were concentrated in the central ghetto and another few thousands in the "International" ghetto. Over three thousand people crowded together in the "Glass House" and six thousand children and their educators were accommodated in the children's houses under the protection of the International Red Cross. Budapest was under siege and gradually disconnected from the sources of supplies from the surrounding areas. The population suffered from a severe lack of food, medicines and heating materials. The predicament of the Jews was even worse due to the restrictions in movement and the wild behavior of the mob patrols of the Arrow Cross which endangered every pedestrian and all the means of transport in the capital. Within the framework of "Department A" of the International Red Cross, the Zionist Relief and Rescue Committee worked hand in hand with the Zionist underground. They cooperated with the well known people in the fields of purchase and transport in order to buy and store very large amounts of food products from any possible source. The Zionist underground undertook the mission of supply, transport and delivery of food under the protection of its members who operated in borrowed uniforms and equipped with forged documents. The first priorities were to deliver the food to the children's houses, the "Glass House" and to supplement the meager rations of the ghetto residents. These operations were financed by the aid money received by the Relief and Rescue Committee from foreign sources as well as from well-to-do Jews who were promised that their money would be reimbursed after the war. In this way famine was avoided and the predicament of the Jews of Budapest was alleviated.

Aid to the local resistance groups
Hungary was the only country in occupied Europe where the relatively small Zionist underground gave significant assistance to local non-Jewish resistance groups and to other units and organizations that rescued Jews by providing forged documents, money and other means.

The activities in the "Glass House"
The Zionist youth movements were in charge of the internal organization of life in the "Glass House" on 29, Vadász Street which was under the auspices of the Swiss consulate. About three thousand Jews found refuge and were fed there. A branch of the "Glass House" was established on 17, Wekerle Street where some of the operations were undertaken.

In fact, the Holocaust of the Hungarian Jews took place during ten months, from March 1944 to January 1945, date of the liberation of Budapest by the Red Army.
According to the official data of the Hungarian government, during the Holocaust, 575,000 Jews were murdered, accounting for 60% of the whole Jewish population in the country at the outbreak of the war.

LIST OF ZIONIST YOUTH MOVEMENTS
AND OTHER ORGANIZATIONS THAT TOOK PART IN THE
UNDERGROUND WORK AND ACTIVITIES IN HUNGARY

"Ihud Mapai"

"Mapai", the workers' party in Eretz Israel, was founded in Palestine in 1930 as the merger of two parties: "Hapoel Hatzair" and "Ahdut Avoda". The word 'ihud' was added to the name of the party operating abroad. This was a party with a Zionist-socialist ideology. The central figure of the party in Hungary at the beginning, in 1933, was Dr. Dénes Béla, a doctor, one of the prominent activists of the Jewish community in Budapest and a member of the Hungarian Zionist Association's leadership. Other prominent activists were Hillel Danzig, a journalist who visited Eretz Israel in 1939, Kiss Katalin, Weiler Ferenc and Dr. Beneschofsky Ilona. The party was active in Hungary until 1949.

"Beitar" (Yosef Trumpeldor's Alliance)

"Beitar" was an activist-Zionist youth movement with a right-wing ideology. It was founded in 1923, in Riga, Latvia, as a youth movement of the Revisionist Zionist Organization, which in 1935 became the New Zionist Organization. The movement spread in Poland and in other European countries and its leader was Ze'ev Jabotinsky. The movement was based on three principles: the establishment of a Jewish State, active self-defense and halutziut, i.e. to be the leaders of the way. The essence of Zionism was perceived in raising 'one flag', i.e. the national flag, and "Beitar" rejected socialist Zionism, which advocated both national and social flags. The movement was in favor of a commanding hierarchy within its ranks. "Beitar" founded settlements in Eretz-Israel (Palestine), was active in illegal aliya and in the opposition to the British Mandate in Eretz-Israel (Palestine).

In Hungary "Beitar" was founded in the 30's and, until it was expelled in 1935, it was a sports association within the framework of the Zionist Organization. Afterwards it operated as an independent youth movement and set up branches in Budapest and other towns in Hungary. The education units of "Beitar" were called "Tzror" where there was one youth leader and ten to twelve members. Youngsters could only join the movement after passing 'new recruit tests'. Adult members of the movement also did military training.

During the Second World War the movement dealt with self-defense and rescue. It set up five bunkers in Budapest, one of which, in the city suburbs, was discovered by the fascists and its members killed in a shooting battle. After the liberation (1945) "Beitar" developed many activities among the youngsters and encouraged them to make aliya. The movement was in constant confrontation with the Zionist institutions operating in Hungary. Sometimes they cooperated but generally "Beitar" operated in a separate framework. In 1948, after a "Beitar" emissary was arrested by the communist government, the movement stopped operating overtly and went underground.

"Bnei Akiva"

"Bnei Akiva" was the youth movement of "Hapoel Hamizrahi". It was founded in 1929 in Jerusalem. The movement's ideology was religion and Zionism. "Bnei Akiva" set up branches in Eretz Israel (Palestine) and in the whole world. In Eretz Israel it founded kibbutzim and moshavim. In Hungary the movement started with the establishment of the "Hashomer Hadati" movement in 1930. In the congress held in 1932 it was decided to change the name of the organization to "Bnei Akiva". The prosperous years of the movement's activities were 1939 and 1940, when kinim were set up all over Hungary and many members went to agricultural and urban hahsharot.

In 1942 the movement transferred tens of its members, mainly speakers of Hungarian, from Slovakia to Hungary. After the Germans invaded Hungary on 19.3.1944, the movement started to deal with rescue operations. Its members produced and distributed forged documents and set up bunkers. Most of the bunkers were apartments used as hiding places for the members. Some of the movement's members were armed but the weapons were meant for self-defense and not for active operations. "Bnei Akiva", in cooperation with other movements, operated in the "Glass House" and its members lived in the attic which was called the 'Bnei Akiva attic'. From the summer of 1944 the movement worked within the framework of the tiyul, distributed money to the needy and delivered food to the hungry Jews in the capital city. Many "Bnei Akiva" members were caught, tortured and incarcerated in prisons and some were murdered by the fascists.

"Dror Habonim"

"Dror Habonim" was a Zionist-socialist movement that was founded before the First World War in Russia and that engaged mainly in self-defense. After the Bolshevik revolution its center was transferred to Poland and in 1925 it joined the "Left Poalei Tzion". It set up branches in a lot of countries and founded many settlements in Eretz Israel (Palestine). The Hungarian "Dror Habonim" movement was founded in 1939 as a result of the merger of "Dror" and "Hehalutz Hatzair" but already in the 30's it operated under various names. At the beginning of 1944 there was an additional merger between "Dror", "Hehalutz Hatzair" and "Habonim". After 1946, as a result of a split, "Dror Habonim" joined "Ahdut Avoda" whereas the second faction, "Netzah Habonim" joined "Mapai".

"Hanoar Hatzioni"

"Hanoar Hatzioni" was a Zionist youth movement and a branch of the "Hatzionim Haclali'im" Organization. The movement was founded in 1930 in Poland. It founded kibbutzim and agricultural settlements in Eretz Israel (Palestine) as well as the "Haoved Hatzioni", which had branches both in Eretz Israel and in the Diaspora.

In Hungary this youth movement had a deep influence on the Jewish youths as part of the Zionist-democratic block and it had branches and hahsharot inside and outside Budapest. The "Haoved

Hatzioni" movement, which at the beginning had members up to the age of forty, operated in Hungary already before but mainly after the Second World War. In 1944 the leaders of the movement were Dr. Sigfried Roth, Mordehai Weisz and Dr. Adonyahu Bilitzer.

"Hatzionim Haclali'im"

The "Clal-Tzioni" movement started to develop in 1907 and supported the 'Basel Plan' of the Zionist Organization. In 1935 the first party congress was held in Cracov, Poland.

In Hungary the party operated before WW II, during and after the war. After the war the movement went by the name of 'The Block of the Tzionim Haclali'im Hademokratim' that comprised several organizations among which the "Hanoar Hatzioni" movement. Prominent activists of the party were Dr. Nagy László, Béla Schwarz and Dr. Nátán Sándor-Alexander who were among the central activists of the Zionist underground in Hungary. The party operated in Hungary until 1949.

"Mizrahi"

Religious Zionism, that was called "Mizrahi" and considered itself a spiritual center, held a convention, in preparation for its first congress, in 1902 in Vilna. In 1904 the first world convention of "Mizrahi" was held in Pozsony (Bratislava). The center was transferred to Germany and its leaders were Rabbi Berlin, Rabbi Fischman and Moshe Schapira. In 1922 "Hapoel Hamizrahi", whose youth movement was "Bnei Akiva", was founded in Jerusalem. Religious Zionism, with "Mizrahi" at its head, took a central place among the Zionist movements in Hungary and at different times it made up about a third of its members. Already in 1902 orthodox Jewry declared that Zionist-religious activities were forbidden. This prohibition was renewed in 1927 but still the Zionist idea was well received among the religious circles. Prominent activists of the "Mizrahi" movement in Hungary and its delegates in the community and Zionist institutions were Salamon Mihály, Fraenkel Jenő and Dr. Ungár Béla. The "Mizrahi" movement operated in Hungary until 1949.

"Hashomer Hatzair"

The "Hashomer Hatzair" movement was founded in 1913 in Galicia and Vienna. It operated amidst the Jewish youth as a scout's movement but with an ideology that was based on three principles: social equality, national independence and cultural revival. The movement spread all over Europe and set up branches in all continents. The young members of the movement were educated towards fulfillment in Eretz Israel (Palestine) and communal living in a kibbutz. The movement had a Marxist ideology and identified with the struggle of the workers world movement. "Hashomer Hatzair" dedicated itself especially to educational activities and created new educational methods. Its main educational guidelines were: Judaism is not only a religion but also a people; the young Jew has social responsibility; the movement's way of life is best expressed in life on a kibbutz. The movement's club was called a ken. The members of the movement were divided into age groups with a youth leader and a work plan including Jewish history, literature, knowledge of Eretz Israel (Palestine), the history of Zionism and chapters of the working class history. The Hungarian "Hashomer Hatzair" movement was founded in 1927 by Dr. Havas who arrived in Budapest from Transylvania. The first group consisted of eight members. In 1930 the first six members made aliya within the framework of Kibbutz I (Ma'abarot). In 1932 the movement already had 1,000 members and 15 hahsharot. In 1931 a group for Kibbutz II (Ramat Hashofet) got organized. During its existence in Hungary the movement had thousands of members and tens of kenim and hahsharot all over the country and hundreds of its members made aliya, founded new kibbutzim or joined existing ones. During WW II "Hashomer Hatzair" dealt with a variety of rescue and self-defense operations. When the communist regime in Hungary fell apart in 1989 the movement was reestablished and is still active.

"Gordonia Maccabi Hatzair"

"Gordonia Maccabi Hatzair" was a youth movement with ideological affiliations to "Mapai". In Hungary it operated at first mainly among the alumni of the Jewish high school who were studying at institutions of higher learning. In 1938 it became a national movement. A year later the national leadership was elected and a first group of Zionists even made aliya within the framework of Aliya Bet. Members who were refugees from Slovakia integrated the movement's leadership. "Gordonia Maccabi Hatzair" took an active part in the rescue and resistance operations. After WW II the movement dealt with the rehabilitation of the remaining refugees and the preparation of youngsters for aliya and their journey to Eretz Israel (Palestine). In order to carry out these missions, widespread educational work developed in peer groups, children's houses and hahsharot. The Zionist olim founded the movement's kibbutz, Tze'elim, but within a short period of time, as a result of a movement's decision, the members were sent to revitalize Kfar Hahoresh while many others joined other existing kibbutzim, especially Metzuba.

Paratroopers

Already in 1942 the Hagana planned to infiltrate fighters from Eretz Israel (Palestine) into the German occupied countries mainly to organize resistance and encourage aliya. The institutions of the kibbutz movement even presented candidates for the mission. However, only in 1944 were the paratroopers from the Yishuv sent to Europe after training within the framework of the British army. Some of the paratroopers were to parachute in Romania and Yugoslavia in order to cross the border into Hungary. The leaders of the Yishuv considered the rescue of Jews as of ultimate importance while the British planned to help the prisoners of war and conduct espionage operations using the paratroopers who spoke the languages of the countries of destination.

"The Shimoni Group"

The group was called after Dov Shimoni and dealt with the running of the hospital on 14, Rákóczi Street outside the ghetto (from 16.11.1944). Many Jews, forced labor workers of the Shimoni Group and foreign draftees, found refuge in the hospital as patients, members of the medical staff and first aid team.

Communists

The Hungarian communists and members of the workers unions had contacts with the Zionist underground, especially with members of "Hashomer Hatzair". They had connections with the Demény Group, with groups of the Communist Party loyal to Moscow and with liberal groups (Fábry). Joseph Meir, a member of "Hashomer Hatzair", had connections with the workers' groups from the beginning of the war and after the rise to power of Szálasi, he set up an operation group by the name of Megyeri, which was his underground nickname. The Zionist underground supplied forged documents to the opponents of the Hungarian regime while these helped the underground people by giving them shelter and accommodation in the workers' neighbourhoods of the Hungarian capital. They also cooperated in the supply of weapons and in the planning of armed operations.

"The Gordon Circle"

The "Gordon Circle" was a group of adults with ideological affiliation to "Hashomer Hatzair". It already operated before WW II and also during the Holocaust. The circle existed only in Hungary. It dealt with social and Zionist activities. The circle was called after Aharon David Gordon, born in Russia in 1856, a philosopher of the Zionist working movement who lived in Deganiya as an agricultural worker. The members of the circle represented "Hashomer Hatzair" in the Zionist institutions. Prominent figures in the "Gordon Circle" were Lajos Fodor, Cvi Ernő Szilágyi, Jenő Kolb, Moshe Rosenberg and Zoltán Weiner.

"The Borochov Circle"

The "Borochov Circle" was a group of young people up to the age of 30-35 with an ideological affiliation to "Hashomer Hatzair". This circle existed in Hungary only. It was officially founded after WW II and replaced the "Gordon Circle". The circle was named after the Zionist-Marxist philosopher Dov Ber Borochov, born in Ukraine, one of the founders of the "Poalei Zion" movement who lived from 1881 to 1919. The circle held lectures, seminars, debates as well as cultural and social activities. Its members represented "Hashomer Hatzair" at the Zionist institutions. Prominent figures of the circle were Dr. István Kulcsár and Dr. Frigyes Nógrádi.

THREE JOINT OPERATIONS

Rescue from prison

At the end of December 1944 the encirclement of Budapest was completed and all the roads leading out of the city were in the hands of the Red Army that had also captured the Buda hills. Eichmann left Budapest, the danger of deportation to the death camps passed but the Jews in the city were trapped and had no way of escaping. Those who were in the ghetto and those living in Protected Houses were subject to the wild behavior of the fascists who broke into houses, shot, killed and led lines of Jews to the banks of the frozen Danube in order to shoot them and drown them. The city was bombarded day and night by the Russians with planes, canons and mortars. Windows were broken, there was no heating or food and the water and electricity systems had collapsed.

In November three bodies of the Zionist underground were still operating on 52, Baross Street in the offices of the International Red Cross. Rafi Friedl-Benshalom, member of "Hashomer Hatzair", managed the foreign and political relations. Neshka and Tzvi Goldfarb, members of "Dror", dealt with the bunkers and hiding places of their movement and Yoshko Mayer-Meir, a member of "Hashomer Hatzair", maintained contact with the Hungarian anti-fascist circles, the activists of the workers unions and the communists. The office on Baross Street was under observation by the Hungarian security forces. On December 6, Neshka and Tzvi Goldfarb and Vili Eisikovicz were caught in an underground meeting and, on December 8, Asher Arni, who was also a member of "Dror Habonim" and the contact person for the bunkers, was caught too. The bunker on Hungary Boulevard fell in a short shooting fight. Ernő Székely "Marci" was shot and killed and another two comrades were wounded. 65 "Dror" members were incarcerated in the central military prison on Margit Street, tortured and interrogated, especially Neshka Tzvi and Vili who were transferred to the Sopronkőhida prison near the Austrian border.

A few weeks later, on December 21st, the underground forgery laboratory on Erzsébet Boulevard was discovered and three members of "Hashomer Hatzair", Miki Langer, Avri Feigenbaum-Andrei Fábry and Dávid Gur-Grosz, who were on the site, were caught and taken to the nearby district headquarters of the Arrow Cross Party. The interrogators used cruel torture and as a result Miki killed himself. David and Avri were transferred to the central military prison on Margit Boulevard where many members of the Zionist youth movements were already being detained.
Members of "Dror Habonim" and "Hashomer Hatzair", in cooperation with other movements' activists, decided to do their best to free their comrades. From an Arrow Cross man, by the name

of Tony, who had a Jewish girlfriend and was willing to help the underground members, they heard about the "big catch", detainees in the prison on Margit Boulevard. It was obvious to all that there was a real risk that all detainees would be executed.

Yitzhak Herbst and Moshe Alpan (Pil), members of "Hashomer Hatzair", found an officer in the Hungarian army who, for a reward of 300 Napoleon gold coins, was willing to release the prisoners. A feverish operation for obtaining the requested amount was set into movement. It was a huge amount at any time but even more so under conditions of blockade and endless dangers, but within a few days it was collected.

On December 23rd, on Christmas Eve, the fascist gendarmes who guarded the prisoners, left the prison in an attempt to escape through the Russian lines, and only the prison guards remained in the place. However, the gendarmes returned a few hours later because the encirclement had already closed the whole city and there was no way of leaving or entering it. With the return of the fascists the life of the prisoners was at an even greater risk.

In the afternoon of December 25th, the prisoners were taken out into the prison courtyard and lined up. An army officer, accompanied by two armed sergeants, faced them and started calling prisoners' names. According to the expression on the faces of the wardens and the soldiers, there was no doubt about the fate of the prisoners whose names were called. The list also included the names of comrades who were not incarcerated in the prison. It was significant that the list was made based on assumptions only. None of the prisoners moved from his position until the officer called the name of Rapos Farkas Tibor. Rapos was the name under which David Grosz was registered when he shared apartment with his friend Moshe Pil-Alpan. Anywhere else he used the name of Tibor Farkas. Pil was the only one to know this name. David immediately realized that Pil was involved in the compilation of the list and he stepped forward. His comrades were surprised but followed his example. The Hungarian officer and his soldiers led the group out of the prison gate, through the empty streets almost up to the Lánc Bridge (the chain) over the Danube and from there to 17, Wekerle Street, a branch of the Swiss legation where underground activists operated. At the building entrance Rafi Friedl, Moshe Pil, Peretz Révész, Joel Palgi and other comrades were waiting for them.

The following day the Hungarian officer repeated the operation and released an additional 97 prisoners, among whom members of the Hungarian Zionist and communist movements. The group was taken to one of the Protected Houses on 32, Pozsonyi Street.

"I know you, you are a Jew!"

On 16.10.1944, the day after coup of Ferenc Szálasi, a retired army officer and the leader of the Arrow Cross party (Nyilaskeresztes párt), the rampaging of the hoodlums started. Most of them were 15-16 years old. In Népszinház Street and near the Teleki Square there were German 'Tiger' tanks that fired at one of the houses. In that same building lived deserters from the forced labor units and Jewish refugees from Poland who were excited about the news that the Hungarian ruler, Horthy, had announced that his country was quitting the German axis. The refugees thought that indeed the war was over and they fired at a group of Arrow Cross men who passed their house. The refugees, who had no command of Hungarian, did not know that, in the meantime, there had been a fascist upheaval who answered to Horthy's commands. In response to the firing, units of the German and Hungarian armies with tanks took position in front of the house and fired. The poor refugees were killed by the mortars and the soldiers' shooting. Tens of shot and pulverized bodies were scattered in the street.

Many Jews were gathered Street in Yellow Star Houses in Népszínház. The fascists took advantage of the liquidation of the Polish refugees to harass the rest of the Jews.

Efra Teichman-Agmon and Joseph Meir, underground activists and members of "Hashomer Hatzair", decided to go to one of the houses in the street in order to rescue Yehuda Alpár, a comrade from the movement. Efra wore the uniform of a railway officer whereas Yoshko wore a mixed uniform of a soldier and an Arrow Cross man. Both of them wore an armband with the Hungarian fascist emblem.

They entered their friend's house pointing their guns. The other tenants were already gathered in the courtyard and were waiting to be taken out to the street and maybe to be executed. Efra and Yoshko were joined by two Arrow Cross men equipped with submachine guns who wanted to take part in the extermination of the Jews.

"Let us do the job" Yoshko told them resolutely, "Go somewhere else!". When they heard the decisive tone and, maybe due to the fact that Efra and Yoshko were older, the two fascists left.

"Where is the Jew Alpár?" shouted Efra at the concierge.
"He left yesterday already", was the answer.
"You are lying!" said Yoshko while pointing his gun at the concierge's chest.
"I will take you to Alpár's mother and she can confirm my words", the concierge answered.
Yehuda's mother was brought to them, fell to their feet and started to beg for her life. Still, she confirmed that her son was not at home but she did not recognize the two friends and was terrified.
"Where is he now?"
"I don't know" said the mother in tears "but believe me that he did not commit any crime".
Yoshko and Efra could not reassure her because they were afraid that their real identity would be discovered. They were devastated by the fact that they had to scare their friend's mother and the other Jews.
"Stay here and don't move! Go down to the cellar and don't get out!" Efra ordered the Jews in the courtyard "and in time we will take care of your son!" he said to Yehuda's mother.
"Stinking Jews!" Yoshko shouted.

The two were about to leave the house when a group of Arrow Cross men came towards them.
"There is no need for you to come in" Efra told them, "We have already finished the job".
The two friends started walking down the street. They intended to enter another house in order to prevent the fascists from carrying out their scheme. Suddenly two thugs wearing hats with the Arrow Cross emblem approached them.
One of them pointed at Efra: "By chance aren't you from Kisvárda and isn't your name Teichman?"
Efra looked at him in shock. It was the son of his hometown neighbors.
"Have you gone mad?" Efra said.
However, the hoodlum did not let go. He appealed to the people in the street and shouted:
"Look, this is a Jew! This one wearing a uniform is a Jew! I know him, he used to live in our street!".
People started to gather around them and Efra was unable to retreat.
"How come you are wandering the streets", shouted Yoshko at the thugs. "Come with us to the headquarters and we will give you work there!"
"That is a Jew! Look, that is a Jew!" the thug continued to scream hysterically.
"Take them to the police where they will find out who they really are".
"Maybe they are really both Jews?"
"Let's undress them!"
These remarks and others were heard among the crowd. The situation was getting desperate. The circle of people closed in on Efra and Yoshko. They felt their end was near whether by the incensed crowd or the fascist hoodlums.

Suddenly, two men wearing the Arrow Cross uniform appeared, drew their guns and pressed them into the backs of the two comrades. "Make way!" they ordered the crowd. "Step aside and make way!" The crowd cleared a narrow path. "We will take them to the headquarters and there we will find out who they are. If they are Jews, they will pay a high price!" they said while pushing the two captured men and added: "And you, Forward!"
A tramway passed in the street with on board Tzvi Goldfarb and his friend Neshka, two members of "Dror", who were also members of the Zionist underground. They saw Efra and Yoshko, whom they knew, being led by two uniformed men whom they also knew.
"Let's get off and see what happens there, maybe they will need some help", Neshka told Tzvi.
Yoshko and Efra marched with their escort behind them.
The four men proceeded quickly, walking or running, and the crowd was left behind but the two thugs followed them...
"Get away! Let us do our job!" shouted one of the escorts to the thugs who went their own way.
Neshka and Tzvi, seeing that the danger had passed, left the site.
The four men went into a side street and there fell in each other's arms. The two Arrow Cross men were in fact Betzalel Adler and Patyu Weingarten (Mordehai Carmi) members of the "Dror Habonim" movement and underground activists.

Two together - The "Glass House" - Rescue attempts

The "Glass House" was located on 29, Vadász Street (hunter in Hungarian), a quiet street in the exclusive 5th district of Budapest. Near the house there were government offices, foreign countries' embassies. On one side was the Parliament and the Danube River and on the other side the Basilica Church and the city center.

This was a two storey building, among 4 and 6 storey ones, owned by Arthur Weisz, a Jew and one of the Jewish community's respected members, a well-to-do glass merchant. The house looked different from the other houses mainly because of its wide glass walls. Weisz' office as well as his private apartment were on the top floor, while the goods storage rooms were on the ground floor and in the basement.

There was also a wide inner yard in the back of which there was a building used by the workers as well as workshops for repairs.

Arthur Weisz agreed to let the Swiss consulate use the premises and, already in 1944, the department of emigration of the Swiss consulate and the foreign interests was set up there. The use of the house for the needs of the Jews was made possible thanks to Karl Lutz who was the Swiss consul in Budapest. Lutz agreed to the issue of 7.800 Swiss Protection Documents but the forgery laboratories of the youth movements issued many more documents and distributed them to anyone who asked for them. Lutz probably knew of this operation but turned a blind eye. The Hungarian government authorized the use of all the unused certificates for the emigration of Jews from all over Europe. At the beginning only "clerks" stayed in the house on Vadász Street. After 15.10.1944 Alexander Grossmann opened the doors to everyone. The Swiss emblem was displayed on the gate to the house and, as a branch of a foreign consulate, it was considered as an exterritorial space (outside the borders of uncertified persons).

Soon the house turned into a refuge for Jews running away from the forced labor units some of whom intended to make aliya. The German and Hungarian authorities, who were interested in calming down the atmosphere after the deportations from the country towns, gave their consent to the existence of the house under the protection of Switzerland for the "emigration of Jews to Palestine".

Before the Hungarian authorities gave the authorization, Lieutenant Colonel Ferenczy of the gendarmerie, who had a bad reputation and was known for his cruel deportation operations, visited the place. Moshe Krausz met him and the atmosphere was businesslike. Ferenczy said to Krausz: "In this house only candidates for emigration to Palestine will be registered and you will be responsible for it".

The people living on the premises were equipped with real Swiss documents which gave them maximum protection under the circumstances in those days in Budapest. The paperwork in preparation for aliya was given to Mihály Salamon and a staff of clerks. Arthur Weisz and his lawyer, Rudolf Mezei, were added to the management of the house.

At the beginning 60 people stayed at the house: the managers, the clerks and their families. However, the number of dwellers grew at an amazing speed and within days, about 600 Jews were staying there. After the liberation of Pest (18.1.1945) almost 3,000 people found refuge there. The chances of survival under Swiss protection worked as a magic stick on the persecuted and the information about the house spread quickly.

Tens of members of the Zionist youth movements found refuge in the "Glass House" and each movement was allocated a special place. The distribution of the places was done without any formal decision but in a natural way. In one part of the basement members of "Hashomer Hatzair", "Dror" and "Maccabi Hatzair" were accommodated. Another part of the basement was called "the Orthodox basement" where traditional adult Zionists found refuge and in the attic the members of "Hanoar Hatzioni" and of "Bnei Akiva" were accommodated.

The organization of the "Glass House" itself and of life there became a difficult and unique mission. This position was imposed on Alexander Grossmann, a member of "Hashomer Hatzair". He worked around the clock and had sleepless nights because his wife and children were deported to the camps. Grossmann also took care of the people's financial welfare. He built connections with food wholesalers and with Hungarian officers who were in charge of the food warehouses. He bought from them products in return for dollars and the commitment to pay them after the war. Meals were prepared in the courtyard. The sanitary conditions were bad and long queues formed day and night in front of the few toilets.

With the increasing flow of Jews who wanted to enter the "Glass House", there were increasing arguments between the representatives of the Zionist youth movements and Arthur Weisz. The movement members argued that every Jew should be allowed to enter the "Glass House" without taking into consideration the crowdedness and the tough conditions because it was a case of life and death. Weisz, on the other hand, argued that accepting more people would endanger the lives of those already staying there and put at risk the whole Swiss protection issue.
On one occasion the confrontations came to the point that one of the youth movements' members took a vase from Weisz' desk and threw it to the ground.
Moshe Krausz, who was a witness, declared: "both of you are right".

After only a few weeks the "Glass House" could not contain any more people. Alexander Grossmann moved to the nearby Wekerle Street in order to open a 'branch'of the house on Vadász Street.
The job of managing the "Glass House" was imposed on Simha Hunwald who had just returned to the city after running away from a forced labour unit. Hunwald suffered long and cruel torments as only five Jews survived from his unit of 242. He was enlisted already in 1942, sent to Ukraine,

escaped once and managed to reach the Hungarian border where he was caught and returned to his unit. He ran away again and succeeded in reaching Budapest. He immediately joined the underground activities. Hunwald, one of the "Hashomer Hatzair" leaders, had leadership and organization skills so it was natural that he should be the manager of the "Glass House". Like Grossmann, his predecessor, he had bitter arguments with Arthur Weisz about accepting more Jews into the house. Hundreds of people assembled each day in front of the gate of the "Glass House" and begged for shelter. The relationship between the two worsened.

On November 23rd at 5 o'clock in the morning, there were sounds of guns hitting the gate. One of the guards hurried to wake Arthur Weisz who got dressed and arrived at the gate. He went out on the street where he confronted a gendarme lieutenant escorted by a squad of soldiers. "We have an order to look for weapons" the lieutenant announced.

"I firmly protest the violation of the diplomatic status of this house" said Weisz while pointing at the sign on the gate.

"I have a written order" the lieutenant insisted.

"And I have a written certificate from your commander, lieutenant colonel Ferenczy", replied Weisz.

The lieutenant hesitated, turned to his soldiers and told then to leave the place. He turned around and mumbled: "Don't worry, I will return".

On 1.1.1945 a unit of Arrow Cross men with Pál Fábry at its head appeared in front of the gate.

"I want to speak to Arthur Weisz" he said aggressively.

Weisz came down from his office and stood behind the gate guard. "Here I am", he announced. He knew Fábry who was the commander of a military unit whose base was in the neighborhood. "What is the matter?" he asked.

"Mr. Weisz", Fábry said politely, "I request that you follow me. My fellow officers and myself want to discuss with you issues related to the consulate house."

Weisz hesitated and did not answer.

"You had better come with me for your own sake and the sake of the people living here. I give you my word as a Hungarian officer that nothing bad will happen to you."

"I want to consult my friends and will return at once" replied Weisz.

"Don't go on any account! You cannot trust them! Find an excuse or offer him a bribe or food" his friends, Mezei and Salamon, advised him.

"I am going", Weisz suddenly announced. He left the house and got into Fábry's car. The car drove in the direction of the Parliament. From that moment Weisz's traces disappeared.

It was late at night. The small black car of the consulate with the Swiss emblem on its doors came through the gate. Simha Hunwald got out of the car. The minute he saw the people's faces he understood that something had happened.

"Arrow Cross men with Fábry, the officer, took Arthur away. We clearly told him not to go", he was told. "We contacted everyone we could, the police, the Swiss consulate and even the Arrow Cross headquarters. No one knows anything about him", Mezei told him.

"I will find him", Simha announced. "I am leaving".

"At this time? It is night..."

The black car disappeared in the darkness.

Hunwald did not come to the "Glass House" for three days but every day he made sure to give a sign of life and said he was continuing to search for Weisz. On January 4th at 2 o'clock after midnight he suddenly appeared at the house and woke Salamon.

"I think I have found Arthur's traces" he said. Salamon sat down on his bed. "Arthur was taken to the City Headquarters on Városházi Street". Salamon's face turned pale. That place had a bad reputation and there were no people there that could be bribed.

"I have already made contact with them through the Swiss. I am going there now."

"No!" Salamon exclaimed, "Not now and not you! Tomorrow morning we will send a messenger there."

"Tomorrow will be too late." Hunwald got up, put on his coat and left.

On January 6th in the morning, the consulate's black car approached the "Glass House". The driver was at the wheel and next to him sat Simha Hunwald wearing a leather coat and a brimmed hat posing as a consulate official by the name of Hans Kűhne. In front of the house stood Fritz, the messenger boy and an Arrow Cross man checking his papers. As the car approached the house, the gate opened. The messenger boy tried to take advantage of the opportunity and run into the house but the Arrow Cross man was faster: he drew his gun and shot at the boy who fell to the ground in a pool of blood. Simha Hunwald got out of the car.

"I am Hans Kűhne, an official of the consulate. I demand that I be allowed to take the wounded man to the hospital!" he said determinedly to the Arrow Cross man and his friends.

There was silence for a moment as if the hoodlums were backing down.

Then the fascist officer approached Hunwald, put his gun to his chest and ordered him to get into the consulate car. The officer, accompanied by two of his men, sat down in the car. On the back seat there was a bag with five hundred forged documents.

On January 10th, a policeman appeared at the "Glass House" and delivered a hand written letter to Salamon. "I am in the cellar of the Police Headquarters, do whatever it takes to set me free. I was tortured but did not reveal anything. Have you received any sign of Arthur? I will try to hold on. Simha."

The policeman said he was late delivering the letter because he was afraid of going out on the streets due to the bombardments.

Simha Hunwald was shot dead on January 8th and buried in a mass grave.

Arthur Weisz was murdered in unknown circumstances.

UNDERGROUND ACTIVISTS
NAMES AND BIOGRAPHIES

Adler Betzalel
Born in Irhóc (Vilhivci) on 9.5.1924
Died on 12.7.1988
Member of "Dror Habonim"

Lacking Hungarian citizenship, the Adler family was deported in 1941 to Kamenetz-Podolsk. The family survived the massacre of Jews which took place there, returned to Irhóc and Betzalel joined the "Hehalutz Hatzair" movement. In 1942 he arrived in Budapest and became active in the then outlawed "Dror" movement. In 1944 Betzalel underwent weapons training. He obtained authentic Aryan papers and legally registered in a police station. Under Neshka Goldfarb's guidance, he went on missions to provincial towns and forced labor camps, where his fellow members were being held, to supply them with documents and money, thus facilitating their escape. He also supplied equipment for members who were supposed to cross the border into Romania by means of the tiyul. Upon the rise to power of the Arrow Cross Party on October 15th, 1944, Betzalel started wearing the fascist party uniform. Together with Patyu-Martin Weingarten (Mordehai Karmi), he rescued Ephra Agmon and Joseph Meir from being lynched by a crowd on Népszínház Street. He participated in the establishment of bunkers, served as a liaison officer and, riding a motorcycle, he supplied food to those hiding in the bunkers. Betzalel rescued a group of Jews who were being taken by fascists for execution on the banks of the Danube. He was caught and taken to the Arrow Cross headquarters on Andrássi Street 60, where he was brutally tortured but managed to escape. He was eyewitness to the capture of Neshka, Zvi Goldfarb, and Vili Eisikovics in December 1944.

After the liberation in January 1945, he was instructed by his movement to volunteer for service in the Red Army. In 1948 he was demobilized with the rank of lieutenant. From 1951 he lived in Germany where he died. Betzalel is survived by his wife, son and daughter.

Adler Mordehai
Adler György
Born in Miskolc, on 20.5.1920
Fell in the Negba battle on 12.9.1948
Member of "Hashomer Hatzair"

Mordehai joined the movement at a very young age and was active in its local ken. He studied dentistry. For a while he joined the outlawed Socialist and Communist parties. In 1941 he enlisted in the Hungarian army from which, due to his Jewish origin, he was transferred to a labor unit. In 1944 he deserted, arrived in Budapest and stayed at the "Glass House" on Vadász and Wekerle Streets. Mordehai underwent weapons training and escorted food deliveries to children's homes around the city. After the liberation he was a member of the hahshara in Kibbutz Ehad BeMay.
In 1946 he made aliya and settled in Kibbutz Ma'anit. He later became a member of Kibbutz Yasur and served in the IDF. Mordehai took part in the Acco and Negba battles. In the battle for Negba he volunteered to rescue wounded soldiers who were trapped in a minefield, and was killed when he stepped on a mine. He was buried in the Kibbutz Negba mass grave.

Adler Mordehai
Ádler Mátyás
Born in Dunaszerdahely (Dunajská Streda) in 1915
Died on 7.5.2000
Member of "Hashomer Hatzair"

His family being religious, Mordehai studied in a Heder and a Yeshiva. Prior to his membership in "Hashomer Hatzair", he was a member of "Mizrahi". He studied printing in Bratislava. In 1942, at the time of the first deportations from Slovakia, he helped dozens of his comrades in the movement and other Jews to cross the border to Hungary. In April 1942, while attempting to travel to Budapest, he was arrested by the police in Komárom. He was interrogated about his activities and tortured but did not give away any information. The police took his father as a hostage and together they were transferred to the Garany detention camp where he stayed for three months. While his father remained in the camp, Mordehai was taken back to Komárom for forced labor. He was then transferred to Budapest where he worked as a porter along the banks of the Danube. He had contact with the Zionist underground movement. Thanks to forged documents he managed to escape to Romania by means of the tiyul. Mordehai arrived in Eretz Israel (Palestine) in 1944 and worked as a printer.

Adler Nesher
Ádler Ferenc
Born in Budapest, in 1923
Perished in Auschwitz, in 1944
Member of "Hashomer Hatzair"

Nesher studied at the Jewish high school in Budapest. In 1942, he organized the smuggling of members of his movement from Slovakia to Eretz Israel (Palestine). Nesher was captured and arrested in the Garany detention camp. During the years 1943-1944, he was a member of the "Hashomer Hatzair" leadership. He was captured again in his attempt to cross the border to Romania and deported to Auschwitz where he perished.

Adoram Ya'akov
Friedman Károly
Born in Kassa (Košice) on 10.12.1925
Died in 2003
Member of "Bnei Hakiva"

Ya'akov arrived in Budapest in 1944, adopted an Aryan look and joined the underground activities of his movement. His work consisted of keeping in touch with other members, finding accommodation and forging and distributing forged documents. He also took care of the refugees who arrived in Budapest by supplying them with money, clothes and food. He took part in audacious rescue activities such as the rescue from the Gestapo of the Mizrahi leader in Hungary, Avraham Samuel Benjamin Fraenkel.
In 1946 Ya'akov made aliya on the "Max Nordau" ship and was arrested and detained by the British Forces for a month and a half in the quarantine camp in Atlit. He received a medal for fighting the Nazis and their collaborators.

Agmon Efraim (Efra)
Teichman Ernő
Born in Kisvárda, in 1922
Member of "Hashomer Hatzair"

Efra was raised in a traditional Jewish family and was the oldest of eight children. At the age of sixteen he joined "Bnei Akiva" and later "Hashomer Hatzair" within whose framework he worked for the underground.
In 1943 he was drafted to forced labor service, but managed to evade it and joined the underground activities in Budapest. From March 19, 1944, he dealt with "Aryanization", visited Jewish communities in order to assist them and warn them of their expected fate. Between June and August he took part in the tiyul activities, and was in charge of contacts between Hungarian members of the movement in labor camps and jails and the underground. He used the name Imre Benkő, and wore a railway officer's uniform. He was one of the liaison people with the Pál Demény communist underground.

Efra distributed forged documents. Under the auspices of the International Red Cross, he was one of the founders of children's houses established by the underground. He supplied food and equipment to those houses, as well as to the central ghetto in the seventh district, the "Glass House" in Vadász Street, and its branch in Wekerle Street, and other starving Jews in the ghetto.

After the liberation he continued his work with the children, and assisted in organizing the illegal immigration of the "Hashomer Hatzair" movement members to Eretz Israel (Palestine). In 1946 Efra was a member of a delegation to the Zionist Congress in Basel.
Efra made aliya at the end of 1946. At first, he stayed in Kibbutz Ein Dor and later became a member of Kibbutz Ha'ogen, where he lived until 1971.

Efra is a member of the Society for the Research of the History of Zionist Youth Movements in Hungary. He resides in Mevaseret Tzion and owns a private import company.

Agmon Tzipora, 'Tzipi'
Schechter Franciska
Born in Técső (Tyacsiv) on 13.8.1920
Died on 17.10.1966
Member of "Hashomer Hatzair"

"Tzipi" was member of the movement as of 1938. In 1940 she moved to Budapest where she stayed at a hahshara and worked in the field of education in a hostel for apprentices at Zöldmáli Street. In the winter of 1943, suffering from arthritis, she was hospitalized. After the German occupation of Hungary on 19.3.1944, she joined the underground activities. Her assignment was to find apartments suitable for hiding and to distribute forged documents and money all around Hungary, in ghettos and forced labor camps. She participated in a daring action to liberate a member of her movement, Juca, who was detained, hit and tortured in a Gestapo basement at the Topolya detention camp.

After the liberation, "Tzipi" looked for Jewish children and transferred them to children's houses. She worked as a supervisor and gave the children in the movement's children's houses assistance and loving care.

In 1947 she made aliya. At first she and her husband Efra lived in Ein Dor and then settled in Kibbutz Ha'ogen. Due to the conditions that prevailed in the underground in Hungary, her illness was not properly treated at the time, and her arthritis turned into a heart disease. She died on the operating table.

Dr. Alexander Esther
Neuman Vera
Born in Budapest in 1929
Died on 24.4.2005
Member of "Hashomer Hatzair"

Esther came from a family of orthodox rabbis. Refugees from Slovakia and Poland found refuge in her father's house. In 1941 she joined the "Hashomer Hatzair" movement.

In the summer of 1944, after the German invasion of Hungary, Esther was caught by a Hungarian policeman who suspected her of being Jewish and of trying to avoid being deported. She succeeded in running away from him by jumping off a running tramway. In the movement Esther underwent a short course in the use of weapons and in evasion.

In the winter of 1944-1945 she was caught again by Arrow Cross men while on her way to distribute forged documents but again succeeded to escape.

After Szálasi came to power on 15.10.1944, Esther stayed at the "Glass House" on Vadász Street, which was under Swiss protection. She served as a Swiss messenger and distributed forged documents to Jews around the city. Again she was caught with a bag full of forged documents but managed to escape. Later, due to a Hungarian informer who knew her before the war, Esther was arrested and taken to the district headquarters of Arrow Cross on 2, Szent István körút (Saint Ishtvan Boulevard) but managed to run away because that very same night there was heavy bombing and the emergency exit was left open.

In 1949 Esther made aliya and served in the IDF as an officer.

She founded a family and studied economics both in Israel and abroad. She was a consultant in economics for several ministers in Israeli governments.

She resided in Mevaseret Tzion.

Alpan Moshe (Pil)
Elefánt Márton
Born in Bazin (Pezinok) in 1918
Died on 30.1.2006
Member of "Hashomer Hatzair"

Pil was one of the most prominent figures in the Hungarian Zionist youth movements underground. His parents, Marcus Elefánt and Reisman Frieda, lived in Várna (Varin) and in Bazin (Pezinok) in Slovakia. His parents, his older sister, Rozy, and her husband, were deported to Auschwitz. His parents died but his sister survived. His two younger sisters, Ella and Shoshana, were active in the Hungarian underground.

In 1936 Moshe graduated from the Jewish high school in Munkács. Until 1939 he studied Law and Philosophy at the University of Prague. He joined the "Hashomer Hatzair" movement and worked in education and organization. Moshe also trained members for aliya in the framework of the hahsharot. He served in a forced labor unit and in 1941 became a teacher for Jewish children who were not allowed to study in Slovak schools. In 1942, when the deportation of Slovakian Jews started, Moshe went underground, obtained forged documents and, as a member of the central committee of the movement, organized illegal activities. Since he spoke Hungarian fluently, on January 19th, 1944, the movement decided to send him to Budapest where he joined the underground activities. At the beginning Moshe used the fictitious name of Michael Solsky, a Polish refugee, and later he operated under the names of János Szabó and Mihály Rajec. He mainly dealt with providing assistance to refugees from Slovakia and Poland.

After the German occupation of Hungary on 19.3.1944, Moshe was a prominent activist in the Organization for the protection and rescue of Jews. In the argument among the different movements on the issue of the building of bunkers, he expressed his opposition, arguing that in light of the reality in fascist Hungary the bunkers would be deadly traps for their occupants. Moshe dealt with the return-tiyul in view of a period of relative calm there, as well as the tiyul. He often traveled to the border himself.

Moshe represented his movement in various forums of the underground and of Hungarian Jewry.

After 15.10.1944, when the Arrow Cross Party formed the government, Pil was mainly engaged in rescuing people serving in forced labor units and Budapest Jews. He took part in the establishment of children's houses where thousands of Jewish children, many of whom orphans, found a shelter.

In December 1944 Moshe was the soul and organizer of the liberation strategy of members of the Zionist youth movements underground from the central military prison on Margit Boulevard. After the liberation, in January 1945, he engaged in the rehabilitation of the movement and in helping those returning from concentration and extermination camps.

Moshe was active in the organization of the illegal aliya within the framework of Aliyah Bet.

In 1946 he made aliya with his wife, Tova Diamant, an underground activist, and joined Kibbutz Ha'ogen.

At first Moshe worked in the fields and later became the manager of the kibbutz rubber factory. Between 1958 and 1974 he was a member of the "Koor" (the umbrella organization of the Histadrut industry enterprises) directorate. In the same period, in 1962, he went to London where he studied economics.

From 1965 to 1967 he served as the Israeli attaché for Economics Affairs in East Africa. From 1974 Pil was an independent consultant in the fields of industry and economics.

In recent years he has served as the chairman of the Museum for the Heritage of Hungarian Speaking Jewry and a member of the directory of the Society for the Research of the History of Zionist Youth Movements in Hungary. He was a resident of Kfar Saba.

Alpan Tova
Diamant Gertrude
Born on 4.1.1924
Died on 8.8.1995
Member of "Hashomer Hatzair"

Tova was a member of "Hashomer Hatzair" from 1939. In 1944 she illegally moved from Slovakia to Hungary. Relatives helped her obtain Hungarian citizenship documents. In January 1944 Tova met Moshe Pil (Alpan) and joined the activities of the movement in Budapest. After the Germans invaded Hungary on 19.3.1944, Tova changed her identity to Anna Schmidt and joined the Zionist youth movements underground. She served as a liaison person between the members of the movement, distributed forged documents, looked for accommodation for refugees, took Jewish children out of the ghetto and transferred them to children's houses under the protection of the International Red Cross. In January 1945 Tova was rescued by the Red Army. In September 1945 she married Moshe Alpan.
She made aliya with her husband in July 1946 and joined Kibbutz Ha'ogen.

Alpar Yehuda
Alpár György
Born in Budapest in 1928
Member of "Hashomer Hatzair"

Yehuda joined the movement when he was a teenager. In the summer of 1944 he and another three members of the movement, were sent to South Transylvania in order to try and open a new route for the tiyul. They were all captured and sent to the Nyiregyháza ghetto and later to Debrecen where they were imprisoned in the wagons of a train bound for Auschwitz. When the train arrived to Slovak territory, three of them, Tzvi Lipkovics, Hillel Hacohen and Yehuda Alpar, managed to jump off. Tzvi Lipkovics was killed by his chasers but his two friends managed to reach Prešov. They made contact with a Jewish doctor who obtained Slovak documents for them from the "Hashomer Hatzair" movement in Slovakia.
Hillel Hacohen remained in Slovakia and joined the Slovak revolt but Yehuda Alpar returned to Budapest and stayed in the family apartment on Népszínház Street in a Yellow Star House. Later he arrived at the

"Glass House" on 29, Vadász Street, from where he was liberated on 18.1.1945.

Yehuda made aliya and joined Kibbutz Givat Oz. Later he left the kibbutz and settled down in Australia.

Dr. Am-ad Tzvi
Schwartz György
Born in Kaposvár on 31.3.1921
Member of "Maccabi Hatzair"

Tzvi was a member of the movement's leadership. He gave assistance to the refugees from Slovakia and Poland who arrived in Hungary. He dealt with the tiyul. He was caught by the Hungarian secret police and interrogated. He stayed in the Garany detention camp for a year. After the invasion of Hungary on 19.3.1944, Tzvi was one of those who were in favour of members of the movement going underground, mainly comrades born in Hungary.

Tzvi made aliya in 1947. He completed his doctorate in sociology. He is a member of Kibbutz Metzuba.

Amir Amram
Grünwald Alfréd
Born on 1.2.1923
Died on 3.6.1998
Member of "Hashomer Hatzair"

Amram came from a well-to-do, strictly traditional family who were in the timber business. He studied at a yeshiva and also learned carpentry. He joined "Hashomer Hatzair" and lived with his comrades in a "Heim" (a shared rented room) where he met his girlfriend and future wife, Marcsa Spinner. He gave assistance to the refugees who arrived from Slovakia to Hungary. Amram was enlisted in a forced labor unit. Marcsa and Efra Teichman (Agmon), who were central activists in the movement, tried to help him escape from service in the forced labor camp in Tata and to arrive in Budapest in order to join the Relief and Rescue Committee train to Switzerland. Amram and his friend, Mordehai Fraenkel, were late and the train left without them. Eventually, Amram succeeded in crossing the border, reaching Romania and, from there, with Marcsa, Eretz Israel (Palestine). He joined Kibbutz Ein Dor.

Amir Miriam
Spinner Mária "Marcsa"
Born in Párkány (Štúrovo) in 1922
Member of "Hashomer Hatzair"

Miriam's parents were enlightened people with leftist opinions. They were business people in Érsekújvár (Nové Zámky). In 1938, after the Hungarian invasion, Miriam joined the "Hashomer Hatzair" movement with the encouragement of her mother who took part in some of the activities. The adult members of the movement founded the Sela Organization within whose framework Miriam went on an agricultural hahshara. In 1942 she moved to Budapest where she met her future husband, Amram Grünwald (Amir). Miriam helped with the absorption of Jewish refugees arriving from Slovakia. After the Germans invaded Hungary on 19.3.1944, she engaged in obtaining authentic documents from the Population Registry offices and modifying them for those who needed them. She helped refugees from Poland from whom she heard about the extermination of Jews. Miriam sent forged documents to her parents but they were afraid of escaping from the ghetto. Together with Amram, who had run away from service in a forced labor unit, and with the help of comrades from the movement, especially Moshe Pil (Alpan), she arrived in Nagyvárad (Oradea) and crossed the border into Romania.
Miriam made aliya and joined Kibbutz Ein Dor.

Angelusz Moshe
Angelusz György
Born in Párkány (Štúrovo) in 1924
Member "Maccabi Hatzair"

Moshe was active in the underground within the framework of the movement. He was engaged in the production and distribution of forged documents. He managed to obtain documents from Hungarian printing workers who were members of the leftwing parties. He worked on Mérleg Street, Percel Mór Street and in the "Glass House" on Vadász Street. He lives in Canada.

Arányi Asher
Arányi István
Born in Újpest in 1924
Died on 2.2.2003
Member of "Dror Habonim"

Asher trained the members of the underground in the use of weapons. He evaded being enlisted into forced labor. He procured forged documents and helped the members of his movement to escape from forced labor camps. He traveled to country towns in order to take Jewish families out of the ghettos before they were deported to extermination camps. He traveled to the border zone in the Carpathian Mountains with a bag full of forged documents in order to try and give them to the Jews being transported on the trains to exterminations camps. However, these Jews refused to run away believing they were being sent to labor camps.

Asher smuggled Jews into Romania via the Hungarian border and often went to the border himself. In the border town of Nagyvárad (Oradea) he was arrested by the Gestapo, interrogated for eight days and told he would be executed. However, after a month he was released, he returned to Budapest and started liberating people from forced labor camps.
Arni had contacts with the Swedish Red Cross, the International Red Cross as well as with the parachutists that went on mission to Europe on behalf of the Yishuv in Eretz Israel (Palestine). He took part in building bunkers that were meant to take in underground fighters.
Asher was caught again on 8.12.1944 by Hungarian policemen when he was in possession of a gun. He was interrogated for three days but did not reveal his real identity. He was lucky again and he survived. After the liberation he worked for the aliya of comrades in the movement and children.

When Asher made aliya, he was arrested by the British and held captive in Cyprus for ten months. He was freed on 14.9.1947 and joined Kibbutz Ma'agan. Later he was among the founders of Kibbutz Beit Ha'emek. Asher held various key positions in this kibbutz, in "Hanoar Ha'oved" (Working and Studying Youth Union, the Histadrut youth organization) and was sent to Persia (Iran) by the Jewish Agency on a Zionist mission. He was awarded the Kaplan Prize.

At his death in Kibbutz Beit Ha'emek, he left a widow, three children, thirteen grandchildren and four great-grandchildren.

Arbel Yitzhak 'Bukszi'
Baumöhl István 'Bukszi'
Born in Csaják on 9.9.1925
Member of "Hanoar Hatzioni"

In May 1944 Yitzhak was enlisted in a forced labor unit. In September the unit was transferred to Budapest and he contacted members of the movement who were underground activists.

Yitzhak escaped from the labor unit and arrived at the "Glass House" on Vadász Street. He joined a unit called "Personal Sacrifice" under the leadership of Alexander Nathan. This unit's role was to protect the house from the Arrow Cross hooligans. Each member of the unit had his own personal firearm. In the end though there was no need for any armed confrontation. Within the framework of the movement Yitzhak helped organize groups of Jewish orphaned children and took care of them.

Even after the liberation in January 1945 Yitzhak continued to work with the children until 1948 and brought them to Israel. He served as the general secretary of the movement.

Yitzhak made aliya within the framework of a group of volunteers in the Haganah. He is a member of Kibbutz Cabri.

Arieli Zehava
Wertheimer Ágnes
Born in Pozsony (Bratislava) on 19.12.1925
Member of "Beitar"

Zehava joined the "Beitar" movement in Nitra in 1941 after having been expelled from Bratislava. In 1942 she was faced with deportation to Auschwitz but Count Eszterházy, the representative of the Hungarian minority in the Slovak Parliament and a friend of the family, helped her to hide for months and later smuggled her into Budapest.

After the Germans invaded Hungary on 19.3.1944, Zehava worked with the underground mainly distributing forged documents and making contact with the underground activists.

In June 1944 she travelled to Kassa to give forged documents to comrades. In Budapest Zehava was caught twice by the Germans, tortured by the Gestapo but managed to escape. She stayed in hiding places and in bunkers on Hungary Boulevard and in the Budapest Institute of Technology where there was a one and a half meter high bunker between the ceiling of the second storey and the floor of the third storey.

In October 1944 Zehava moved to the "Glass House" on 29, Vadász Street. She caught scarlet fever and was hospitalized. She was rescued in January 1945 by the Red Army. In 1946 Zehava married Tibor Klein - Arie Arieli.

In 1948, after 22 months in Paris, she made aliya. She assisted in the preparation of the vessel "Altalena".

She lives in Haifa.

Asael David
Auslaender Dezső 'Kis Oszi'
Born in Ungvár (Uzshorod) on 14.6.1924
Died on 13.2.1983
Member of "Bnei Akiva"

David joined the movement at the age of twelve. After graduating from high school, he studied at a yeshiva in Ungvár. He engaged in obtaining Aryan documents for his comrades in the movement who arrived in Budapest. On 30.5.1944 he was caught, together with his friend David Friedman, while in possession of many forged documents, Hungarian money and foreign currency. They were both interrogated by the Hungarian police and the Gestapo. After a three month imprisonment, with the help of comrades, they managed to run away. David at once resumed his underground activities and engaged mainly in the forgery of Protection Documents and their distribution. After the liberation David was a member of the central leadership of the movement and represented it as a delegate at the 22nd Zionist Congress in Basel.

David made aliya in 1946, volunteered for service in the Hagana and was wounded in the Ramla-Lod battles. In 1949 he married Tova Schlesinger. He was a teacher and a headmaster. David was sent on a mission to France by the Jewish Agency. From 1959 to 1962 he was the manager of the Center for Religious Education in Jerusalem. In the last seven years of his life he served as the chairman of the Religious Council in Ramat-Gan.

Garany detention camp, 1943.
From left, standing: Adler Nesher,
Am-ad Tzvi, Israel Shimon, Klein
Anna, Herman Uri, Ármin, Eisenberg
Moshe. Sitting: Funk Arie, Füredi
Avri, Lavi David.

"Maccabi Hatzair" at the Garany
detention camp, 1943.
From left: [-], [-], Porat Dov, Scheffer
Joseph.

Garany detention camp, 1943.
Members of "Hashomer Hatzair".
From left, top row Adler Nesher,
Funk Arie, Hunwald Simha.
Sitting in the front: Herman
Uri, Füredi Avri, Lavi David,
Eisenberg Moshe, Weiss Levi.

Members of "Dror" at
an outing, 9.5.1943.

Asael Tzvi
Auslaender Herman 'Nagy Oszi'
Born in Ungvár (Uzshorod) on 21.12.1919
Died on 21.10.1991
Member of "Bnei Akiva"

Tzvi was active in the "Bnei Akiva" ken in his town. He was among the first students of the Jewish high school in Ungvár. In 1941 he went to a hahshara in Budapest. In 1943 Tzvi was enlisted in a forced labor unit and wounded. In 1944 he escaped. Tzvi was an underground activist. He arrived in Arad, in Romania. In 1945 Tzvi was a member of the central leadership of his movement.

He made aliya. He was a high official in the religious department of the Jewish Agency. Tzvi went on various missions abroad for the Jewish Agency.

Atsmon Hanna
Neuwirth Lili
Born in Nagymegyer (Veľký Meder) in 1921
Member of "Maccabi Hatzair"

Hanna was active in bringing Jewish refugees from Slovakia to Budapest. She provided them with accommodation, basic equipment and money. After the German invasion of Hungary on 19.3.1944, Hanna visited forced labor camps and brought forged documents and money to her comrades from the movement so they could escape. After May 1944 Hanna took part in the tiyul operation and within this framework she escorted groups to Oradea (Nagyvárad). She managed to cross the border and join her husband who was already in Romania and from there too she helped refugees.

Hanna made aliya and joined Kibbutz Metzuba where she is still a member.

Atsmoni Ruth
Reich Edit
Born in Rákospalota on 27.8.1926
Member of "Dror Habonim"

Ruth studied at the Jewish high school in Budapest. In 1940 she joined the movement. She gave assistance to refugees, members of her movement, who arrived in Budapest from Slovakia, Poland and the Carpatho-Ruthenia region. Ruth obtained authentic documents from the Population Registry offices and distributed them. She left Hungary on the train of the Relief and Rescue Committee.
Ruth made aliya and joined the garin in Kvutzat Kinneret. In 1946 she and her comrades moved to Ein Zeitim. She resides in Nahariya.

Atzmoni Joseph 'Dagi'
Schwartz József
Born in Budapest in 1923
Died on 4.10.1968 in a road accident
Member of "Dror Habonim"

In 1919, during the short rule of Béla Kún, Joseph's father was a member of the Supreme "Soviet". At a young age Joseph joined the "Dror" movement and was active in the fields of culture and scouting. He was sent to country towns in order to enlist new members to the movement. After the Germans invaded Hungary on 19.3.1944, Joseph was enlisted in a forced labor unit. After a short period of time he escaped and integrated the underground work. He was sent to Romania within the framework of the tiyul but was caught and incarcerated in the Kistarcsa detention camp. Joseph escaped from the camp by hiding in a dirty laundry cart. He returned to Budapest and the underground activities and hid in the bunker on Hungary Boulevard. In the middle of December the bunker was discovered and its occupants were taken to the prison on Margit Boulevard where Joseph was interrogated, tortured but eventually liberated with a group of friends in a daring operation of underground activists of the Zionist youth movements, on 25.12.1944.
After the liberation, he gave assistance to orphaned Jewish children in the children's houses and dealt with aliya. In 1949 he made aliya himself and joined Kibbutz Parod. He was a youth educator and active with the leftwing movements, the "Sneh" group and the Israeli Communist Party. He had to leave his kibbutz and moved to Holon with his family.

Avidor Yardena
Polák Gizella
Born in Budapest, in 1925
Member of "Hanoar Hatzioni"

Yardena obtained various Aryan documents, mainly by using the Population Registry offices. She visited the offices pretending to look for fictitious names and from the list she was given she wrote down names of real Aryans. Later, a member of the movement (in most cases, a young woman) came into the office and asked for a copy of an authentic document, bearing one of the names taken from the list.
Yardena fled to Romania. From there she made aliya.

Bakos Andor
Berger Andor 'Bicege'
Born in Budapest on 25.5.1923
Died in 1988
Member of "Hashomer Hatzair"

Andor was an intellectual. He studied mathematics and physics at university in Budapest but was forced to interrupt his studies due to the anti-Jew laws. He joined the movement at the age of seventeen. His instructor was Arie Ya'ari Hunwald. After the German invasion of Hungary on 19.3.1944, Andor took part in the underground operations of the movement and was sent on various missions. After the liberation, in 1947 he left the movement and joined the Hungarian communist party. Andor finished his studies as a construction engineer and took part in the building of the underground train in Budapest.

Dr. Balázs Alice Tova
Edinger Alice
Born in Budapest in 1928
Died in Budapest in 1999
Member of "Hanoar Hatzioni"

In 1944 Tova moved from the Yellow Star House where she lived in Budapest to the "Glass House' on Vadász Street. She adopted the identity of a refugee, Erzsébet Csovsky, who arrived from Transylvania, joined the underground operations and distributed forged documents. Later

Tova moved to a girls' boarding school under the auspices of the Calvinist Church. She worked in children's houses, took part in the smuggling of Jews out of the ghetto and distributed forged documents as well as medicines to those who needed them.

Tova lived in Hungary and was a university lecturer.

Bar Sela David
Bisseliches Péter
Born in Budapest on 7.9.1923
Died in Israel in December 1999
Independent

David's father was the chairman of the Hungarian Zionist Association. After the Germans invaded Hungary, he was enlisted in a forced labor unit and served in Miskolc. He deserted and arrived in the "Glass House" in Budapest. He was Simha Hunwald's assistant. David distributed protection documents of the Swiss consulate. When the Arrow Cross men raided the "Glass House", he hid in one of the rooms, made contact by telephone with the outside world and succeeded in asking for help from Swiss agents and other people. After the liberation, within the framework of his father's metal factory, he worked for the reconstruction of the Danube bridges that were destroyed during the war. David made aliya in June 1949. He worked in several factories and in the Air Force Industry. David wrote a diary about the year 1944, which can be found in the "Moreshet" archives in Givat Haviva.

Barak Judith
Bischitz Judit
Born in Balassagyarmat in 1921
Member of "Hashomer Hatzair"

Judith joined the movement at the age of ten together with her older sister, Leah. In 1938 she moved to Budapest and from there she was sent to a hahshara in Izbég to prepare for aliya to and life in Eretz Israel (Palestine). About a year later, after the hahshara group was dismantled, Judith returned to Budapest. She belonged to the "Sela Organization". As of 1942 she helped with the absorption of Jewish refugees arriving from Poland and Slovakia to Budapest. After the Germans occupied Hungary on 19.3.1944, Judith supplied forged documents and prepared a bunker for refugees in one of the capital's suburbs. At the end of June 1944, she left Hungary on the train of the Relief and Rescue Committee.

In September Judith made aliya. She was member of a garin first in Kibbutz Negba and then in Kibbutz Ein Dor. Judith left the kibbutz in 1947 and in 1948 she married Barak Shmuel. She was a handicrafts teacher. She lives in Kiriyat Tivon.

Bar-Joel Joseph
Kandel László
Born in Debrecen in 1924
Member of "Hanoar Hatzi'oni"

In March 1944 Joseph was living in Debrecen and, as an apprentice in a printing house, he produced forged documents and distributed them to the members of youth movements as well as to refugees from Slovakia. In April 1944 Joseph was mobilized into a forced labor unit in Cegléd but in September he escaped with seventeen of his friends and arrived in Budapest where he joined the underground activities. Joseph went to the "Glass House" and from there he distributed forged documents all around the city. He was arrested and interrogated but managed to get released thanks to a Swiss "Schutzpass" (a Protection Document). He then returned to the "Glass House" to continue his activities until the liberation in January 1945. After the war Joseph was a member of the National Leadership of "Hanoar Hatzi'oni". In 1946 he led a group of children to Eretz Israel (Palestine) via Belgium and Cyprus. Joseph made aliya in 1947, was drafted into the army and demobilized with the rank of lieutenant colonel. He resides in Herzliya.

Barmat Yoheved
Barmat Judit
Born in Érsekújvár (Nové Zámky) in 1924
Perished in Auschwitz in 1944
Member of "Hashomer Hatzair"

Thanks to forged documents provided by the movement, Yoheved arrived in Budapest in 1943 and took part in illegal activities. She assisted refugees from Slovakia.. After the German invasion on 19.3.1944, Yoheved procured authentic documents from the Population Registry in Budapest. Yoheved worked with a friend, Nesher Adler, in bringing members of the movement from country towns to the capital city. In the summer of 1944, with a group of friends, she tried to cross the border into Romania within the framework of the tiyul. They were all caught. All her friends' efforts to release them failed. Yoheved was deported to Auschwitz where she perished.

Baron Miriam
Stern
Born in Kolozsvár (Cluj) on 6.6.1924
Member of "Dror Habonim"

Miriam arrived in Budapest in 1941. She stayed at an illegal hahshara of "Habonim" (which later became "Dror Habonim"). She smuggled refugees, members of the youth movements and other Jews to Romania within the framework of the tiyul. Miriam acted under various false names. She was arrested but released. At the end of 1944 she arrived in Eretz Israel (Palestine). Miriam was one of the first members of Kibbutz "Ein Zetim".

Dr. Bar-Tzvi Moshe
Schweiger Miklós
Born in Zenta (Senta) on 29.11.1905
Died on 13.8.1963
Member of "Ihud Mapa'i"

Moshe was the son of the Orthodox Rabbi in his town. He studied law in Zagreb and was head of the Jewish Academics Union, "Judea". After graduating he opened a law firm. He was known as a brilliant orator in Hungarian, German and Serbo-Croatian.

After the Vojvodina area was occupied by the Hungarians in April 1941, Moshe fled to Budapest and made contact with Joel Brand and his circle. He was appointed by the representatives of the Jewish Yishuv who operated in Istanbul as head of the "Committee for Defense" of the Zionist youth movements in Budapest. However, the representatives of the youth movements chose Moshe Rosenberg over him.

After the German invasion of Hungary on 19.3.1944, Moshe was arrested by the German security forces who claimed he was Stalin's brother-in-law. When the truth emerged, the Germans were afraid to admit their mistake and Moshe was sent to the Mauthausen Camp where he was detained for over a year with important political prisoners. At the end of April 1945, the S.S. officer Becher, one of Eichmann's main assistants, released him and gave him the suitcases and valuables that the passengers of the train that left Budapest at the end of June 1944 gave to the Relief and Rescue Committee as payment. Bar-Tzvi handed the suitcases over to representatives of the C.I.C. Later, when the agents of the Jewish Agency received these suitcases, they found only a third of the original content.

Moshe made aliya, volunteered to the IDF and served on the judge advocate staff. He passed the bar examinations for practicing law in Israel and worked for the judicial department of the "Histadrut" He was also a member of the "Mapa'i" court of justice.

Prof. Barzel Alexander
Vas Alexander 'Alex'
Born in Budapest in 1921
Died on 29.6.2005 in Kfar Hahoresh
Member of "Maccabi Hatzair"

Alexander was a member of the movement from 1939. He assisted his comrades, who arrived in Budapest as refugees from Slovakia, to adjust to their new life. In October 1942 he was enlisted in a forced labor camp. In June 1944 Alexander deserted and joined the underground activities of his movement. Among other things he produced and distributed forged documents and made contact with his comrades in the underground. At the end of June he left Hungary on the train of the Relief and Rescue Committee. In 1944 Alexander married Shoshana Steiner.

Alex made aliya in September 1945. He was a member of 'Kfar Hahoresh' and held various positions on the kibbutz. From 1952 to 1954 he served as the general secretary of "Hanoar Ha'oved" (Working and Studying Youth Union, the Histadrut youth organization). In 1971 he got his PhD in Philosophy and worked as a professor at the Technion.

Barzel Shoshana
Steiner Zsuzsa
Born in Pozsony (Bratislava) in 1924
Member of "Maccabi Hatzair"

In the spring of 1938 Shoshana helped Jews who were deported from "Burgenland" and were aboard a ship anchored on the Danube in Bratislava. In 1941 she settled down with her family in Budapest, where she gave assistance to the refugees who arrived from Slovakia. Since she had an Aryan appearance, Shoshanna was given the task of obtaining authentic Christian documents. In 1944 she traveled around Hungary and visited ghettos in order to warn the Jews of their fate, to distribute forged documents and to accompany friends to Budapest. In June 1944 she helped her husband (Alex Barzel Vas), whom she had married in April, to run away from a forced labor unit and reach Budapest. Shoshanna left Hungary on the train of the Relief and Rescue Committee.
Shoshana made aliya in 1945 and was one of the founders of Kibbutz Tze'elim. She has been a member of Kibbutz Kfar Hahoresh since 1948.

Baumer Joseph 'Yoshko'
Baumer József
Born in Nagymihályi (Michalovce) on 20.12.1914
Died in 2001
Member of "Hashomer Hatzair"

Joseph's parents were pious Hasidim Jews and Joseph studied in a Yeshiva. In 1939 he became member of the Hasomer Hatzair movement's leadership in Bratislava and as the coordinator of the Hehalutz organization. He dealt with the aliya of young people from Slovakia.
In 1940 Joseph traveled to Budapest in order to enlist in the Hungarian movement and help refugees. In 1941, before the invasion of Yugoslavia by the Germans, Joseph and some of his friends tried to open an aliya route from that country. They were caught, freed, caught again and arrested and then returned to Slovakia. In 1942 Joseph moved to Budapest with Mimish (Yitzhak Herbst) in order to organize help for many Slovak refugees who were members of the movement who arrived illegally in Hungary.
In the summer of 1943 Joseph contacted Menahem Bader, a member of Kibbutz Mizra and the representative of the Jewish Agency in Istanbul,

who sent money to the Relief and Rescue Committee which operated in Budapest.

Joseph represented the movement in the Eretz Israel Office. In 1944 he obtained a certificate, travelled to Romania and from there made aliya. He was a member of Kibbutz Ha'ogen.

Beck Mordehai
Beck Tibor
Born in Érsekújvár (Nové Zámky) on 15.4.1925
Member of "Hashomer Hatzair"

After receiving mobilization orders for forced labor, Mordehai asked members of the movement in Budapest to send him forged documents with which he reached Budapest. He was an underground activist and ran all kinds of errands. At the end of June 1944, Mordehai left Hungary on the train of the Relief and Rescue Committee.

He made aliya and became a member of Kibbutz Negba.

Becker Zehava
Sáfár Alena
Born in Kassa (Košice) on 30.6.1921
Member of "Beitar"

Zehava joined the movement in Košice at the age of fourteen. For a while she was active in Miskolc and arrived in Budapest in March 1944.

She was the main assistant of Andy Freiman, who was the commander of "Beitar" and in charge of the underground operations. Zehava was a liaison officer among the members of the movement, helped build bunkers and buy weapons. For a while she worked in the "Glass House" on 29, Vadász Street.

She made aliya in 1949 and in 1950 she married Shmuel Becker.

Bem Lili
Born in Szeged
Executed in 1941
Member of "Hashomer Hatzair"

Lili was a member of a "Hashomer Hatzair" ken in Újvidék (Novi Sad).
At the onset of the Hungarian invasion of the area she took part in the
organization of activities against Hungarian occupation and in sabotage
groups. On 20.9.1941 Lili was caught by the Hungarian gendarmerie
while carrying a weapon, judged in a military court and publicly hanged
in Újvidék.

Ben-David Mordehai
Horovitz Tibor
Born in 1923
Died in 1995
Member of "Hanoar Hatzioni"

In 1944 Mordehai was enlisted in a forced labor unit. In October 1944,
after the Arrow Cross Party formed the government, he deserted, arrived
in the "Glass House" on Vadász Street and joined the "Hanoar Hatzioni"
movement. Within the framework of his activity in the underground,
holding forged documents in the name of Gyüre Miklós, he carried food
to the Protected Houses, to two bunkers and to the hungry ghetto of
Budapest. He was arrested several times but with his documents as a
worker for the International Red Cross he managed to escape and resume
his activities.
Mordehai made aliya, served in the IDF and was demobilized with
the rank of colonel. He wrote an autobiography "Parsot Susim" (Horse
Hooves).

Ben-David Yehuda
Elfer Oszkár
Born in Kassa (Košice) on 7.10.1926
Member of "Hashomer Hatzair"

Yehuda was brought up in an orthodox Jewish family. On 16.4.1944
he fled to Budapest carrying authentic Christian documents bought
from a friend in his hometown. Yehuda intended to leave Hungary on
the train of the Relief and Rescue Committee but at the Jewish Center

he met Rafi Benshalom, who enlisted him in the underground. He took part in the rescue of Jewish young men from the forced labor units and in moving people from the Yellow Star Houses. Yehuda was caught in November 1944 while trying to rescue Jews from a "transport" at the railway station in Újpest, a suburb of Budapest. He was tortured with electric shocks but after a few days he managed to escape and resumed his activities with the underground until the city was liberated by the Red Army in January 1945.

Yehuda made aliya at the end of 1945 and joined Kibbutz Yehiam where he stayed until 1957. He resides in Jerusalem.

Ben-Porat Hava
Auslaender Kató
Born in Nyirbátor on 9.6.1924
Member of "Hashomer Hatzair"

In 1943 Hava was sent to Ungvár in order to set up the "Hashomer Hatzair" ken there. In 1944 she smuggled Jews into Romania (tiyul) in the Nagyvárad area. Hava was caught together with Eli Sajó, a member of "Maccabi Hatzair" and sent to Auschwitz and other extermination camps.

After the liberation Hava stayed first in Sweden, then in Cyprus and made aliya in 1947. She lives in Kibbutz Ga'aton.

Ben-Porat Joseph, 'Yusuf'
Schőnberger József
Born in Budapest on 23.9.1923
Member of "Hashomer Hatzair"

Between 1940 and 1943, Joseph took care of groups of children within the framework of the "Hashomer Hatzair" movement. He was enlisted in a forced labor unit but managed to escape. Joseph joined the underground and was sent to work in the children's house on 90, Dob Street which was under the protection of the International Red Cross in Budapest. After the liberation Joseph was in charge, in Germany, of a group of about 200 children who were going to make aliya. He himself made aliya in 1947. Joseph is a member of Kibbutz Ga'aton. For many years he was a teacher. He is now in charge of the kibbutz archives. Joseph is also an artist.

Benshalom Rafi
Friedl Richárd, Frigyes
Born in Kolozsvár (Cluj) on 6.5.1920
Member of "Hashomer Hatzair"
Died in 5.9.1996

Rafi's father died when he was three years old. In 1931 he moved to Germany with his mother and brother and then, in 1933, they moved to Bratislava. At the age of fourteen Rafi joined the "Hashomer Hatzair" movement and in 1937 he was sent to Prague to set up a ken there.

Rafi was enlisted in the Slovak army and served as a photographer. In 1941 he went underground in Trenčín. On the last night of 1943 the council of the movement decided that Rafi, together with Pil (Alpan), who both spoke Hungarian, would move to Hungary in order to work in the underground in the organization of the movement and the rescue of Jews. After the German invasion on 19.3.1944, Rafi represented the movement and the Zionist youth movements underground in the Jewish Zionist institutions. He had contacts with the military, the police and non-Jewish opposition groups. Rafi, who spoke fluent German and looked Aryan, excelled in negotiations and in making allies. He freed prisoners from jails. Tamra, his girlfriend, who later became his wife, was a loyal partner in his activities.

After the liberation of Hungary, Rafi moved to Prague and founded the Eretz Israel office. In 1947 he made aliya with Tamar and his son Danny and joined Kibbutz Ha'ogen. Rafi was an active member of his kibbutz and of the Kibbutz Artzi. He enrolled in the Israeli Foreign Service and served as the first secretary at the Israeli Embassy in Czechoslovakia and as the Israeli Ambassador in Mali, Cambodia and Romania.

In 1977 his book "We Struggled for Life" was published (Moreshet and Sifriat Hapoalim Publishing House). In this book Rafi documented and described the Zionist youth movements underground operations in Hungary (the English translation and the new edition in Hebrew were published in 2001). He was a member of the Society for the Research of the History of Zionist Youth Movements in Hungary.

Benshalom Tamar
Brunner Kató
Born in Budapest in 1921
Died on 28.1.2003
Member of "Hashomer Hatzair"

Tamar's family moved to Dunaszerdahely (Dunajská Streda) which was then in Czechoslovakia.
In 1938 she joined the "Hashomer Hatzair" movement. She learned photography and worked as a photographer.
At the beginning of March 1944 Tamar moved to Budapest and started working for the underground. She was sent to Bácska where a large group of refugees from Poland was concentrated. She brought them money, forged documents and assisted them in whatever they needed for their stay in Hungary. After the German invasion on 19.3.1944, Tamar continued her underground activities and was sent to country towns in order to make contact with other members of the movement. In the border town of Kassa she rescued people from the ghetto. With the beginning of the tiyul to Romania, Tamar was sent to the border town of Nagyvárad (Oradea) and helped the young men cross the border. Since the police were following her, she returned to Budapest and continued her work with Rafi, her future husband.
In July 1944 Tamar traveled to Vienna in order to follow the train of the Relief and Rescue Committee. She arrived at the Strasshof camp and returned from there with vital information and letters from the detainees. She was freed in January 1945 and in December of the same year Tamar moved with her husband and their son to Prague where Rafi was in charge of the Eretz Israel office.
Tamar made aliya in 1947. She was a member of Kibbutz Ha'ogen.

Ben-Shlomo Márta
Gut Márta
Born in Nagymihályi (Michalovce) on 4.6.1922
Member of "Hashomer Hatzair"

At the beginning of 1942 Marta hid with a Christian family. In May of the same year she crossed the border to Hungary illegally. She bought Aryan documents and worked in a hat factory. In May 1944, after the German invasion of Hungary, because someone informed on her, Marta was arrested and detained in the prison on Markó Street. She was freed by members of the "Hashomer Hatzair" movement working with the underground. She arrived in the "Glass House" where she got forged documents and rented an apartment with her brother Mark's girlfriend on Paulai Ede Street. Mark was caught by Arrow Cross members and executed.

Márta was liberated in January 1945 and in March she made aliya. She joined Kibbutz Ha'ogen. Márta married Moshe Ben-Shlomo (Miki Fleischman). In 1951 they left the kibbutz and moved to Nahariya.

Ben Tzvi Yona 'Jani'
Friedmann János
Born in Kisvárda in 1927
Member of "Dror Habonim"

In 1943 at school Yona declared that, because of the anti-Jews laws of the Hungarian government, he refused to be Hungarian. As a result, he was expelled from all the schools in the area. Yona moved to Budapest. After the Arrow Cross Party rose to power in mid-October 1944, he arrived at a house on 90, Dob Street where a children's house was set up for Jewish children collected around the city. About one thousand children and adults found refuge in this house. Yona's job was being a guard at the gate. He served as a liaison between the dwellers of the house and the management. After the liberation in 1945 he was active in his movement. Yona made aliya in April 1948 and stayed in various kibbutzim. He resides in Beer-Sheva. He was the manager of a development company and a teacher at the Administration College in Beer-Sheva.

Ben-Yitzhak Eliezer
Kaufman Sándor
Born in 1926
Died in 1971
Member of "Hanoar Hatzioni"

Eliezer came from a working class family in a village near Pécs. In 1944 he was enlisted in a forced labor unit but after about a month he was released and worked in a factory. Eliezer joined the underground and helped free Jews from forced labor camps mainly in the Székesfehérvár area to where he traveled three times. He was also active in Budapest in the Swiss legation and in one of the centers of underground activities on 17, Wekerle Sándor Street.

Eliezer made aliya and was a member of Kibbutz Yehiam until 1952.
Later he worked with the police force as an officer.

Ben-Ze'ev Avigdor
Farkas Viktor
Born in Rahó (Rahiv) on 22.5.1926
Died in 31.7.2004 in Israel
Member of "Maccabi Hatzair"

Avigdor served in a forced labor unit, managed to escape, reach Budapest
and arrive at 17, Wekerle Sándor Street which was a branch of the Swiss
consulate and one of the centers of the underground youth movement
operations. Avigdor joined the underground activities and was one of
the founders of the "Hospital" on Vilmos Császár Boulevard located in
the cellar of the Zichy cinema to provide a hiding place for the activists.
Thanks to his Aryan appearance (light hair and blue eyes) and wearing
an overall with the Nazi insignia, Avigdor went every morning to the
Vígszinház Theater in order to receive the daily password which was
needed for walking freely in the city streets. He then gave the password
to his friends on Wekerle Street. After the liberation Avigdor continued
his activities in the movement and provided food for children who had
survived. In an effort to make aliya, he crossed the border into Romania
and arrived in Bucharest where a hahshara unit was being set up. From
Romania he travelled to Yugoslavia. In Belgrade he was informed that
his sister, Leah, had returned from Auschwitz and was in Budapest. He
traveled back to the Hungarian capital and found his sister in a severe
condition. He helped her to recover and enrolled her in the movement.
Avigdor lived in Herzliya.

Berger Mihael 'Michael'
Born in Pozsony (Bratislava) in 1924
Died in 1945
Member of "Hashomer Hatzair"

From 1942 Michael was a "Hashomer Hatzair" ken leader in Budapest. In
1944 he was engaged in organizing hiding places. Michael was caught and
taken for interrogation to the Gestapo headquarters on Schwab Hill in Buda.
He was deported to Auschwitz and died in the Gusen camp in Austria.

Berger Naftali Nathan, Rabbi Dr.
Born in Szatmár in 1911
Died in the USA in 1964
Member of "Mizrahi"

Nathan studied in yeshivot with famous rabbis and at universities in Hungary and Germany. He was a doctor in philosophy. Nathan was an enthusiastic Zionist activist, a brilliant speaker and talented publicist. After the Germans invaded Hungary on 19.3.1944, he engaged in saving Jews. On one of his missions he was caught by the fascists and cruelly beaten. In 1949 he moved to the United States where he was a teacher and the head of a yeshiva. Nathan never recovered from the beatings he suffered during the war and that speeded up his death.

Berko Dov
Berkó Béla
Born in Nagyszőllős (Vinohragyiv) on 23.9.1922
Member of "Dror Habonim"
Died in 1997

At the age of sixteen Dov joined the "Hehalutz" movement in Huszt. In 1941 he arrived in Budapest, joined "Dror Habonim" and took part in the illegal activities of this movement. He assisted the refugees who arrived in Budapest. In October 1943 Dov was drafted to a forced labor unit. In July 1944 he received forged documents from the movement so that he could escape. However, Dov hesitated for fear that his friends who remained in the unit would be punished. In November though he decided to escape after all and arrived in Budapest. He was caught by Arrow Cross men and sent to concentration camps in Austria and Germany. Dov was liberated in May 1945.
In 1947 Dov made aliya and was one of the founders of Kibbutz Parod.

Berko Nahman
Berkó Károly
Born in Nagyszőllős (Vinohragyiv) in 1927
Member of "Dror Habonim"

In 1942 Nahman went to Budapest in order to learn to be an electrician and made contact with other members of his movement. After the Germans occupied Hungary on 19.3.1944, he became an underground activist and received forged documents from Vili Eisikovics. Following Tzvi Goldfarb's instructions, Nahman engaged in obtaining Aryan documents, smuggling Jews into Romania and building bunkers. In August 1944 he tried to cross the border into Romania. He was caught, interrogated and put on a deportation train but managed to escape while the train was near Budapest. Nahman arrived in the underground center of the movement in Baross Street. Donning a Levente uniform, he ran various errands mainly supplying food to the bunkers. He was arrested again and sent to the prison on Margit Boulevard. He was transferred to the border with Austria where he was forced to do bomb clearing. Nahman was released by the Red Army at the end of March 1945.

He made aliya in 1946 and was one of the founders of Moshav Beit Hanina (1950).

Bernáth Joseph
Member of the "Shimoni Group"

Prof. Bettelheim Avraham
Bettelheim Frigyes
Born in Győr in 1923
Died in 2004
Member of "Hanoar Hatzioni"

Avraham was active in Győr and the surroundings from 1939 mainly with finding hiding places for refugees from Slovakia. He studied at the University of Szeged in 1943 and 1944. With the German invasion of Hungary Avraham had to stop studying and enlist in a forced labor unit. He fled, arrived in Budapest and joined the underground. He settled in the "Glass House" on Vadász Street, distributed documents to those who needed them and supplied food to the bunkers. After the liberation Avraham accompanied groups of members of the movement to Italy. For about a year he was active with the B'riha on the Austria-Italy border. In 1946 Avraham boarded a ship on his way to Eretz Israel (Palestine) but the vessel was intercepted by the British and its passengers were taken to Cyprus.

In 1947 he arrived in Eretz Israel (Palestine) and was one of the founders of Kibbutz Mavkiyim (today a moshav). In 1951 he resumed his studies. Avraham was a professor at the University of Adelphi in Canada and was the dean of the Department of Chemistry.

Biederman Moshe 'Oszi'
Biederman Oszkár
Born in Sajószentpéter on 1.8.1924
Died in 1977
Member of "Hanoar Hatzioni"

In Budapest Moshe studied in a high school affiliated with the Rabbinical Seminar. After the German invasion of Hungary on 19.3.1944, he was allowed to walk freely in the streets of Budapest thanks to his father who fought in the First World War as an outstanding officer in the Hungarian Army. Moshe took advantage of the situation to collect information, deliver messages and to contact the Jews who were living in Yellow Star Houses. He worked in the "Glass House" on Vadász Street distributing documents and hiding weapons.
Moshe was liberated in January 1945 and made aliya in 1948.
Moshe was a member of Kibbutz Kfar Glücksohn where he worked as a teacher and the principal of the nearby school.

Dr. Bilitzer Adonyahu
Dr. Bilitzer Dezső 'Dajnus'
Born in Debrecen on 4.7.1913
Died on 17.5.2005
Member of "Hanoar Hatzioni"

Adonyahu studied at a Seminar of Rabbanim in Budapest and was a member of the student union "Maccabea". In June 1944 he joined the movement's underground activities under the fictitious name of Dunka László. Adonyahu went to Debrecen in order to take his family to Budapest since it was easier to hide in the capital city. . However, except for one of his sisters, his family did not want to leave Debrecen.

Adonyahu traveled to Debrecen again twice with the same purpose until it was too late to save his family. He was caught but managed to escape and return to Budapest.

He distributed forged documents that arrived from the forgery laboratory of the Zionist youth movements underground and other sources thanks to David Grünwald ("Coca") and supplied food to the bunkers.

He worked from the office of "Hanoar Hatzioni" which was located in the building of the International Red Cross on József Boulevard.

On October 15th, 1944, the day the Arrow Cross fascist party rose to power in Hungary, Adonyahu was caught in front of the "Glass House" on 29, Vadász Street while holding a bag full of documents. He was taken to the Gestapo headquarters on Svábhegy Hill and brutally beaten but he argued that he was only a messenger. From the Gestapo headquarters he was taken to the Tolonchász prison.

Adonyahu was freed thanks to a safe pass given to him by a lawyer for the Zionist movement, Dr. Beregi. After the liberation he continued with the rescue operations.

Adonyahu made aliya. He worked as a school headmaster and was also sent on an educational mission to South America.
He passed away in Jerusalem.

Bisseliches Moshe
Bisseliches Mózes
Born in Galicia in 1878
Died in Israel in 1970
Member of "Hatzionim Haclali'im"

In 1888 Moshe arrived in Budapest with his family. He studied at the Rabbinical Seminary and at the Budapest Institute of Technology. In 1903 he founded the student union "Maccabea". During WW II Moshe gave assistance to refugees from Poland and Slovakia and helped the pilots who were imprisoned. After the war he took part in the reconstruction of the bridges over the Danube River. In 1948 Moshe served as chairman of the Hungarian Zionist Association before it was outlawed. In 1949 he made aliya.

Blau Haim

Blau Sándor
Born in Vágsellye (Šal'a) in 1924
Killed in 1944
Member of "Maccabi Hatzair"

Haim was Ya'akov Böeri's brother. He studied in a Yeshiva in Galanta. In April 1944 he was enlisted in a forced labor unit. Haim deserted and joined the Zionist youth movements underground. He served as a liaison officer between the "Glass House" on Vadász Street and the Protected Houses under the auspices of neutral countries. About ten days before the liberation of Budapest by the Red Army he, and his friend Meir Kárpáti, were told to contact and supply food to a group of comrades who had been caught in bunkers but recently freed by the underground from the military prison on Margit Boulevard and were in hiding. Kárpáti and Blau left the "Glass House" with two parcels of food but never delivered the goods and disappeared. One conjecture is that they were arrested by an Arrow Cross patrol and executed on the banks of the Danube River. Another conjecture is that they died in the cellar of the Royal Palace in Buda, which served as the German headquarters.

Blau Malka

Blau Málka Magda
Born in Miskolc in 1920
Perished in Auschwitz in 1944
Member of "Hashomer Hatzair"

Malka was a member of the Miskolc ken. She moved to Budapest with her sister Yehudit.
After the Germans entered Hungary on 19.3.1944, she operated under false documents. Malka was caught and deported to Auschwitz.

Blau Sarah 'Aduma'

Blau Sári
Born in 1922 in Vágsellye (Šal'a)
Perished in Auschwitz in 1944
Member of "Maccabi Hatzair"

Sarah's family lived in Vágsellye (Šal'a) near the Slovakian-Hungarian border. The location of the town was extremely important in the smuggling of Jewish refugees over the border into Hungary. "Aduma" took part in this smuggling, waited for the refugees at the railway station, gave them overnight accommodation and, the following day, took care of their transfer to Budapest. Sarah worked with the underground until she was arrested.

One of the refugees who was caught gave her name and address to his interrogators. "Aduma" was deported to Auschwitz where she perished.

Blau Yehudit Lili
Blau Judit Lili
Born in Miskolc in 1923
Perished in Auschwitz in 1944
Member of "Hashomer Hatzair"

Yehudit was a member of a "Hashomer Hatzair" ken in her hometown. She moved to Budapest with her sister Malka.
After the Germans entered Hungary on 19.3.1944, she operated under false documents. Yehudit was caught and deported to Auschwitz.

Blum Pnina
Kaufman Magda
Born in Kassa (Košice) on 9.6.1925
Member of "Bnei Akiva"

In 1941 Pnina and her family were sent to the Garany detention camp because they could not prove their Hungarian citizenship. They were deported to the east, to Tchortkov. Pnina managed to return to Budapest, got hold of forged documents and worked for the underground. She distributed forged documents, maintained contact with her comrades and helped Jews leave Hungary illegally. After the liberation Pnina took care of orphaned Jewish children and prepared them for aliya. Her parents perished in the Holocaust.
Pnina made aliya in 1947. She lives in Kiryat Ono.

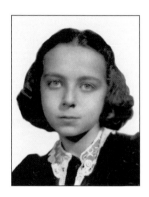

Böér Shosha
Somló Zsuzsa
Born in Budapest in 1929
Member of "Hashomer Hatzair"

As a high school student Shosha was a member of the "Hashloshim" group which was affiliated to the "Hashomer Hatzair" movement. In April 1944 her family villa was requisitioned by the Germans and Shosha moved to a Protected House. She took part in the underground activities. She did errands for the movement, especially the transfer of forged documents. Shosha succeeded in smuggling her father from the forced labor camp to a hiding place. In November 1944 she moved to a nunnery and continued her underground activities.
Shosha is a member of Kibbutz Ga'aton.

Böeri Ya'akov
Blau Károly
Born in Vágsellye (Šaľa) in 1926
Member of "Maccabi Hatzair"

In April 1942 Yaakov crossed the border into Hungary with his three sisters. They were caught and returned to Slovakia but on their second attempt they succeeded in crossing the border without being arrested. Ya'akov engaged in the forging of documents. In December 1944 Ya'akov was caught, interrogated for a week and tortured but did not reveal anything about his connection to the underground. He was transferred to the Tolongház prison where he was detained for three weeks. Ya'aakov managed to escape and on 18.1.1945 he was liberated by the Red Army.
He made aliya and is a member of Kibbutz Kfar Hahoresh.

Brand Hansi
Hartman Hajnalka
Born in Budapest in 1912
Died on 9.4.2000
Member of "Ihud Mapa'i"

Hansi came from a traditional and Zionist family. In 1928 she joined the "Shomer" movement which later became the "Hashomer Hatzair" but when it became part of the "World Movement", she quit and was among the founders of "Netzah" (Scout Zionist youth movement).

In 1931 Hansi was a member of an "Ihud Mapa'i" mission to Vienna in order to meet other similar movements in Austria. She was engaged in educational activities and in setting up hahsharot.

In 1935 she married Joel Brand.

As of 1941 Hansi gave assistance to Jewish refugees who arrived in Hungary from Germany, Austria, Poland and Slovakia. Hansi and Joel's house and hearts were open to all the refugees, many of whom asked for their help.

On 19.5.1944 Joel went on a mission to Istanbul for the Relief and Rescue Committee, with the support of Adolf Eichmann, in order to present to the representatives of the Yishuv the deal of "Goods for Blood". Before his departure, Joel introduced Hansi to Eichmann, who entrusted her with being the contact person between the Jews and himself.

In addition to her role as liaison officer Hansi obtained and distributed forged documents and helped hide the forgery laboratory. On May 27th she was arrested by the Hungarian secret police who wanted information about the laboratory, the documents and, especially, about her husband's mission to Istanbul. Hansi was interrogated and tortured but did not reveal anything. About Joel's mission, she maintained that he was traveling in order to buy provisions for the Germans. In the end she was released due to the intervention of the Germans who did not want the Hungarians to know the details of Joel's mission.

After her release Hansi resumed her activities and dealt mainly with financial matters in order to insure the existence of the children's houses.

At the beginning of January 1945 Hansi and her two sons went into hiding with a Christian family until the city was liberated by the Red Army.

The whole family made aliya. At first they lived in Kibbutz Givat Haim but later settled down in Tel-Aviv. Joel published his book "On a mission for the sentenced to death" and, together, they published another book, "The Devil and the Soul".

Brand Joel
Brand Jenő
Born in Naszód (Năsăud) in 1906
Died in 1964
Member of "Ihud Mapa'i"

Joel was one of the most prominent figures in the rescue of Hungarian Jews. His father was the founder of the telephone company in Budapest. When Joel was ten, his family moved to Germany and settled down in Erfurt. After he graduated from high school, Joel traveled across the United States. In 1932 he returned to Erfurt. In 1933 he was arrested for leftwing activities and spent a year in prison. In 1934 Joel was expulsed from Germany for being a Jewish Hungarian citizen. In 1938 his mother and sisters fled Germany and arrived in Budapest.

Joel was a "Poalei Tzion" activist, was elected to the central committee of "Ihud Mapa'i" and to the executive committee of the Zionist Organization in Hungary. Together with his wife, Hansi, he gave assistance to the refugees who arrived from Germany and Austria and later from Poland and Slovakia. He was a member of the Relief and Rescue Committee and, as such, he made contact with the representatives of the Jewish Yishuv in Eretz Israel (Palestine) who were based in Istanbul.

After the German invasion of Hungary on 19.3.1944, Joel had contacts with the S.S., mainly Adolf Eichmann, in order to save Jews' lives. Due to his personality and his perfect German, in the eyes of the Germans he was an appropriate representative. On 8.5.1944 Eichmann invited Joel to a meeting and made him an offer: the lives of a million Jews in return for supplies and money. Eichmann even suggested that Brand travel abroad in order to make contact with Jewish organizations and close the deal.

Brand arrived in Istanbul on 19.5.1944 while his wife and two sons were held hostages in case he did not return to Hungary. However, he was not allowed to enter Istanbul, was arrested by the British and transferred to Cairo where he was imprisoned. Brand sat in an Egyptian prison from the end of May until October 6th. On October 7th, 1944 he arrived in Eretz Israel (Palestine) where he met with central figures of the Jewish Yishuv. He blamed them for not giving him any assistance. Teddy Kolek, Eliahu Golomb and others replied that his mission was not a failure since it made it possible to break the wall of silence in London, New York and around the free world.

Joel Brand's activities are described in detail in his book "On a mission for the sentenced to death". Brand died in Frankfurt in 1964 from a heart attack while testifying against Nazi criminals.

Braun Yitzhak
Braun Ferenc
Born in Sopron on 25.3.1922
Member of "Hanoar Hatzioni"

Yitzhak was among the very first members of the movement in the Sopron area. He completed some hahsharot and took part in the winter camp in Balatonboglár in 1943. He distributed forged documents. In the summer of 1944 Yitzhak went on a tiyul to Romania.
In Israel Yitzhak worked for El-Al (the Israeli Airlines). He resides in Tel-Aviv.

Breuer Meir
Breuer Géza
Born in Miskolc in 1923
Disappeared/murdered in 1944
Member of "Hashomer Hatzair"

Meir was member of the Miskolc ken of Hashomer Hatzair. He was an upholsterer. Meir was mobilized for forced labor, escaped and arrived in Budapest. He worked for the underground, delivering food to the children's houses and the Budapest ghetto. In December 1944 Meir left Wekerle Sándor Street with a delivery of food and disappeared.

Broshi Dov
Borsodi Tibor
Born in Budapest in 1923
Died in 2003
Member of "Hanoar Hatzi'oni"

In December 1943, in the "Hanoar Hatzi'oni" camp in Balatonboglár, Dov organized underground operations together with other members of the movement, who had arrived from Poland as refugees. He took part in the organization of the bunker of the movement in Szeplőcsepkőbarlang in Buda. In March 1944 Dov traveled to country towns to warn his comrades there of the imminent danger for Jews.
Dov crossed the border into Romania and arrived in Eretz Israel (Palestine). Dov was an economist and worked for Bank Leumi. He was appointed to the Committee for the Inspection of Atomic Energy in Vienna and was a department manager. Thereafter, he retired.

Charody Judith
Ritscher Ilona
Born in Kiskunhalas in 1927
Member of "Hanoar Hatzioni"

At the time of the German invasion she was living in Budapest with her family. She studied at a business school and trained in typing and stenography. She printed papers and documents and often worked around the clock to meet the demand. On 26.6.1944 Judith was caught with her sister and taken to the Gestapo headquarters on Schwabs Hill. She was interrogated for two weeks. For some days she was incarcerated with Hanna Szenes. Judith was transferred to Kistarcsa and eventually she and her sister were released with the help of the International Red Cross because they were minors. Judith worked in one of the children's houses established by her movement. For a while she stayed in a bunker and transferred weapons. Judith and her sister applied to the post office in the capital and were hired. The uniform and authentic documents made it possible for Judith to walk around freely, work in the Protected Houses, children's houses, ghetto and bunkers. She collected wandering homeless Jewish children and took them to the children's houses.
Judith resides in Australia.

Dr. Cohen Nissan
Dr. Kahan Niszon
Born in Lemberg (Lvov) in 1883
Died in 1949 in Israel
Member of "Hatzionim Haclali'im"

Nissan was a lawyer. He devoted most of his time to Zionist activities. He was one of the founders of the student unions "Ivriya" and "Maccabea" and later of various aid organizations for refugees who arrived in Hungary. In 1941 he engaged in helping deportees from Kamenec Podolsk who did not have Hungarian citizenship. After the Germans invaded Hungary in March 1944, Nissan was a member of the Jewish Council in Budapest. He was in favour of rescue operations in the country towns with the help of the Zionist youth movements. Nissan was a delegate for his movement in Zionist congresses. He left Hungary on the train of the Relief and Rescue Committee and arrived in Eretz Israel (Palestine) in 1945. He worked in the legal department of the Keren Kayemet LeIsrael.

Demény Pál
Born in Budapest on 29.8.1901
Died in Budapest on 14.1.1991
Member of the Communist Party

Demény Pál was a writer and a politician. He was member of the Hungarian Communist Party from 1919. He was the editor of the first underground newspaper. Demény Pál was arrested several times by the Hungarian Police. The prosecution demanded he be sentenced to death but the court only condemned him to imprisonment. Demény Pál was among the founders of the new communist movement that stood for independence from Moscow. In 1944, after the German occupation, the various factions of the Communist Party united, planned a civil revolt and armed rebellion in Budapest. Demény cooperated with the members of "Hashomer Hatzair" who provided him with forged documents for deserters from the army and those who were being persecuted mainly for political reasons. Demény helped the Zionist underground in finding hiding places, food and weapons.

After the liberation of Budapest, in February 1945, Pál was arrested by the pro-Soviet government on charges of allegedly being an informer for the fascist police. He was sentenced to four and a half years in prison but was not released after serving his term. In 1953 Pál was tried again and this time condemned to ten years in prison on charges of being a traitor to the homeland. In 1957 he was exonerated from treason and in 1989 also from being an informer. In 1990, after the change of the regime, Demény Pál was a representative of the Socialist Party in the Hungarian Parliament. He died in the conference room of the Parliament.

Deutsch Rahel
Tornay Ágnes
Born in Nyiregyháza on 12.1.1924
Member of "Hashomer Hatzair"

Rahel joined the movement where she met her future husband, Ya'akov Deutsch.
In 1942 she moved to Budapest with Ya'akov and gave assistance to the Jewish refugees who arrived from Slovakia to Hungary. Because of her mother's illness Rahel returned to her hometown and passed on all the information she had about the extermination of Jews in the countries

occupied by the Germans. Most Jews did not want to believe her and only some of the youngsters were willing to assume a borrowed identity. Rahel returned to Budapest and, after some time, she found refuge on the estate of Christian acquaintances.

At the end of June 1944 Rahel and Ya'akov left Budapest on the train of the Relief and Rescue Committee and arrived in Switzerland. In 1945 they received certificates, made aliya and joined Kibbutz Ein Dor.

Deutsch Ya'akov
Deutsch Miklós 'Bub'"
Born in Nyiregyháza in 1922
Member of "Hashomer Hatzair"

Ya'akov was the only child of a devout Jewish family who owned a large bakery. He joined the "Hashomer Hatzair" movement. He excelled in various sports. Ya'akov met his future wife, Rahel (Tornay Ágnes) at an early age. When he was fifteen, his father died.

In 1942 Ya'akov moved to Budapest with Rahel and joined his comrades in the movement there. Ya'akov gave assistance to the Jewish refugees who at the time were arriving from Slovakia to Hungary. He gave one of the refugees his own documents and when he returned to Nyiregyháza to get new ones, he was arrested and taken to prison in Budapest. He was released by his family who hired a lawyer who convinced the judges that he had acted genuinely. Ya'akov was sentenced to returning to his hometown and to report to the police on a daily basis.

Ya'akov told the leaders of the community all he had learnt from the refugees about the extermination of Jews but they did not believe him. He saved the youngsters who were willing to hide and receive forged documents. After the German occupation of Hungary on 19.3.1944, he returned to Budapest with Rahel and, after some time, they found refuge on the estate of Christian acquaintances.

At the end of June 1944 they left Hungary on the train of the Relief and Rescue Committee and arrived in Switzerland. In the spring of 1945 Ya'akov and Rahel made aliya with certificates. They joined Kibbutz Ein Dor.

Diósi Ya'akov
Diósi Jenő
Born in Eperjes (Prešov)
Died in 1970
Member of "Maccabi Hatzair"

In 1943 Ya'akov joined the underground activities. In 1944 he was one of the people in charge of finding escape routes to Romania He escorted the fugitives to the border and equipped the bunkers that were set up in Budapest.
After the liberation Ya'akov made aliya.

Doron Amir
Fodor Imre
Born in Lőcse (Levoča) on 25.5.1923
Died on 3.12.2001
Member of "Hanoar Hatzioni"

Amir graduated from high school in Budapest.
After the German invasion of Hungary on 19.3.1944, he worked with the Jewish council and simultaneously joined the rescue activities of the Zionist movement under the auspices of the International Red Cross in Baross Street and József Boulevard. Donning a German uniform Amir carried forged documents to various places and gave them to those who needed them. Together with a German deserter, he took part in the release of Jews from the grip of Arrow Cross men. At the end of November 1944 Amir organized a refuge for activists of the movement in a residential building and the defense of the house by men who had escaped from forced labour units.

After the war Amir took part in the organization of the B'riha mainly on the Hungarian-Romanian border.

In 1948 he made aliya, served in the IDF and later in the police force from which he was discharged in 1979 with the rank of Brigadier General Amir died in Israel.

Dotán Joseph
Vajda József
Born in Nagymegyer (Vel'ký Meder) in 18.6.1923
Member of "Hashomer Hatzair"

Joseph studied in Bratislava and Moravská Ostrava. He joined "Hashomer Hatzair" in childhood. In 1943 he was conscripted into the Hungarian army and later into a forced labour unit. Towards the end of the war he was transferred to Germany, escaped and arrived at the "Glass House" on Vadász Street in Budapest. In the underground Joseph dealt with organization and defense, safeguarding the weapons and their distribution in case the place were attacked. Joseph also prepared lists of Protection Documents and their distribution. After the liberation he was active in the children's houses that were set up in order to rehabilitate the children and to prepare them for aliya. Joseph dealt with illegal aliya and escorted groups of Jews from Hungary to Romania. He made aliya and resides in Ramat Gan.

Efrati Tzvi
Frőhlich Herman Sándor
Born in the town of Hajdunánás in 1923
Died in 1991
Member of "Hashomer Hatzair"

Tzvi was born in a Jewish Orthodox family. In 1927 his family moved to the city of Debrecen and in 1933 they moved to Budapest, where he studied at the Jewish high school. In 1944 he was enlisted in a forced labor unit, escaped and found refuge in the "Glass House" on Vadász Street. He supplied food and forged documents. After the liberation he joined Kibbutz Ehad BeMay and made aliya illegally on the vessel "Knesset Israel" that was intercepted by the British and he was sent to Cyprus. During a struggle with British soldiers he was wounded in the head.
He arrived in Eretz Israel (Palestine)in 1947 and in 1948, together with his friends, he founded Kibbutz Ga'aton. He worked as a nurse in a hospital.

Dr. Eichler Hava
Fischer Edit
Born in Budapest in 1923
Member of "Hanoar Hatzioni"

Hava joined the movement at the age of fifteen. During the years 1942 and 1943 refugees from Slovakia and Poland stayed at her parents' home. After the German invasion of Hungary on 19.3.1944, she stayed with her family at a Yellow Star House and kept in touch with the members of the movement.

She joined the underground and distributed forged documents to comrades in the country towns and in the tiyul. After Szálasi came to power on 15.10.1944, Hava stayed at the "Glass House" on Vadász Street and continued to take part in the underground activities.

She made aliya illegally in 1946 on the "Biriya" vessel. Hava is a history teacher with a doctorate degree. She did research on the activities of the Zionist Youth Movements in Hungary. She resides in Ramat Gan.

Einhorn Asher
Einhorn Anschel
Born in Irhóc (Vilhivci) on 17.6.1915
Died in April 1986
Member of "Dror Habonim"

From 1933 Asher took part in Zionist activities in the Carpathian Mountains as a member of "Hehalutz Hatzair". That same year he was sent to Alsókalocsa (Kolocsava) for training towards aliya. He served as the leader of the Técső area and set up new hahsharot.

At the end of 1937 Asher was enlisted in the army. From 1935 to 1939 he was an activist for "Hehalutz Hatzair". In 1942 he was arrested in his residential town, Aknaszlatina (Szolotvina) because of his Zionist activities and was interrogated for ten days.

At the beginning of 1944 Asher dug bunkers in Kökenyes (Ternove) and built a stock of military equipment, arms and ammunitions.

On 20.4.1944 Asher was deported to Auschwitz.

After the liberation he returned to Budapest and was chosen as a member of the movement's central committee and sent to the Carpatho-Ruthenia region to work with the Jewish youths, bring them to Budapest and prepare them for aliya. In Budapest he trained olim, organized a seminar in Yiddish and was also one of the lecturers.

On 9.7.1945 Asher made aliya with his family on the "Exodus" ship. He lived for a short period of time on a kibbutz but later became one of the founders of Moshav Omer.

Asher wrote a book: "Aviv Aharon" (The Last Spring) about Máramaros Jewry.

Einhorn Menahem
Born in Irhóc (Vilhivci) on 2.10.1920
Died on 20.11.2000
Member of "Dror Habonim"

In February-March 1944 Menahem dug bunkers in the Máramaros district with the "Dror Habonim" group.
He made aliya and died in Israel.

Eisenberg Hava (Weisz)
Gábor Éva
Born in Békéscsaba on 25.10.1923
Member of "Hanoar Hatzioni"

Hava joined the movement in 1943. In 1944 she was released from a forced labor camp and arrived in Budapest. Together with Mordehai Weisz she distributed Protection Documents, found locations for bunkers and was sent on various missions on behalf of the underground. Hava was liberated while staying in the "Glass House" and married Mordehai Weisz.
She made aliya in 1947. Hava worked with the Committee for Atomic Energy in Nahal Sorek and in the Israeli Embassy in Washington. She resides in Herzliya.

Eisenberg Moshe
Eisenberg Miklós
Born in Budapest in 1922
Died in 1943
Member of "Hashomer Hatzair"

Moshe was brought up in a religious Jewish family. He studied in a teachers' college. At the beginning of 1940 he joined the Sela Organization of "Hashomer Hatzair". Moshe assisted in the absorption of refugees that arrived to Budapest from Slovakia and Poland.

Due to the arrest of Simha Hunwald, one of the movement's leaders, at the end of April 1942, he and other members were also arrested and sent to the Garany detention camp where he stayed for thirteen months. Because of his great sensitivity, he lost his strength and committed suicide.

Eisikovics Ze'ev
Eisikovics Wilhelm 'Vili'
Born in Nagybocskó (Velikij Bicskiv) in 1924
Member of "Dror Habonim"

Ze'ev was the eldest of three brothers. His father, who was active in the communist party, was arrested in 1942 by the Hungarian counter-espionage, tortured and killed.

In 1941 Ze'ev moved to Budapest and studied electronics. At the beginning of 1944 he joined the "Habonim" movement. In May 1944 he was enlisted in a forced labor unit to build a railroad. He escaped and joined the underground. Ze'ev learned the trade of seal forging, produced and distributed forged documents. He took part in preparing bunkers and weapons training. On 7.12.1944 Ze'ev was caught together with Neshka and Tsvi Goldfarb and imprisoned in the military jail on Margit Boulevard. After a week of interrogations and torture he was moved to the town of Sopron. Interrogators that followed him to Sopron told him that within eight days he would be hanged. However, in the end, together with his two friends, he was returned to Budapest to the Margit Boulevard jail. On 25.12.1944 Ze'ev and other detainees were released thanks to the daring rescue operation of underground activists. After the liberation he continued to be active in his movement with legal and illegal aliya.

In August 1946, in Italy, Ze'ev boarded a ship bound for Eretz Israel (Palestine). However, the ship was intercepted by the British and its passengers were taken to Cyprus. In 1947 he arrived in Eretz Israel (Palestine) and joined the hahshara in Kibbutz Daphna and Ein Harod. Ze'ev volunteered to the IDF and served in the 13th battalion of the Golani Brigade. He took an officer's training course. After being demobilized Ze'ev joined Kibbutz Gardosh, called Parod nowadays, and became the first regional commander. He left the kibbutz together with his wife Yaffa and settled in Vienna where he set up a noble metals export company. He is retired and resides in Vienna.

Eisinger Baruh
Eisinger Ferenc 'Feri'
Born in Kárpáthalas (Vištuk), on 20.6.1927
Member of "Maccabi Hatzair"

In 1940 following the coming to power of the fascists in Slovakia, Baruh was expelled from school. In 1941 and 1942 he worked on a farm. In 1942, with his three sisters, Baruh crossed the border into Hungary but they were caught and returned to Slovakia. On their second attempt, though, they succeeded in reaching the capital. In Budapest, under a fictional name and with forged documents, he worked in an oil factory until 1944. He served as the liaison officer of the forged documents laboratory located on Rózsa Street and later on Baross Street. In December Baruh was caught because the man he ordered forged seals from informed on him. He was arrested and tortured but did not break down and did not give away any information. Baruh was transferred to different prisons but managed to escape. He reached one of the Protected Houses under the auspices of the Swiss legation and met other members of his movement.
Baruh was released on 18.1.1945. He now resides in the USA.

Dr. Eppler Elisheva Elizabeth
Eppler Erzsébet Erzsi
Born in Budapest in 1921
Died in Israel on 4.2.1999
Member of the "Gordon Circle" - "Borohov Circle"

Elisheva studied at the Sorbonne in Paris where she got a doctorate. She was an expert in French culture. From 1942 she worked at the National Library in Budapest. On 20.3.1944 Elisheva was invited by Samu Stern, who was the leader of the Jewish community in Budapest, to join his staff. She worked as the liaison officer between the leaders of the various communities and the Zionist youth movements working in the underground. Elisheva worked in the "Glass House" on Vadász Street and with the Swiss legation on Szabadság Square. After the liberation she resumed her work at the National Library in Budapest. In 1947 she did research at the British Museum in London. From 1954 Elisheva worked in the archives of the World Jewish Congress. She published a great number of books and articles in the fields of literature, culture and Judaism. She made aliya and died in Israel.

Epstein Sarah

Weisz Sára
Born in Nagymegyer (Vel'ký Meder) on 21.12.1925
Member of "Hashomer Hatzair"

In 1942 Sarah moved to Budapest. She helped refugees from Slovakia by supplying them with food cards and forged documents. Sarah left Hungary on the train of the "Relief and Rescue Committee". Her daughter was born in Switzerland.
Sarah arrived in Eretz Israel (Palestine) in September 1945. She is a member of Kibbutz Negba.

Epstein Yehoshua

Epstein Zsigmond
Born in Tiszafüred on 8.7.1924
Member of "Hashomer Hatzair"

In 1940 Yehoshua joined the "Hashomer Hatzair" movement. He was active in the underground. He left Hungary on the Relief and Rescue Committee train.
On 2.9.1945 he arrived in Eretz Israel (Palestine). Yehoshua, his wife Sarah and their daughter Shosha, who was born in Switzerland, joined Kibbutz Negba.

Even Eliezer, Dr.

Köves László
Born in Székesfehérvár, in 1923
Member of "Hanoar Hatzioni"

Eliezer joined the movement in 1933. In as early as 1938 he engaged in obtaining documents for Jews from Slovakia and their relatives who found refuge in Hungary. Together with his father, Eliezer helped two families who managed to escape from the Dachau concentration camp and arrived in Hungary.
In 1943 he took part in the organization of the Balatonboglár camp, in order to train members of his movement for underground and resistance activities. The training camp instructors were members of "Hanoar Hatzioni" who entered Hungary illegally. On 1.4.1944, Eliezer was drafted into a forced labor camp. Together with his comrades he helped

a group of Serbian inmates to escape. In August 1944, Eliezer escaped, via Komárom, to Budapest, holding forged documents for himself and ten of his comrades. During a period of three months he was among the suppliers of food to the ghetto and the Protected Houses in the city.

Dr. Even is a teacher, lecturer, and researcher at the "Hadassah" Institute of Educational Research in Jerusalem. In 1988, he went to Hungary on a Zionist mission. He was honored with a special award for his achievements in disseminating the Hebrew language. He is a member of the World Zionist Organization's Executive Committee.

Fábián Tibor
Member of the "Shimoni Group"

Prof. Fábry Andrej 'Feigi'
Feigenbaum Endre
Born in Kolta in 1919
Member of "Hashomer Hatzair"

Andrej joined the movement in 1929. In 1930 his family moved to Bratislava where he continued to be active in the movement. In March 1942, with the beginning of the deportations, mainly of girls, from Slovakia, Andrej was sent by the movement to Budapest. He met Samu Stern, head of the Jewish community in Budapest, told him about the deportations and asked for his help in absorbing refugees arriving in Budapest from Slovakia. Stern categorically rejected his request saying: "I will allow no intruders to endanger the relative safety of Hungarian Jews". In 1943 Andrej was arrested by the police, moved from one prison to another and sentenced to imprisonment on charges of forgery and slipping across the border. Andrej escaped from prison and arrived at the

"Glass House" on Vadász Street. He immediately joined the underground activities and was part of the team in the forgery workshop. In December 1944, when the workshop was discovered, Andrej was arrested with David Gur and Miki Langer. He was interrogated, tortured and about to be executed. He was liberated in a daring operation of the Zionist underground.

After the liberation he organized children's houses for the hungry orphaned Jewish children outside Budapest. For about six months he managed the children's house in Békéscsaba. He returned to Budapest and worked in the children's department of the International Red Cross.

In 1946 he traveled to Prague, registered at the university and completed his studies as an agricultural engineer. He published many researches and acquired an international reputation. He was a professor at the Prague University. He has been retired since 1989. He resides in Prague.

Fast Otilia (Tila)
Feldman Otilia
Born in Munkács (Mukacsevo) on 31.7.1919
Died in 1991
Member of "Hashomer Hatzair"

Otilia came from a religious Jewish family. Her father died when she was eleven years old. She joined the movement at an early age. In 1939 Otilia was a member of a hahshara unit "Al Hahoma" (On the wall) in Bratislava. She arrived in Budapest and gave assistance to the refugees arriving from Slovakia. After the Germans invaded Hungary on 19.3.1944, she dyed her hair in order to give herself an Aryan look. Otilia managed to cross the border into Romania within the framework of the tiyul.
At the end of 1944 she arrived in Eretz Israel (Palestine) and joined Kibbutz Ha'ogen.

Fast Shmuel
Fast Miklós
Born in Eperjes (Prešov) on 2.7.1919
Member of "Hashomer Hatzair"

In 1942 Shmuel crossed the border from Slovakia into Hungary. He operated in the underground together with his wife, Otilia. Shmuel moved to Romania within the framework of the tiyul, was arrested there by the police but because he asked to meet a representative of the Slovak embassy he succeeded in getting released.
Shmuel made aliya and joined Kibbutz Ha'ogen.

Fay Péter
Fischer Péter
Born in Palánka (Backa Palánka) on 30.11.1913
Died in London on 13.7.2000
Member of "Hashomer Hatzair"

After the Germans invaded Hungary, Péter arrived in Budapest and joined the Zionist underground activities as an employee of the International Red Cross. As of September 1944 he dealt with the rescue of Jewish children, taking them out of the ghetto and bringing them to safe places in children's houses on Budafoki Street. He took part in other activities too.

Federit Árpád
Born in Pécs in 1891
Died in Israel in 1971
Member of the "Gordon Circle"

Árpád was an officer in the Hungarian army during WW I. He was a sportsman and a sports businessman. He approached the Zionist movement and the "Gordon Circle". He sent his son to Eretz Israel (Palestine) in 1941 with a "Hashomer Hatzair" group. Árpád saved Jewish children from Slovakia. His apartment served as a workshop for forged papers where Shraga Weil and David Gur worked for a while. In the summer of 1944 he left Hungary on the train of the Relief and Rescue Committee. Árpád made aliya and joined the Sh'ar Yashuv settlement.

Members of "Bnei Akiva", 1943.
From left, top: Rosenfeld Yitzhak, Asael Tzvi, Spiegel Sanyi.
Middle: Asael David, Kadari Menahem Tzvi. Front: Seidel Tzvi,
Yacovi Menahem.

Members of "Hashomer Hatzair",
Kassa, 1942.
From left, top row: Altmann
Miriam, Eisikovics Yardena, [-],
Fodor Malka, Fodor Mordi, Levavi
(Komlós) Dina. Front: Halpern
Patyu, Eisikovics Eli, Altmann Eli.

Members of "Dror Habonim" ("Hehalutz Hatzair"), 1943.
From left, standing: Prizant Tzvi, Rosenbaum Moshe, Joseph
Sitting: Rosenbaum Shmuel, Golani Dov.

"Hashomer Hatzair" winter camp, Kóspallag, December 1943.
From left, top row: Epstein Yeshayahu, Ben-dor Tova, Epstein Sarah, Klein Moshe, Sharoni Tzivonit, Gur David, Kilon Moshe, Netzer Miriam, Fischer Avri, Schechter David, Shlomi Judith, Lipkovics Tzvi. Bottom: Ronen Miriam, Kama Yirmiyahu, Berger Michael, Ronen Avraham, Reichman Ezra.

Feigenbaum Benjamin
Born in Kispári in 1923
Died in 1981
Member of "Bnei Akiva"

Benjamin was active in the movement in Kassa from 1940. In 1944 he was enlisted in a forced labor unit, deserted and arrived at the "Glass House". He was an underground activist. After the liberation he worked in the education of children who had survived the Holocaust. He made aliya with the children via Cyprus in 1946. On the way he married Sarah Steiner. In Eretz Israel (Palestine) he continued his educational work.

Felsenburg Baruh
Born in Budapest in 1926
Member of "Maccabi Hatzair"

Baruh joined the movement in 1942. Together with some comrades he did agricultural work in a village until they were forced to run away as they were suspected of being Jews. Baruh returned to Budapest and took care of his paralyzed mother. His father was enlisted in a forced labor unit.
In the summer of 1944 Baruh started working for the underground. He maintained contact with comrades who were serving in various forced labor camps all over Hungary, brought them money and documents so that they could escape.
After the liberation he joined his father who had emigrated to France.
In the mid 50's Baruh returned to Hungary. He committed suicide.

Fettmann Yeshayahu
Fettman Tibor
Born in Nyirbátor in 1924
Member of "Hashomer Hatzair"

The Nyirbátor ken of "Hashomer Hatzair" was established in 1936. The movement operated under the auspices of the rabbi of the "Status Quo" community, who loved the Hebrew language and had Zionist feelings, on the premises of the synagogue under the name of "Hanoar Ha'ivri".
In 1940 Yeshayahu moved to Budapest and worked as a watchmaker. He stayed at the Zöldmáli hostel for apprentices and integrated the illegal

activities of the movement. At the beginning of 1944 he was sent to Debrecen to operate the local ken and to organize self-defense. On the day the Germans invaded Hungary, on 19.3.1944, he was staying in Budapest. Following the instructions from the movement's leadership, he obtained for himself authentic Christian documents from the Population Registry. Yeshayahu and his brother, Haim, wearing "Levente" uniforms, traveled in order to release their parents and two sisters from the Nyirbátor ghetto and bring them to Budapest. Their parents and sisters refused to go with them and were deported to Auschwitz.

Yeshayahu was meant to leave Hungary within the framework of the tiyul but in the end he left on the train of the Relief and Rescue Committee and on 7.12.1944 he arrived in Switzerland. In September 1945 he made aliya legally and joined Kibbutz Negba. Later he settled down in Holon.

Fischer Avri
Born in Pozsony (Bratislava) in 1924
Perished in Auschwitz in 1944
Member of "Hashomer Hatzair"

Avri was an instructor in the Budapest ken from 1942. After the Germans invaded Hungary on 19.3.1944, he engaged in finding hiding places. Together with Dan Zimmerman and Yitzhak Herbst-Mimish he forged documents on a large scale and distributed them. He was caught and deported to Auschwitz where he perished.

Fischer Ernst
Fischer Ernő
Born in Endrőd in 1924
Died on 6.6.2000
Member of "Hanoar Hatzioni"

In 1939, due to the family's difficult economic situation, Ernst was sent to Budapest to learn the goldsmith's craft in the hostel for apprentices. On 15.5.1944 he was enlisted in a forced labor unit. After some time he escaped from the camp, arrived in Budapest and joined his movement's underground activities. Carrying forged documents, he joined the auxiliary unit of the Hungarian army "Kiska" for the defense of Budapest and was given a weapon. When the suspicion arose that there were Jews among the enlisted, a physical inspection was carried out but Ernst managed to avoid it. Donning a military uniform, Ernst went on various missions around Budapest. He escorted Jews who were led on the streets and cooperated in saving them. During the last days of the war he served as a guard in front of the movement's building on Benczúr Street that was under the protection of the International Red Cross. After the war he continued with his activities for the movement. On his way to Eretz Israel (Palestine) he was taken to Cyprus by the British.

Fleischer András
Member of the "Shimoni Group"

Fleischer György
Member of the "Shimoni Group"

Fleischer Mordehai
Fleischer Pál
Born in Pozsony (Bratislava) on 29.6.1926
Member of "Hashomer Hatzair"

Mordehai went to elementary school and the Jewish high school in Bratislava. In 1941 due to the anti-Semitic decrees he had to interrupt his studies. He joined "Hashomer Hatzair" at the age of ten. In 1942 Mordehai crossed the border into Hungary, was caught and returned to Slovakia. In December of the same year he again tried to reach Hungary but was caught again and imprisoned. This time he was not returned to

Slovakia. He was released in the spring of 1943 and became active in the movement that operated underground in Hungary.

One day after the Germans invaded Hungary on 19.3.1944, Mordehai was told to save the contents of the movement's ken on József Boulevard in Budapest. On 14.4.1944 he was caught again and sent to different detention and forced labor camps. After the Szálasi coup on 15.10.1944 Mordehai escaped and met Moshe Alpan who took him into the underground activities. Among other things Mordehai escorted delivery carts to the ghetto, children's houses and other places.
After the liberation he worked as a translator in Russian and was the instructor of groups of children and youngsters. Mordehai took part in the revival of the movement.

In April 1946 he made aliya on the "Max Nordau" (Smirna) ship which was intercepted by the British and whose passengers were imprisoned in Atlit (Palestine). After his release from the camp, Mordehai stayed for a year in Kibbutz Ma'anit. The garin he was a member of founded Kibbutz Yassur. In the fall on 1947 he volunteered to an infantry unit of the Hagana, escorted convoys and was wounded. After his convalescence, he resumed his military service and took part in many battles. In 1951 he married Trudi.
The family left the kibbutz in 1952. Mordehai is an interior designer and lives in Givatayim.

Fleischer Trudi
Born in Pozsony (Bratislava) on 4.7.1929
Member of "Maccabi Hatzair"

In 1942 Trudi was smuggled by her parents from Slovakia to Budapest. She experienced many hardships as a refugee living under a false name. Trudi was arrested, released and moved from one place to another. With Peretz Révész' help she was added to the train of the Relief and Rescue Committee and, at the end of June 1944, she left Hungary. In September 1945 she made aliya. Trudi enlisted in the IDF and served for two years. In 1951 she married Mordi Fleischer. Between 1951 and 1952 they were members of Kibbutz Yassur. Trudi worked as a medical secretary. She resides in Givatayim.

Fodor Lajos
Friedlander Lajos
Born in Beregszász (Berehovo) in 1883
Perished in 1944
Member of the "Gordon Circle" and of "Hashomer Hatzair"

Lajos was a lawyer and a loyal friend of the "Hashomer Hatzair" movement from the 1930's. He served as the legal consultant for the movement and represented it at Zionist Congresses and in many other events. He was one of the founders of the "Borohov Circle". After the Germans invaded Hungary on 19.3.1944 he was arrested and all the efforts to rescue him failed. He was deported to Auschwitz where he perished. His children, Aladár and Éva made aliya.

Fodor Mordehai 'Mordi"
Fodor István
Born in Kassa (Košice) in 1921
Murdered in 1944
Member of "Hashomer Hatzair"

Mordi was an only child and a relative of the poet Avigdor Hame'iri. He was a member of the movement from an early age. He learned plumbing. Mordi moved to Budapest at the end of 1938 and joined the movement's leadership. He belonged to the Sela Organization. From 1942 he was active in giving assistance to the refugees arriving in Budapest from Slovakia and took part in the underground activities of his movement.
In 1943 Mordi returned to Kassa in order to witness the birth of his son from his wife, Malka Baumőhl. In Kassa he was enlisted in a forced labor unit which was sent to the copper mines in Bor, Yugoslavia where he perished probably in 1944. His wife and son Abraham were shot by the Germans in a forest near Kassa.

Fogel Dov
Fogel Béla
Born in Nagybocskó (Velikij Bicskiv) on 27.9.1927
Member of "Dror Habonim"

Dov arrived in Budapest during Passover of 1942. He met Asher Arni and joined the "Dror Habonim" movement. After the Germans invaded Hungary on 19.3.1944, he dug fortifications in the suburbs of Budapest.

In the fall of 1944 Asher Arni enlisted him in the underground activities of the movement. Dov supplied food and equipment to hiding places and bunkers. After the liberation he took part in finding and taking care of orphaned Jewish children. In 1946 Dov left Hungary and stayed in the Cyprus and Atlit (Palestine) camps. At the end of 1947 he arrived in Kibbutz Ein Harod within the framework of the "Gárdos" Group. He was among the founders of Kibbutz Parod. He wrote a book: "From My Father's House to Parod", 1993.

Foltyn Ella
Foltyn Elefánt Ella
Born in Lazony (Ložin), on 16.5.1922
Died in 2003
Member of "Hashomer Hatzair"

Ella's family lived in Varin (Várna) and later in Bazin (Pezinok). Her father was a dentist.
In 1942 thanks to her father's exemption certificate, Ella was saved from deportation. In 1944 she fled to Hungary. After the Germans invaded Hungary on 19.3.1944, Ella joined the underground and operated mainly as a liaison in the distribution of forged documents. She worked as a German speaking governess for a Bulgarian diplomat.

After the fascist Arrow Cross Party came to power on 15.10.1944, Ella engaged, under the false name of Rapos Mária, in moving Jewish children from the Budapest ghetto area to the children's houses that were set up under the protection of the International Red Cross and in taking care of them. Her brother, Moshe Pil-Alpan, was one of the most prominent underground activists.

After the liberation in January 1945, Ella travelled to Slovakia on a mission for the movement as a clerk of the new Slovak government. In Kassa (Košice) she took care of Jews who returned from concentration camps. From April of the same year she operated in Pozsony (Bratislava) assisting refugees. Ella made aliya in 1949. In 1952 she married Andrew Foltyn and emigrated to the USA.

Foren Ya'akov
Fried Jancsu
Born in Nagyszőllős (Vinohragyiv) on 27.5.1924
Died on 16.11.1999
Member of "Hashomer Hatzair"

Ya'akov became a member of the movement in the late 1930's. After the Germans invaded Hungary on 19.3.1944, he set up a hiding place in his town's ghetto where he hid for three months. When he left his hiding place, he was caught, moved to Beregszász (Berehove) and then to the Mosonyi prison in Budapest. He was freed and arrived in the "Glass House". Ya'akov joined the underground activities and distributed forged documents. After the liberation he was sent to Transylvania in order to rehabilitate the movement.
Ya'akov made aliya and joined Kibbutz Ga'aton.

Fraenkel Avraham
Samuel Benjamin
Fraenkel Jenő
Born in Kisvárda on 4.1.1897
Died in 1986
Member of "Mizrahi"

Avraham fought in WW I with the Austro-Hungarian army with the rank of junior officer. After his discharge from the army he joined the Zionist movement. He started to study medicine but was forced to stop due to the anti-Semitic decrees. He joined the Zionist student union "Maccabea" and later the "Mizrahi" movement. He held high positions in those movements.
From 1943 Avraham gave assistance to Jewish refugees arriving in Budapest. After the Germans invaded Hungary on 19.3.1944, he was arrested by the Gestapo with his wife and his eldest son. His son was released with Kasztner's help whereas Avraham and his wife were set free by Pinhas Rosenbaum and his comrades, members of "Bnei Akiva" wearing the fascist Arrow Cross uniform. Avraham was transferred to the "Glass House" on 29, Vadász Street and served there as a member of the management.
After the liberation he recruited people for aliya. In 1946 Avraham took part in the 22nd Zionist Congress in Basel. In 1948 he made aliya but was asked to return to Hungary in order to lead the movement. He

was arrested by the communists, freed and after a year and a half he returned to Israel.

Fraenkel Gabi
Born in Budapest in 1923
Member of "Dror Habonim"

At the age of fifteen, in Újpest, Gabi joined the "Dror" movement which after some time became "Dror Habonim". As refugees started arriving from Poland and Slovakia, he was operating in Miskolc where he helped in their absorption and obtained accommodation and food for them.
After the Germans invaded Hungary on 19.3.1944, Gabi became an underground activist obtaining Aryan papers and distributing forged documents. He was enlisted in a forced labor unit near Budapest and, while serving there, he still distributed the forged documents to his comrades and traveled to country towns to help the Jews and convince them to escape. When it was found out that his unit was being transferred to a location far from Budapest, Gabi ran away from the forced labor camp. He crossed the border into Romania within the framework of the tiyul.
Gabi made aliya in August 1944. He stayed at the hahshara in Kfar Szold and in Kvutzat Kinneret. In 1947 he was among the settlers of Ein Zeitim.
Gabi fought in the War of Independence and in 1952 settled down in Moshav Ben Ami.

Fraenkel Joel
Born in Budapest in 1925
Fell in the War of Independence in the battle for the Latrun police station
Member of "Dror Habonim"

Joel was a member of the movement in Újpest from the 1940's. He learned tanning and stayed at a "Dror Habonim" hahshara. He gave assistance to refugees, members of the movement, who arrived in Budapest. After the Germans invaded Hungary, Joel was enlisted in a forced labor unit and sent to occupied Yugoslavia. After the liberation he made aliya, joined a garin and took part in the establishment of Ein Zetim. During the War of Independence Joel fought in the Ramat-Yohanan and Haifa battles. He fell in the battle for the Latrun police station. He is buried in the Har HaMenuhot cemetery in Jerusalem.

Fraenkel Lili 'Ahuva'
Born in Brassó (Brašov) in 1906
Died in 1958
Member of "Mizrahi"

Lili was one of the prominent women activists of "Mizrahi". In 1930 she married Avraham Shmuel Benjamin Fraenkel. During the Holocaust she assisted refugees from Poland and Slovakia. Lili was arrested by the Gestapo with her husband and their eldest son. In prison she shared a cell with Hanna Szenes. After the liberation she continued with her Zionist activities. She made aliya.

Fraenkel Mordehai
Fraenkel Miklós
Born in Kisvárda in 1923
Member of "Hashomer Hatzair"

Mordehai's family lived in Kisvárda. His father was a learned person and a Zionist activist. Mordehai joined the movement at an early age. He learned mechanical locksmith's work. He moved to Budapest and, from 1942, assisted in the absorption of refugees, members of the movement, from Slovakia. He lived in a commune of the Sela organization. In 1944 Mordehai enlisted in a forced labor unit but after a while he escaped and arrived back in Budapest. After the Germans invaded Hungary on 19.3.1944, he went underground. Due to an informer he was arrested and taken to the Sárvár camp. The attempts of his comrades in the movement to rescue him failed and eventually Mordehai was deported and stayed at various concentration camps. Thanks to his professional skills he managed to survive. After the liberation he returned to Budapest, resumed his activities for the movement and in 1947-1948 he was an instructor in a Hagana training camp in Hungary. He made aliya in October 1948 with his wife Miriam Fleischman and joined Kibbutz Ga'aton. Later he left the kibbutz and lives now in Kiriyat Tivon.

Fraenkel Shmuel
Fraenkel Sándor
Born in Kisvárda in 1918
Died in 1990
Member of "Hashomer Hatzair"

Shmuel studied at the Jewish high school in Munkács. In 1939 he was drafted in the Hungarian army and, at the end of his service in 1941, he was enlisted in forced labor unit that was sent to Ukraine. In 1943 due to an illness, he was sent back to Hungary and joined the movement's activities.

After the Germans invaded Hungary on 19.3.1944, he went on missions to country towns in order the help Jews escape from the ghetto. He arrived in his hometown, went into the ghetto and managed to say goodbye to his parents who were not willing to take the risk of escaping.
In May 1944 Shmuel moved to Romania within the framework of the tiyul.
He made aliya and arrived in Kibbutz Ma'anit. In his last years he worked in the Givat Haviva archives.

Freiman Avigdor 'Andi'
Freiman András
Born in Kassa (Košice) on 23.9.1922
Died on 4.1.1945
Member of "Beitar"

Andi was the commander of "Beitar" in Hungary. Until the German invasion he took part in the smuggling of Jews from Poland and Slovakia to Budapest.
In March 1944 Andi arrived in the Hungarian capital and immediately started organizing underground cells among the members of his movement. He organized the delivery of forged documents to members of "Beitar" in the country towns. He met the comrades who arrived in Budapest and integrated them in the underground activities. Avigdor prepared shelters and obtained weapons and food.

In April 1944 he was caught with his friend Mendel. They were both taken back to Kassa and added to the thousands of Jews who were to be deported. Andi managed to escape but his friend was sent to Auschwitz.

Andi returned to Budapest and resumed his underground activities. On June 8th he married his girlfriend, Ági. In May he was caught again and imprisoned in the Gestapo headquarters on Schwabs Hill in Buda. From there too he managed to escape after ten days through a prison window. He made contact with the underground of the Hungarian Communist Party and received from them a weapon that was used in the defense of the bunkers. Avigdor was caught a third time with his wife but they both managed to escape. He took an active part in the establishment of bunkers in various parts of the city.

Towards the end of 1944 he and Ági moved to the "Glass House" on 29, Vadász Street. Prior to the liberation of Budapest Andi caught scarlet fever and at the end of December he was transferred to Kőbányai Fertőző Kórház (The Kőbánya Hospital for Contagious Diseases) located in the tenth district. He Red Army conquered the hospital on 2.1.1945 and Andy died in the hospital two days after the Red Army invaded this part of the city on 4.1.1945.

Freiman Tzvi
Freiman Tamás
Born in Kassa (Košice) on 22.11.1926
Member of "Beitar"

In April 1944 Tzvi arrived in Budapest with forged documents he had received from his brother who was the commander of the movement. He prepared forged documents and distributed them. He worked as a photographer and lived in a bunker of the movement in the building of the Institute of Technology in Budapest. Later he moved to the bunker on Hungary Boulevard. Together with his friend, Róbert Offner, he registered in the fascist Arrow Cross Party and received official documents. As an Arrow Cross man he took part in the eviction of Jews from the Protected Houses.

Towards the end of the war Tzvi stayed at the "Glass House" on 29, Vadász Street.
In 1949 he made aliya with his wife, Magdalena Schlesinger. In 1952 he emigrated to Canada.

Friedman Avigdor 'Viki'-Yitzhak

Friedman Viktor
Born in Halmaj in 1914
Died in Jerusalem in 1982
Member of "Mizrahi"

Viki studied at Rabbi Austerlitz's yeshiva in Miskolc and joined the Zionist activities within the framework of "Mizrahi". He moved to Budapest and from 1944 he dedicated all his energy to rescue operations. Viki went on missions to Kassa. From July 1944 he was one of the twenty-four employees at the "Glass House". He distributed Protection Documents (Schutzpass) on the "Death March". After the liberation he continued his public work.
Viki made aliya. In 1951 he joined the administrative staff of the Hadassah Hospital in Jerusalem.

Friedmann David

Friedmann Dezső 'Dévi'
Born in Kassa (Košice) on 10.2.1921
Member of "Bnei Akiva"

In addition to studying at elementary and high school, David strived to learn Hebrew. When he was in the third grade, following the steps of his brother Meir, he joined the "Bnei Akiva" movement. He stayed at a hahshara in Miskolc, moved to Budapest and became a member of the movement's leadership.
After the Germans invaded Hungary on 19.3.1944, he started his underground activities according to the rules decided upon by the leadership:
1) not to cooperate with the Jewish Council established by the Germans; 2) not to wear the yellow star; 3) to use forged documents; 4) to move house frequently; 5) to find hiding places in time; 6) to work in the organization of the escape to Romania (tiyul) and from there to Eretz Israel (Palestine).
During a meeting in a park to organize the smuggling of Jews across the border, David and his comrade, David Asael, were arrested, imprisoned and interrogated. After some time they managed to escape. David resumed his activities and continued to deal with rescue operations. His parents and brother were also in Budapest. On 31.12.1944 two Arrow Cross men broke into his parents' apartment and took them to an unknown place.

They were probably shot on the bank of the Danube.
Some months after the liberation David arrived in Eretz Israel (Palestine), stayed at Wilhelma, Gat Rimon and Hadid. He married Tzipora Magda Hirschfeld. From 1950 and for 36 years David managed the children's Institute "Neve Michael". He lives in Jerusalem.

Pridan Moshe
Friedman Imre
Born in Kassa (Košice) in 1926
Member of "Beitar"

After the German invasion of Hungary on 19.3.1944, Moshe joined the underground rescue operations but was caught due to an informer who was a refugee he had helped. He was taken to the Gestapo headquarters on Schwabs Hill in Buda and interrogated for two weeks. Moshe was then transferred to the central prison in Budapest and from there to the concentration camp of non-Jewish Hungarians in Sárvár. Following an SS inspection visit of the camp, it was found that Jews were also being detained there. They were sent to Auschwitz. Moshe stayed in Auschwitz for about a month until he was sent to the Moldorf camp in Germany. He was liberated by the American army on 1.5.1945. He returned to his hometown and found out that his whole family had perished in Auschwitz.
In May 1948 Moshe made aliya and enlisted in the IDF where he served in the Intelligence. He was demobilized with the rank of captain.
For about thirty years Moshe worked for the Israeli television. He lives in Ra'anana.

Friedmann Meir
Friedmann Tibor
Born in Halmaj in 1925
Member of "Bnei Akiva"

After the Germans invaded Hungary, Meir was taken to the ghetto, escaped and arrived in Budapest. He made contact with members of his movement, equipped himself with forged documents and joined the underground activities. In October 1944 he arrived at the "Glass

House". After the liberation in 1945 he continued with his work for the movement and with the aliya of youngsters. At the beginning of 1950 he arrived in Israel. He was a lawyer approved for trials. He filled high positions in the Finance Ministry of the Israeli government and in private companies. He also volunteered for public work, especially in the field of education.

Fröhlinger Yitzhak
`Kis Tokaj`
Born in Tokaj in 1928
Member of "Bnei Akiva"

Yitzhak was an underground activist and a member of "mi-ha" (a hahshara for teenagers). He moved to Romania on a tiyul. After the liberation Yitzhak returned to Hungary. He made aliya in 1946. He owned an electric appliances shop in Tel-Aviv.

Fuksz Braha
Bilitzer Etel
Born in Debrecen in 1916
Died on 9.9.2004
Member of "Hanoar Hatzioni"

Braha graduated from Jewish high school in Debrecen and started to study nursing. She continued these studies in Budapest and became a certified nurse. She worked in the operating room of the Jewish hospital in the capital. Braha was a member of the movement both in Debrecen and in Budapest. In May 1944 she worked as a servant in a villa near the bunker set up by her comrades in the hilly part of Budapest. Food for the Szeplőshegy bunker was stored in her room. Braha was a member of the movement's leadership. From June she operated in Mérleg Street, obtained authentic seals and prepared forged documents for the young Jews who wanted to escape from forced labor units. In October she joined Department A of the International Red Cross on József Boulevard which was managed by her brother, Adonyahu-Dezső Bilitzer. Braha supplied documents and money to the deserters from forced labor units.
Braha made aliya in 1946 with her husband Shlomo Fuksz. She joined Kibbutz Kfar Glücksohn, moved to Pardes Hanna and later to Be'ersheva.

Funk Arie
Funk Lajos
Born in Csökmő in 1920
Perished in Auschwitz in 1944
Member of "Hashomer Hatzair"

Arie became a member of the movement at the beginning of 1940 and in 1941 he joined the Sela Organization within whose framework he went to a hahshara. After the hahshara was closed, he worked in construction. Arie gave assistance to refugees arriving in Hungary from Slovakia and Poland. After Simha Hunwald, one of the movement's leaders, was caught with other comrades at the end of February 1942, Arie was also sent to a detention camp in Garany. He managed to get released and together with his friend, Judith Scharf (Hartman), he was added to the tiyul to Romania. Both of them were caught on the train. Judith was incarcerated in the Mosonyi prison in Budapest and from there deported to Auschwitz. Arie was taken to the town of Szolnok where the local Jews and Jews from nearby small towns were concentrated and among them his family members. In Szolnok Arie was humiliated and tortured in public and sent with all the Jews to Auschwitz.

Füredi Avri
Füredi István 'Fábri'
Born in Nyíregyháza in 1922
Fell in battle on 27.3.1948
Member of "Hashomer Hatzair"

Avri was an only child. His father was a lawyer and the family was learned and assimilated. Avri was a member of "Hashomer Hatzair" from 1939. He moved to Budapest in 1941. Within the framework of the movement Avri was a member of the "Hebrew Circle" whose members' ambition was to speak Hebrew only. He was a highly cultivated man and possessed leadership skills. He excelled in the field of music as well. In 1942 with the arrival of refugees from Slovakia, Avri was among the first to engage in helping them. He was caught with three comrades and sent to the Garany detention camp. Eventually there were fifteen "Hashomer Hatzair" activists in this camp.
Avri made aliya in 1946 and was a member of the "Ehad BeMay" garin within whose framework he stayed in Kibbutz Ma'anit and Kibbutz Yassur. During the War of Independence he enlisted in the Hagana. He

was sent to escort convoys in the North and to bring the illegal immigrants from the ships to the shore. He fought in various places in the North. He fell in the "Yehiam Convoy" on 27.3.1948 with 46 of his friends as a soldier in battalion 21 of the Carmeli brigade.

Fürszt-Komoly Lea
Born in Veröce (Viroticia) in 1921
Member of "Maccabea" and "Hatzionim Haclali'im"

Lea's family returned to Budapest in 1924. Her father, Nathan Komoly, was the president of the Hungarian Zionist Association from 1940 to 1944, and from 1941 he was the chairman of the Relief and Rescue Committee. Lea took part in underground help activities from the building of the Jewish community on 12, Síp Street. She was sent on behalf of her father on missions with government authorities and foreign legations. Lea distributed the "Auschwitz Report", that was translated into various languages, and which she translated into Hungarian in cooperation with Sarah Friedlander, including testimonies of what was happening in the extermination camp. Lea left Hungary on the train of the Relief and Rescue Committee and arrived in Switzerland. She made aliya in 1946 and married the engineer Fürszt. She worked as a librarian at the Tel-Aviv University and at "Beit Ariella". Lea resides in Tel-Aviv.

Futó-Galambos Sándor
Goldstein Sándor
Born in Debrecen in 1909
Died in 1963
Communist

In 1929 Sándor arrived in Antwerpen, Belgium, on his way to South-America as an emigrant. He remained in Antwerpen and made contact with the local workers' movement. In 1931 he was accepted in the Hungarian section of the communist party in Antwerpen. Sándor was arrested, imprisoned for a year and deported to Paris. In 1935 he returned to Belgium, was arrested and sent back to Hungary. Although he was under police surveillance, he was active in the trade unions and a member of the social-democrat party. In 1936 he organized volunteers for the civil war in Spain and operated in the industrial suburbs of the capital.

After the Germans invaded Hungary on 19.3.1944, Sándor served as the liaison between the central committee of the underground communist party and the "Hashomer Hatzair" movement. These connections led to cooperation in the supply of forged documents from the "Hashomer Hatzair" side, and the finding of shelters for young Jews from the other side. After the liberation in January 1945, Sándor held various management positions in the new Hungarian regime.

Gal Ya'akov
Grünberger Jenő
Born in Geszt on 27.4.1923
Died on 14.1.1977
Member of "Hashomer Hatzair"

When he was five years old, Ya'akov's family moved to Miskolc. His brother, Miki, was a leader in "Hashomer Hatzair" and Ya'akov followed his steps by joining the movement. After the German invasion of Hungary on 19.3.1944, he was enlisted in a forced labour unit, deserted and arrived in the "Glass House" on Vadász Street. Ya'akov took part in the underground activities, ran various errands and escorted food convoys for the children's houses that were under the auspices of the International Red Cross. He joined a group of people under the command of Natan Alexander who moved to the basement of the building next to the "Glass House" with weapons in order, if necessary, to defend the Jews who found refuge there. After the liberation, Ya'akov returned to Miskolc and reopened the "Hashomer Hatzair" ken. In 1948 he made aliya with his girlfriend Edo within the framework of the "Ehad BeMay" garin. Their oldest daughter was born in Italy. Ya'akov took part in the conquest of Acco during the War of Independence. He was among the founders of Kibbutz Yassur.

Dr. Galor Eliyahu
Dr. Gellért Endre
Born in Budapest in 1917
Died in 1997
Member of "Hatzionim Haclali'im" and "Maccabea"

Eliyahu studied at the Jewish high school and in the department of humanities at university. He received his teaching diploma in 1939 in Budapest. As early as 1934 he joined the "Maccabea" movement and was an active member. Before the German occupation on 19.3.1944, Eliyahu helped refugees from Poland and Slovakia find refuge. After the German invasion, he worked from the "Glass House". He engaged in preparing lists of Jews and Protection Documents and taking them to their destination, mainly to the Yellow Star houses. In addition, Eliyahu supplied food to the Jews in the ghetto and often visited them endangering his own life. He took people out of the ghetto while posing as a representative of the Swiss Embassy. After the liberation Eliyahu was the manager of the Education Department of the Jewish Community in Budapest and made sure that a Zionist spirit and the Hebrew language were taught in the Jewish institutions.

Between 1950 and 1955 he was an official in the Israeli legation in Budapest.

Eliyahu made aliya in 1955, was a teacher, a publicist and did public work.

Gárdos Johanan

Gárdos Gyula
Born in Kecskemét in 1920
Member of "Hashomer Hatzair"

Johanan's family was traditional and liberal leaning towards socialism. His father was a follower of Béla Kun and in 1919 carried out a communist regime that was crushed. His father was arrested and did time in prison.

In 1924, after his father was released from prison, the family moved to Bratislava. At the age of fifteen Johanan joined the movement.

From 1939 to 1941 he was a member of the central leadership of the movement and spent some time in a hahshara. With the beginning of the deportations from Slovakia he went underground.

In 1942 Johanan moved to Hungary and took part in the underground activities. At this time he met Lea, his future wife.

In 1943 he succeeded in making aliya in a legal way escorting a group of adolescents who had received the authorization to leave Hungary.

Johanan joined Kibbutz Ha'ogen and has been a member ever since.

Gárdos Joseph

Gárdos József
Born in Újpest in June 1921
Died in Hungary in 1945
Member of "Dror Habonim"

Joseph came from an assimilated Jewish environment. He joined the movement in the 1930's. From an early age he was an instructor and teacher for the younger members. At the age of fourteen Joseph already edited the movement's newspaper. As the refugees from Slovakia started arriving, he met them and took care of them. Some of them he accommodated in his own flat. He helped some refugees find work and others to continue their voyage to Eretz Israel (Palestine). After the German invasion of Hungary on 19.3.1944, Joseph walked around under the fictitious identity of a generations long Christian and later as a citizen of San Salvador. He took part in the rescue of young Jews from the forced labour camps and persuaded Jews to run away from the transports to Poland.

Joseph managed to penetrate the ghettos of Munkács and Huszt carrying forged documents which he gave to the relatives of comrades in the movement. He took part in the planning of the tiyul. He arrived in Arad in Romania, made contact with smugglers and set up "stations" on the route of the fugitives.

After the liberation Joseph returned to Hungary, and took part in setting up children's homes and the revival of the movement. He was in charge of educational activities. At that time he was already very ill but continued his activities until his last day. Kibbutz Gardosh-Parod was named after him.

Gárdos Lea

Tischler Friderika
Born in Hajdudorog on 10.5.1919
Member of "Hashomer Hatzair"

Lea joined "Hashomer Hatzair" at the age of sixteen. She lived in Budapest from 1940 and took part in the activities of the movement. In 1942 she met her future husband, Johanan.

Upon his arrival in Eretz Israel (Palestine), Johanan, who made aliya in a legal way escorting a group of adolescents who had received the authorization to leave Hungary, gave her name and address to Menahem

Bader. Her name was given because due to the movement's illegality it could not have an official address. From then on Lea served as an address for the transfer of money and letters to the movement. She gave forged documents to comrades in the forced labour units.

In the summer of 1944 Lea left Hungary equipped with an authentic Bulgarian passport and sailed to Eretz Israel (Palestine) on the "Bulbul". She joined Kibbutz Ha'ogen and has been a member ever since.

Gedaljevics Avraham
Born in Irhóc (Vilhivci) on 23.1.1923
Died on 30.5.1961
Member of "Dror Habonim"

Avraham was a mason and planned the bunkers that were dug in February and March 1944 by members of the movement in the Máramaros district. He was killed in a car accident in Hungary in 1961.

Gedaljevics Yitzhak
Born in Irhóc (Vilhivci) on 15.7.1925
Member of "Dror Habonim"

Yitzhak belonged to the "Dror Habonim" group that built bunkers in the Máramaros area in February and March 1944.

Gerson Asher 'Bubi'
Gerson Áser
Born in Toplica (Topliţa Mureşului)
Died in 1943
Member of "Hashomer Hatzair"

From an early age Asher was a member of the Marosvásárhely (Tárgu Mureş) ken of the movement. He became the head of the ken and a member of the central leadership in Transylvania. During the Romanian rule over the area Asher was active in the Aliya Bet, was caught, put on trial and imprisoned. In 1941 he was enlisted in a forced labour unit. Asher perished in Ukraine.

Golan Aharon
Glantz
Born in Huszt in 1922
Member of "Dror Habonim"

In May 1944 Aharon received mobilization orders for a forced labor unit but succeeded to avoid them and arrived in Budapest. Equipped with forged documents, he took part in underground activities. Four members, one of whom was Aharon, accompanied by Moshe Alpan, took the train to the Romanian border within the framework of the tiyul. Three of them were caught and only Aharon and Moshe Alpan managed to escape. Aharon crossed the border into Romania.
In August 1944 Aharon arrived in Eretz Israel (Palestine). He was a member of Kibbutz Kfar Szold. He now resides in Rehovot.

Golan (Fettmann) Haim
Fettmann Imre
Born in Nyirbátor on 12.7.1926
Member of "Hashomer Hatzair"

At an early age Haim joined his two brothers, Yeshaiyahu and Joseph, who were members of the local ken of the movement. In 1943 he moved to Budapest, worked as a watchmaker and took part in the activities of the movement.
On 19.3.1944, the day the Germans invaded Hungary, following instructions from the movement, Haim went underground. He obtained authentic Christian documents at the offices of the Population Registry. After ghettos were set up in the country towns, Haim was sent to Debrecen with a bagful of money and forged documents for his comrades in the movement. Five girls managed to reach the capital. Donning a "Levente" uniform, he was sent with his brother Yeshaiyahu to take his parents and sisters out of the Nyirbátor ghetto and bring them back to Budapest. However, they refused to leave and eventually were deported to Auschwitz.
Haim was supposed to cross the border into Romania within the framework

of the tiyul but instead, in June 1944, he left Budapest on the train of the Relief and Rescue Committee and arrived in Switzerland.

In September 1945 he legally made aliya. Haim served for thirty years in the Israel Defense Forces in the armored corps and the supply corps. He was discharged with the rank of brigadier general in 1978. He was then appointed as head of the purchasing and production department in the Ministry of Defense and for five years was head of the purchasing delegation in France.

Haim resides in Ramat-Gan.

Golan (Fettmann) Joseph

Fettmann József
Born in Nyirbátor in 1920
Died in 1995
Member of "Hashomer Hatzair"

Joseph studied in a Yeshiva. In 1937 he founded the local ken of "Hashomer Hatzair".

In 1941 Joseph moved to Budapest. In 1942 he took part in the organization and absorption of Slovak refugees who were members of the movement.

In 1943 Joseph was enlisted in a forced labour camp. He was freed in Vienna in 1945 while hospitalized with typhus. When he returned to Budapest, he became a central activist in the "Borohov Circle" (the political entity identified with "Hashomer Hatzair").

Joseph made aliya. He was a journalist for the "Lamerhav" and "Davar" newspapers and the spokesman for the "Histadrut" and the Tel-Aviv Municipality.

Golani Dov

Glanz
Born in Huszt in 1927
Member of "Dror Habonim"

Dov arrived in Budapest in 1942 and started to learn carpentry. He lived with another five youngsters who were members of "Hehalutz Hatzair", later 'Dror'. He assisted in the absorption of refugees arriving in the capital from Poland and the Carpatho-Ruthenia region. Following the German occupation of Hungary on 19.3.1944, Dov used forged Aryan documents and took part in a variety of underground activities. He built bunkers, organized the escape route to the Romanian border (the tiyul), supplied forged documents and was a liaison person for the members of the underground.

At the end of June 1944 he left Hungary on the train of the Relief and Rescue Committee and, via Bergen-Belsen, he arrived in Switzerland. From there he arrived in Eretz Israel (Palestine)where he joined a group of Aliyat Hanoar in Kibbutz Daphna. Dov was one of the founders of Kibbutz Parod. Later he moved to Kibbutz Givat Brenner. He was drafted and served in the army for two years. Dov fought in the War of Independence.

Dov resides in Kfar Daniel. He is married to Shlomit and they have four children and four grandchildren.

Goldberger Miriam
Scheer Ibolya
Born in Tiszafüred in 1922
Member of "Hashomer Hatzair"

At the age of ten Miriam moved to the city of Debrecen and joined the "Hashomer Hatzair" movement. In 1939 her father's license for a tobacco shop (which he was granted for being an invalid of the First World War) was cancelled and the family moved to Budapest. She was an underground activist for the movement. After the German occupation on 19.3.1944, her husband Yaacov was arrested at his workplace. With the help of the movement Miriam managed to rescue him from the military prison on Margit Boulevard. After hiding for a few days, equipped with forged documents provided by the movement, Miriam and her husband succeeded in crossing the border into Romania while taking with them six children aged 5-6, refugees from Poland, as well as two young boys aged seventeen from the Carpatho-Ruthenia region who did not speak Hungarian. All the way to Bucharest the couple took care of the children giving them medical care, clothes and food.
Miriam made aliya in 1944 and is a member of Kibbutz Ha'ogen. She was a central figure on the kibbutz and in the Kibbutz Artzi institutions.

Goldberger Yaakov
Goldberger Ottó
Born in Kassa (Košice) in 1919
Member of "Hashomer Hatzair"

Yaakov was a member of the "Maccabi" sports association as a pupil, instructor, manager and gymnast. From 1938 he was among the leaders of his movement. In 1939 Yaakov moved to Budapest. He was enlisted in a forced labor unit in the fall of 1940 and released at the end of 1943. On 5.4.1944, after the German invasion, Yaakov was arrested at his workplace and sent to the military prison on Margit Boulevard. In July of the same year he was released but was mobilized for forced labor. Members of his movement equipped him with forged documents and, with his wife, Miriam, he was smuggled into Romania. Ya'akov and Miriam took with them six children aged 5-6, refugees from Poland, as well as two young boys aged seventeen from the Carpatho-Ruthenia region who did not speak Hungarian.
 In November 1944 he made aliya and is a member of Kibbutz Ha'ogen. Ya'akov was a central figure on the kibbutz and in the Kibbutz Artzi institutions.

Goldfarb Neshka
Szandel Ágnes
Born in Tiszabogdány (Bohdan) in 1921
Died on 1.2.2000
Member of "Dror Habonim"

Neshka came from a religious Jewish family. Her father was a Hasid and a reader of prayers in the synagogue. She was orphaned at an early age. Although the Hassidic currents were predominant in the village, Zionism was not banned. Emissaries from Eretz Israel (Palestine), Mordehai Caspi and Shlomo Lipsky, set up a ken of "Hehalutz Hatzair" (which later became "Dror Habonim") in the village and Neshka, aged fifteen, joined the movement. She stayed in hahsharot in preparation for her aliya. In 1939 she and her friends in the hahshara were surprised by Hungarian policemen and taken to Budapest. In the Hungarian capital they were detained for four days and then sent back to their village. In 1940 Neshka left the family home again and arrived in Budapest where the Zionist youth movement was already outlawed. Neshka and her friends lived in a commune. In 1941 she met Jewish refugees from

Poland and, from them, she learned about the deportation of Jews. She devoted herself to helping them.

In 1943 she met Tzvi Goldfarb, who had arrived in Hungary after an eleven month stay in Slovakia. From then on they worked together and did not part. In 1943 Neshka was sent by the movement to the Carpatho-Ruthenia region in order to warn the Jews of the dangers of fascism and to set up new kenim of the movement. After the German occupation of Hungary on 19.3.1944, Neshka was a prominent activist in the underground and stood out for her wisdom and courage. She was engaged in a great variety of activities and missions. On one of her operations she was caught, together with Tzvi and other comrades, interrogated, brutally tortured but did not reveal her secrets. Neshka was sent to the military prison on Margit Boulevard, which was the main military prison in Budapest, then to the Sopronkőhida prison, and again to Margit Boulevard. She was liberated thanks to a daring rescue operation of the Zionist youth movements underground. After the liberation in January 1945, Tzvi and Neshka worked on the rehabilitation of the movement, took care of the remaining refugees and of the orphanages where hundreds of Jewish children found refuge.

In 1949 Neshka made aliya with her husband and was one of the founders of Kibbutz Parod. Her son, Uri, was killed in the Yom Kippur War. Four years later, Tzvi also passed away. Neshka died in 2000.

Goldfarb Tzvi
Goldfarb Cvi
Born in Biala Podlaska (Poland) in 1921
Died in 1977
Member of "Dror Habonim"

Tzvi was one of the outstanding figures of the Zionist youth movements underground in Hungary. He came from an ultra-orthodox family and studied in a Heder and later in a Yeshiva. He joined the "Dror" movement. In 1942 Tzvi was sent by the movement to Slovakia in order to warn the Jews of what to expect from the fascists and to plan resistance and rescue operations. About a year later he moved to Hungary. In the Hungarian capital Tzvi operated under various fictitious identities, as a refugee from the Carpatho-Ruthenia region and as an Italian tourist. Owing to his personality and experience, he became the leader of the movement. Together with friends he smuggled Jews over the Romanian border within the framework of the tiyul, underwent weapons training, set up bunkers and liberated Jews from forced labor camps and prisons. Tzvi Goldfarb was one of the central figures in all these activities. He worked with his friend Neshka Szandel who was to become his wife. During one of the operations Tzvi, Neshka, Vili Eisikovics and other comrades were caught. They were imprisoned, brutally tortured and finally liberated by a daring operation of members of the Zionist youth movements underground from the main military prison on Margit Boulevard. After the liberation, Tzvi and Neshka devoted themselves to caring for the remaining refugees and the organization of orphanages and to taking children to Eretz Israel (Palestine). In 1949 they made aliya and were among the founders of Kibbutz Parod. Their son, Uri, was killed in the Yom Kippur War. Tzvi passed away four years later.

Goldstein Erzsi
Born in Pozsony (Bratislava), in 1927
Member of "Hashomer Hatzair"

In 1943, Erzsi arrived in Budapest with forged documents. Yitzhak Herbst (Mimish) helped her integrate the movement and its underground activities. Following the German occupation of Hungary on 19.3.1944, Erzsi acted as a liaison officer for the members in the underground, supplying them with documents and instructions. For a certain period of time, Erzsi and two other young women kept safe six suitcases containing equipment for the underground laboratory which produced forged documents. Upon liberation in 1945, Erzsi returned to Bratislava where she attended medical school.
Erzsi lives probably in Slovakia.

Goldstein Peretz
Goldstein Ferenc
Born in Lugos (Lugoj) on 14.7.1923
Paratrooper
Perished in Germany in 1944

In 1933 Peretz's family moved to Kolozsvár. In 1937 Peretz joined the "Habonim" movement (Scout halutz youth).
In 1941 he made aliya with Aliyat Hanoar and lived in Kibbutz Afikim for two years. Peretz then joined Kibbutz Kinneret - Kibbutz Ma'agan as a member of the Transylvanian garin. At the end of 1942 he was enlisted in the Palmah and at the beginning of 1943 he volunteered for

a paratrooper mission to occupied Europe. Both at home and in Cairo Peretz went through the selection, practice and training stages.

On 15.4.1944 Peretz, Joel Palgi and two British military men jumped over North Yugoslavia, an area that was under the control of Tito's partisans. On 6.5.1944 he met with his fellow paratroopers from Eretz Israel, Yona Rozen, Hana Szenes, Reuven Daphni and Aba Berdichev who also parachuted on Yugoslav land. Together they arrived at the headquarters of the sixth corps of the partisans in the Papok Mountains. On 19.6.1944 Peretz and Joel Palgi crossed the Drava River and arrived in Hungary. From the day they crossed the border, the Hungarian counter-espionage followed them. Joel and Peretz reached Budapest within a day. First they met Dr. Israel Kasztner, one of the leaders of the Relief and Rescue Committee, and then members of the Zionist youth movements underground.

They were both arrested by the Hungarian police: Joel Palgi on June 27th and Peretz on July 1st. The Germans demanded that the Hungarians hand over the two paratroopers to them and on September 11th Peretz was taken to the Gestapo prison in Fő Street. From there he was transferred to the central military prison on Margit Boulevard in Budapest where Joel Palgi and Hana Szenes were also being detained.

Peretz was interrogated and tortured but did neither reveal any secret information nor the objective of his mission.

As the Red Army was approaching the Hungarian capital, Peretz was transferred to the Komárom prison and from there, on 8.12.1944, to the German city of Oranienburg, north of Berlin. He did forced labor in the Heinkel factory that built planes.

Joel Palgi managed to jump off the train and to return to Budapest where he found refuge with members of the underground until the liberation. The plane factory was bombarded by the allied forces and Peretz was probably killed.

Goldstein Shoshanna
Roth Ágnes
Born in Budapest on 3.1.1924
Member of "Hashomer Hatzair"

Following the German occupation of Hungary on 19.3.1944, Shoshanna engaged in obtaining authentic documents in the offices of the Population Registry in the Hungarian capital. After a friend, Avri Lissauer, was caught, she was afraid her real identity was discovered and she had to flee from one place to another with forged documents. Shoshanna left Hungary at the end of June 1944 on the train of the Relief and Rescue Committee.

In 1945 she made aliya and arrived in Kibbutz Negba which she left in 1946. Shoshanna resides in Ramat Gan.

Goren Herta
Schwartz Herta
Born in Pozsony (Bratislava) in 1931
Member of "Dror Habonim"

In 1942 Herta fled to Budapest with her family as refugees from Slovakia. That same year Herta joined the "Dror" movement whose members equipped her and her family with forged documents and helped them to survive in the Hungarian capital. After the German invasion of Hungary on 19.3.1944, although she was only thirteen, Herta ran various errands for the Zionist youth movements underground. She was sent to meeting places to hand out forged documents and give news. Herta visited bunkers of the movement while carrying a schoolbag. At a later stage she stayed in the bunker on Hungary Boulevard in Budapest. The bunker was discovered and its dwellers fell into the hands of the fascists. Herta was imprisoned and served as a nurse in a military hospital. She was liberated by members of the movement.
Herta lives in Israel.

Greenstein Jean
Grünstein Jenő 'Icu'
Born in Nagyszőllős on 9.7.1924
Non-affiliated

There were six brothers in his family. Jean's father was a dentist. At the time of the German invasion into Hungary (19.3.1944) he stayed in Nagyszőllős. In April, when the Jews were concentrated in the local ghetto, Jean and some of his friends decided to set up a hideout in the mountains. Following the draft of his comrades to forced labor units, the plan was altered and a hiding place was prepared in a basement within the ghetto, where Jancsu Fried (Ya'acov Paran), his sister Ilonka, and Tuli Rosenberg (Anton Roland) found refuge together with Icu. After a few weeks, in August, they all left the basement only to find the entire ghetto abandoned. They were caught by patrolling soldiers who handed them over to the gendarmerie. On their way by train via Kassa to Budapest, Icu managed to jump out of the window but was caught again and transferred to Tolonchάz, where he met his three comrades. He escaped and arrived at the Jewish Community building on 12, Síp Street. Following Adonyahu Bilitzer's advice, he identified himself as a refugee of Schwab (German) origin and joined a German military unit. While wearing the German uniform, he went on various missions, and rescued Jews, mainly women and children, from deportation. He escorted them to the Spanish legation where he met Perlasca, Spain's chargé d'affaires of Italian origin. On the day of liberation (18.1.1945) Jean stayed at the Glass House. In August he immigrated to Eretz Israel via aliya bet, and in 1947 joined the Hagana. Later he served in Pal-Yam, the Marine Corps of Palmah, and completed his service as the deputy commander of the Jaffa port. By the end of 1949 Jean immigrated to the United States and studied at a university.

Dr. Grosinger Sándor
Born in Belényes (Beiuș) in 1913
Passed away
Member of "Hanoar Hatzioni"

Sándor was born in a large pious Jewish family. He studied in a heder in his village and later in Nyiregyháza and Debrecen. He studied at the Rabbinical Seminary in Budapest and learned to be a tailor. Sándor also did a doctorate in history in Budapest. He returned to Debrecen and was Rabbi Meir Weiss' deputy. Sándor taught at the local Jewish high school and was active in the Zionist movement in the framework of "Hatzionim Haclali'im". At the beginning of 1944 he moved to Budapest and joined the "Hanoar Hatzioni" movement. Sándor engaged in obtaining documents. He was the assistant of Ottó Komoly, president of the Hungarian Zionist Association who was at the head of the Relief and Rescue Committee. Sándor's role was to take care of the fugitives from forced labour units. He emigrated to Australia where he died.

Grossman Alexander
Sándor 'Sanyi'
Born in Mezőnagymihály on 3.3.1909
Died on 24.10.2003
Member of "Hashomer Hatzair"

Alexander's family moved to Miskolc. Alexander joined the "Kadima" movement and in 1925, with some friends, he founded the "Blau-Weiss" movement that in 1927 merged with "Hashomer Hatzair". He was among the first members of the movement in Hungary.

Alexander founded a family and had a child. In 1944, with the establishment of the ghetto in Miskolc, he moved to Budapest with the help of a friend who was a police officer. Alexander was sent on a tiyul, caught and incarcerated in various prisons. At the end of September of the same year he was released and arrived at the "Glass House" on Vadász Street and later at a branch of the Swiss consulate on Wekerle Sándor Boulevard.

Sándor was one of the main activists in the underground. His organizing and working skills were extraordinary. In fact he was the manager of the "Glass House" and the representative of the youth movements in the management. When the argument arose about whether to absorb more Jews into the "Glass House" as they might endanger the lives of those already living there, he said: "For the sake of one hundred thousand Jews it is worth to endanger our own lives".

Sándor's wife, child and other relatives were deported to Auschwitz where they perished.

After the liberation, in January 1945, Sándor was the secretary of the Joint in Budapest, a member of the board of the Hungarian Zionist Association and of the "Eretz-Israel" office.

In 1949 he made aliya and was a member of Kibbutz Ma'abarot until 1951.

He worked in journalism and in the publication of books.
He died in Geneva, Switzerland.

Grosz Betzalel

Grosz Gábor (Böci)
Born in Tokaj in 1924
Member of "Hashomer Hatzair"

When Betzalel was nine years old, his family moved to Budapest. He graduated from a business high school in 1942. He first joined the "Maccabi Hatzair" movement and later "Hashomer Hatzair". In May 1944 Betzalel was enlisted in a forced labour unit. He distributed forged documents, received from comrades in the movement, in and outside the camp. The conscripts did dangerous work in sites that were bombarded. Betzalel ran away from the unit and hid thanks to Aryan documents. He went into the ghetto as a Christian, arrived in the "Glass House", distributed forged documents and helped Jews escape.
Betzalel made aliya illegally in 1946. The ship he was sailing on was caught by the British and its passengers were imprisoned in Atlit. After a stay of several months in Atlit, Betzalel was released and arrived in Kibbutz Ma'anit. He was one of the founders of Kibbutz Yassur. Betzalel left the kibbutz and in 1970 he opened an accountancy firm which was active until 1995. Betzalel is retired and resides in Modiin.

Grosz Metuka

Fellner Edit
Born in Debrecen on 29.10.1925
Member of "Hanoar Hatzioni"

Metuka joined the movement at the age of thirteen. In 1942 she was a member of a hahshara in Budapest. After the Germans occupied Hungary, Metuka engaged in obtaining authentic Christian documents in order to distribute them to those who needed them. In the summer of 1944 she went on a tiyul to the Yugoslavian border with refugees from Poland. Metuka was caught by Hungarian gendarmes and imprisoned in the Szeged prison. She was interrogated and tortured by the Gestapo. Metuka was transferred to a prison in Budapest and eventually sent to Auschwitz. After the liberation she returned to Hungary and, in 1946, Metuka made aliya with her husband Yitzhak within the framework of the B'riha. Metuka spent almost a year in a camp in Cyprus. She resides in Haifa.

Grosz Yitzhak
Grosz Ernő
Born in Debrecen on 5.6.1924
Member of "Hanoar Hatzioni"

Yitzhak joined the movement in Budapest at the age of fourteen. In 1942 and 1943 he gave assistance to the refugees arriving from Poland. In May 1944 he was enlisted in a forced labour unit. Yitzhak escaped and joined the movement's activities while equipped with forged Christian documents under the name of Cserkész Tibor. He distributed forged documents to the forced labour camps and to the Protected Houses. He was engaged in obtaining food which he delivered to the bunkers and the "Glass House". After the liberation Yitzhak continued to organize Jews who were liberated from the extermination camps for aliya. He operated between Budapest and Bucharest. After the liberation Yitzhak took part in the organization of 200 Jewish children and accompanied them to Austria and Germany on their way to Eretz Israel (Palestine). In April 1946 he made aliya together with his wife Edit. He was one of the founders of the educational Institute in Alonei Yitzhak, where he and his wife worked for many years. He moved to Haifa where he still resides.

Grünfeld Anikó
Ganz Hanna
Born in Salamás (Sarmaș) in 1923
Died on 7.11.1995
Member of "Dror Habonim"

Hanna joined the movement in 1939. She stayed at the hahshara in Hátszeg (Haṭeg). She studied dental technology. In 1942 Hanna moved to Budapest and was a member of the "Dror Habonim" leadership.
In 1944, after the Germans invaded Hungary, Hanna was active within the framework of the tiyul, smuggling groups of Jews to Kolozsvár, Romania and often traveled from Budapest to the border. In May 1944 Hanna was caught and imprisoned for about two months. Later she was sent to Auschwitz. After the liberation Hanna returned to Budapest and resumed her activities in the movement. From 1946 to 1948 Hanna was the secretary of "Hehalutz". In 1946 she attended the Zionist Congress in Basel.
In 1948 Hanna made aliya.

"Habonim" outing, 1943. Joseph Gárdos - middle row, first from the left (with the mandolin).

Maccabi Hatzair, 1943.
From left, top row: Steiner Miriam, Glück Lea, Csányi Hava, Singer Yaffa, Stern Tamar, Flohr Rahel, Barmat Eli, Robicsek Avri, Felsenburg Baruh, Sajó Eli. Sitting, from left: Surányi Yitzhak, Ben-Zeev Avigdor, Ben-Tzvi Yitzhak, [-], Radó Hava, Russ Haim.

Grünwald David 'Coca'
Grünwald Béla
Born in Vencsellő on 5.5.1925
Died in Israel on 15.5.1985
Member of "Hanoar Hatzioni"

In 1942 David joined the movement in Budapest. Prior to the German occupation of Hungary, he went on missions to provincial towns in order to awaken the local Jews to what lay in store for them. David obtained Aryan documents and distributed them among Jews. On March 19th, 1944, the day the Germans entered Hungary, he was arrested, together with other members of the movement, and detained in a camp (Tolonchá z) where many prisoners were being held. A few days later he was released without any explanation. Other comrades, though, were sent to Auschwitz.

At the beginning of April, David resumed his underground activities. His major assignment was to travel to country towns in order to supply forged documents to members of his movement, as well as to other Jews, and save them from deportation to Poland.

On April 12th, 1944, David traveled to the town of Vencsellő to smuggle his parents out of the ghetto, but they refused to leave. According to his movement's instructions, in May and June, David remained in country towns in order to help the local Jews.

He returned to Budapest on October 12th, where he was caught and imprisoned even before he could continue his activities. He managed to escape on the following day, and resumed his underground work, obtaining and distributing forged documents, and assisting Jewish orphanages. He maintained contacts with underground activists of the Hungarian Communist Party, gave them forged documents and received important information that was necessary for the continuation of the underground activities. He set up bunkers and equipped them. He made contact with an SS lieutenant who helped him to set inmates free (the lieutenant was put on trial after the liberation, exonerated and even praised).

Wearing a fascist uniform, David managed to penetrate the Centre of the Hungarian Legion (Hungarista Légió), and obtain a certificate for the establishment of a hospital. Members of the underground hid in that hospital posing as patients, nurses and doctors.

After the liberation, David continued to work in the movement. In 1949 he made aliya. In Israel he taught physical education.

Grünwald Eliezer

Born in Beregszász (Berehove) in 1923
Member of "Bnei Akiva"

Eliezer was active in the movement from 1942. He stayed at a hahshara in Budapest. Eliezer was enlisted in a forced labour unit and was an underground activist. In 1945 he became a member of the central leadership and engaged in rehabilitating the movement.
Eliezer made aliya. He was a high official in the State Watchdog Office and at the Mizrahi Bank.
Eliezer resides in Jerusalem. His son, Avi, was killed in the Yom Kippur War.

Gur David

Grósz Endre
Born in Okány in 1926
Member of "Hashomer Hatzair"

David was a member of "Hashomer Hatzair" from 1943. With the German invasion on 19.3.1944, he went underground and joined the team that prepared forged documents for the members of all the Zionist youth groups. Over time he was in charge of all forgery activities of documents and seals. The forgery workshop of the Zionist underground supplied forged documents to non-Jewish resistance as well. This operation was the largest in terms of size and variety in occupied Europe. In December 1944 David was caught in the forgery workshop with the whole staff and all the equipment. He was taken to the district headquarters of Arrow Cross and brutally interrogated. One member of the staff, Miki Langer, was murdered on the very first night of the interrogation. Gur was transferred to the central military prison on Margit Boulevard and interrogated by members of the political department of the gendarmerie. He was released at the end of December together with a group of his comrades in a daring operation of the Zionist youth movements underground. Owing to his release, over a hundred other prisoners from the same prison were freed. A total of 117 detainees were liberated. This was an extraordinary achievement.
After the war, from 1945 to 1949, David held central positions in the movement and in the Haganah headquarters. He was the commander of the last B'riha from Hungary. David made aliya in 1949 and joined Kibbutz Ga'aton. He learned civil engineering at the Technion. He owns

an office for the management of engineering projects.

David now resides in Ramat-Gan. He is married, has three daughters and ten grandchildren.

David is one of the initiators and founders of "The Society for Research of the History of the Zionist Youth Movements in Hungary". Since 1984 the Society has been active in commemorating the underground operations of the Zionist youth movements in 1944 and in disseminating information in Israel and in the world about their activities.

Gut Marek
Born in Nagymihályi (Michalovce) in 1926
Murdered in 1944
Member of "Hashomer Hatzair"

In 1941 Marek was drafted to a military work unit in Slovakia. In December 1943 he moved to Hungary, was caught and detained in the Tolonc prison. He escaped and joined the underground activities. Marek saved the lives of members of the movement and other Jews. Thanks to his Aryan appearance he was able to move around freely in the streets of Budapest while wearing an Arrow Cross uniform. On his way to deliver forged documents, in December 1944, he was caught by Arrow Cross men and executed.

Gutmann Sándor
Born in Kassa (Košice)
Murdered in 1944
Member of "Beitar"

Sándor lived in Budapest from 1944 and was an underground activist. The Laciköz bunker where he was staying was attacked by Arrow Cross men and gendarmes. He and his friends tried to break out of the bunker but were killed in a firearm battle with their attackers. His friend Schwartz Frigyes and another seven friends from the city of Miskolc, whose names are not known, were also killed.

Hadas Shoshanna
Morvai (after her marriage: Vadász) Zsuzsa
Born in Makó on 17.10.1922
Member of "Hashomer Hatzair"

Shoshanna joined the movement in her hometown in 1929. She graduated from high school in 1940 and travelled to Budapest. In 1941 she stayed in a hahshara. In 1942 Shoshanna gave assistance to refugees, comrades from the movement that arrived from Slovakia. In cunning ways she obtained authentic documents for them. Shoshanna was active in the hostel for youngsters on Zöldmáli Street where young refugees also found refuge. After the German invasion of Hungary on 19.3.1944, upon her parents' request, she travelled to see them but was caught, arrested and taken to the Strasshof camp and from there to Theresienstadt. After the war Shoshanna returned to Budapest and worked in a children's boarding school where Jewish children, who during the war had found refuge with Christian families or in convents, were gathered. Shoshanna made aliya in 1950 with her husband Miklós and her son Gabriel.

Hakohen Hillel
Born in Komárom (Komárno) on 2.5.1925
Died in Israel in 2003
Member of "Hashomer Hatzair"

Hillel joined the movement in 1936 and in 1942 he moved to Budapest. After the Germans occupied Hungary on 19.3.1944, he and another three comrades were sent to South Transylvania in order to open a new route for the tiyul to Romania in the direction of the city of Brassó (Brašov) beyond the Hungarian border. They were all caught. Hillel was transferred to Debrecen and put into a wagon whose destination was Auschwitz. When the train reached Slovakia, he and some of his friends managed to escape by jumping off the train. Hillel reached the town of Eperjes (Prešov), made contact with comrades from his movement and traveled to Bratislava. Ten of Hillel's comrades who escaped with him were caught and executed.

In August 1944 the Germans entered Slovakia in order to crush the rebellion that erupted in the Banská Bystrica area. Hillel Hakohen joined the partisans and, with the outbreak of the Slovak uprising, fought with the paratroopers who arrived from Eretz Israel (Palestine) and among them Haviva Reick.

On October 31st his camp was attacked by the Germans. His comrades were killed but Hillel survived by pretending to be dead. He lay wounded for four days until his partisan friends found him and took him to a cabin in the mountains. Ukrainian soldiers who worked for the Germans found him there. Thanks to the forged documents he carried, they did not find out his real identity. Hillel was transferred to the hospital in Banská Bystrica and underwent several operations on his leg. In May 1945 he was liberated by the Red Army.

In 1947, with forged documents, he arrived in Eretz Israel (Palestine) as a pilgrim. He moved to Zürich to study medicine. He was a neurosurgeon. Hillel returned to Israel in 1995.

Halász Joseph

Halász József
Born in Pozsony (Bratislava) on 24.2.1924
Perished in Auschwitz in 1944
Member of "Hashomer Hatzair"

Joseph was a member of the movement from 1939. In 1942 he moved to Hungary and became an underground activist. In 1944 he returned to Slovakia and joined the partisans. Joseph took part in the Bukovec battle. He was caught (Haviva Reick was also caught there) but managed to escape and reach Bratislava. Joseph fell ill and was hospitalized. He was caught in the hospital and deported to Auschwitz.

Halevi Hava

Ritscher Éva
Born in Kiskunhalas in 1929
Member of "Hanoar Hatzioni"

When the Germans occupied Hungary on 19.3.1944, Hava obtained a forged Christian document. Her family moved to a "Yellow Star House". Hava distributed Protection Documents to those who needed them. On June 26th, Hava and her sister decided to cross the border into Romania. They were caught and incarcerated in various prisons for over two months and in one of them they met Hanna Szenes. As they were minors, they were released at the beginning of September by the International Red Cross. After her release Hava joined the underground and distributed documents at railway stations where Jewish forced labor workers passed through. She managed to rescue and hide some of them. She gathered Jewish orphans and took them to the children's houses in the responsibility of the Zionist youth groups. Hava succeeded in getting a job at the post office, received a uniform and carried documents and letters between the "Glass House" and Wekerle Street, the branches of the Swiss consulate and the centers of underground activities. In the same way she helped the residents of the ghetto. Hava managed to give some Protection Documents to the Jews who were on the Death March and save them.

Hava made aliya. She resides in Ashkelon.

Halevi Joel
Hacker Pál
Born in Sopron on 13.2.1927
Died in 1994
Member of "Hanoar Hatzioni"

Joel was one of the first members of the movement in his town. At the age of fifteen he went to Budapest and studied agriculture and gardening at the agricultural school MIKÉFE. Joel was active in the movement's hahshara. On 20.3.1944, the day after the Germans invaded Hungary, he was caught and taken to the Kistarcsa detention camp. Two months later he was allowed to enlist in a forced labor unit that was transferred to the copper mines in Bor, Yugoslavia. Joel managed to run away and join Tito's partisans where he served as a saboteur. As the Red Army approached, Joel moved to Romania and made contact with comrades from the movement. He stayed at an agricultural farm.

At the end of 1945 Joel made aliya and joined Kibbutz Kfar Glücksohn. He married Hava Ritscher. In 1947 he left the kibbutz, enlisted in the army and served as a saboteur during the War of Independence. Later he worked in the educational institute Nitzanim and in Ashkelon.

Hantos Hadasa
Singer Edit
Born in Budapest in 1924
Member of "Hanoar Hatzioni"

Hadasa grew up in an orthodox Jewish family. She joined the movement at an early age. She studied to be a kindergarten teacher. After the German invasion of Hungary on 19.3.1944, she equipped herself with Christian papers. Hadasa stayed in the town of Gyöngyös where she took care of children and among them the grandchildren (who were half Jewish) of Árpád Szakasits, one of the leaders of the Hungarian Social-Democrat Party. Hadasa returned to Budapest posing as a refugee, was caught and taken to the Arrow Cross Party headquarters but managed to escape. Hadasa arrived in the ghetto and then at the "Glass House" on Vadász Street where she operated within the framework of her movement. After the liberation she escorted a large group of Jewish children to Debrecen for their rehabilitation. Hadasa made aliya in 1945. She took part in the hahshara in Kibbutz Ramat Yohanan. From 1949 she worked as a kindergarten teacher. In 1952 she got married to Dr. Yitzhak Hantos, who was born in Budapest and is now a retired judge. They reside in Kiryat Ono.

Harari Yehuda
Wertheimer Ernő
Born in Debrecen on 24.1.1922
Died on 21.10.1996
Member of "Hashomer Hatzair"

In the years 1941 and 1942 Yehuda lived in a "Hashomer Hatzair" commune in Budapest. In 1943 he was enlisted in a forced labor unit. In October 1944 he escaped with sixteen of his friends thanks to forged documents supplied by the movement and at once joined the underground activities in the "Glass House".
Yehuda made aliya in 1945 and was a member of Kibbutz Yehiam.

Harari Yisrael
Hochhauser Zoltán
Born in Kassa (Košice) in 1921
Member of "Hashomer Hatzair"

Yisrael lived in Budapest from 1941. He was sent by the movement to country towns on an information mission in order to warn the Jews of what to expect from the Germans and the Hungarian fascists. The family house in Kassa served as a refuge, a meeting place and a station for all the passing refugees, members of the movement, who moved from Slovakia to Hungary. In March 1944 Yisrael received mobilization orders for forced labor in a unit that was about to leave for the Ukrainian front. He disobeyed the order and succeeded in crossing the border into Romania. From there he continued his journey to Eretz Israel (Palestine).

Yisrael was the first of all the Zionist youth movements' members to slip across the border and, thereby, opened the season of the tiyulim to Romania.

He is a member of Kibbutz Ein Dor.

Harel Menahem
Kőnigsberg Herrmann
Born in Bilke (Bilki) on 8.1.1930
Died on 27.6.1990
Member of "Hashomer Hatzair"

Menahem came from a traditional Jewish family. At the end of 1943 he parted from his family and traveled to Budapest where his older brother and sister lived. They sent him to the town of Sárvár where he stayed under the protection of a local friend.

After the German invasion of Hungary on 19.3.1944, as the Jews were concentrated in the ghetto, Menahem fled from Sárvár and arrived in Budapest again. In the capital he witnessed the suffering of the Jews and the dangers they were facing. Menahem asked to be rescued and arrived at the "Glass House" on 29, Vadász Street. With the help of a "Mizrahi" activist who knew him, he succeeded in entering the House where he joined "Hashomer Hatzair". From David Gur, who was in charge of the forgery laboratory, Menahem received documents bearing the name of Peter Pranitz, a Greek Orthodox Christian, who had fled from the Carpatho-Ruthenia region out of fear of the Russians. In the "Glass House" he was ordered to go out in the streets and distribute forged documents to the Jews. Menahem did this a few times at the risk of his own life.

He was a member of Kibbutz Negba.

Hartman Judith
Scharf
Born in Kisvárda on 15.12.1921
Member of "Hashomer Hatzair"

Judith joined the movement at a young age. Her two sisters made aliya already in the mid-1930's. In 1942 and 1943 she maintained contact with the Garany detention camp inmates and even visited the site. At the beginning of the persecution of Jews, Judith arrived in Budapest and joined a group of young women, members of the movement. After the German occupation of Hungary on 19.3.1944, she went, together with her boyfriend, Arieh Funk, on a tiyul. They were captured on their way to the Romanian border. Arieh was deported to Auschwitz, and Judith was sent to a detention camp in Budapest. All attempts to rescue her failed and she was deported to Auschwitz. Upon her liberation, on 8.5.1945, she returned to Budapest.

In 1947, Judith made aliya, and became a member of Kibbutz Ha'ogen.

Heffner Dézi
Heffner-Reiner Dézi
Born in Budapest on 10.1.1927
Member of "Dror Habonim"

At the age of twelve Dézi was a member of "Maccabi Hatzair" and later joined the "Habonim" movement. She assisted refugees from Poland who found a hiding place in her family house on 45, Hársfa Street in Budapest before moving to another place or leaving for Romania. Dézi obtained documents from the offices of the Hungarian Population Registry. She was sent to the Gestapo headquarters in Buda in order to help the prisoners there. Dézi was also sent to country towns in order to find hiding places in case there was a need for them. She left Hungary on the train of the Relief and Rescue Committee to Bergen-Belsen and from there to Switzerland.

Dézi made aliya and is a member of Kibbutz Givat Brenner.

Heffner Imre 'Hefi'
Born in Újpest in 1924
Fell in the War of Independence
Member of "Dror Habonim"

Imre joined the movement in 1938. As refugees arrived from Poland and Slovakia, he gave them assistance. After the German invasion of Hungary on 19.3.1944, Imre went underground with the other members of the movement who had not been enlisted in forced labor units. Imre traveled to the Miskolc ghetto, handed out forged documents to comrades whom he smuggled into Budapest. In July 1944, he crossed the border into Romania within the framework of the tiyul and in August of the same

year, he arrived in Eretz Israel (Palestine). Imre was one of the founders of Kibbutz Ein Zeitim and in 1947 he moved to Kvutzat Kinneret.
He fought in the War of Independence and was killed in the battle for the Tzemah police station.

Herbst Judith 'Juca'
Weisz Judit
Born in Kökényes (Ternove) on 26.12.1912
Died on 8.12.1974
Member of "Hashomer Hatzair"

Judith was active in the movement and the Zionist underground in Hungary during World War II. She was caught by the Hungarian fascists and the Gestapo, brutally tortured but did not break and did not reveal any secrets of the underground. The torture left her with scars and irreversible damage to her health which she lived with until her last day. In 1944 she married "Mimish", Yitzhak Herbst.
Judith made aliya in 1948 and joined Kibbutz Ha'ogen. Later she left the kibbutz and moved to Tel-Aviv. She was an art teacher, an artist and displayed her creative work in various exhibitions.

Herbst Yitzhak 'Mimish'
Herbst Imre
Born in Eperjes (Prešov) in 1916
Died on 8.2.1978
Member of "Hashomer Hatzair"

Yitzhak joined the movement at an early age. In 1935 he started to study medicine in Prague but in 1938 he had to discontinue his studies due to the worsening of the conditions for the Jews.
Yitzhak's older brother, Jenő, who was a communist activist, was arrested and deported in 1942. Yitzhak was also in danger and had to escape to Hungary. When he arrived in Budapest, Mimish joined the aid and rescue operations for the refugees from Slovakia and Poland. In 1943 Mimish was caught, arrested and brutally tortured. His health was damaged by the torture. He was released and resumed his rescue operations.
After the German invasion of Hungary on 19.3.1944, he was one of the main activists of the Zionist youth movements underground. In June 1944, together with his wife Judith, he was supposed to cross the border

into Romania within the framework of the tiyul in order to make aliya. They were both caught by the Hungarian gendarmerie and were detained in the Szeged prison. Mimish managed to escape but Judith remained in the custody of the Gestapo and was cruelly tortured. Mimish succeeded in liberating her in a daring operation with the help of Tzipi Schechter (Agmon) and Milan, a Serbian.

Mimish continued his underground activities until the end of the war. According to his friends he got the nickname of "Mr. Underground". After the liberation Mimish was active in the Aliya Bet.

He made aliya in 1948 and joined Kibbutz Ha'ogen.

In 1950 he moved to Tel-Aviv with his family. He worked as a photographer. Of the many films he made, one of the first Israeli films, "Burning Sands", is famous.

For many years Mimish suffered from the physical damage caused by his arrest in 1943.

Herman Shlomo
Herman Slomo Ladislav
Born in Újvidék (Novi Sad) in 1925
Perished in Auschwitz in 1944
Member of "Hashomer Hatzair"

In 1941, after the Hungarian occupation of Újvidék, Shlomo took part in the movement against Hungarian occupation by writing slogans, scattering nails on the roads in order to impede the movement of the Hungarian and German armies and distributing leaflets. He was caught and sentenced to death but since he was a minor, the sentence was converted to incarceration. Shlomo was imprisoned until 1944, then deported to Auschwitz where he perished.

Herman Uri
Herman Endre
Born in Budapest in 1923
Perished in 1944
Member of "Hashomer Hatzair"

Uri studied at the Jewish High School in Budapest. In 1938 he joined the "Hashomer Hatzair" movement. His instructors were Arie (Hunwald) Ya'ari and later David Yahin. In 1942 Uri was recruited to help members of the movement that arrived from Slovakia as refugees. He and his friends were arrested by the Hungarian secret police and sent to the Garany detention camp. Uri was released in 1943 and after the German invasion of Hungary on 19.3.1944, he took part in the underground activities as a member of the leadership. On 28.5.1944 he was caught again, taken to the Gestapo headquarters on Schwabs Hill (Svábhegy), interrogated and tortured but did not give away any information. He was transferred from one detention place to another until he was taken to the Sárvár detention camp. From there Uri was deported to Auschwitz and then to another camp after which his traces disappeared.

Heser George
Heser György
Born in Szabadka (Subotica) in 1922
Died in 1943
Member of "Hashomer Hatzair"

George was a member of the movement's ken in Újvidék (Novi Sad). He took part in the anti-fascist movement and the organization of sabotage units. In February 1942, George was caught, tried in a military court and sent to do forced labor in Ukraine escorted by a punishment unit. He perished there.

Hollaender Yaakov
Hollaender Jakab
Born in Nagyszőllős (Vinohragyiv) on 30.1.1923
Member of "Hashomer Hatzair"

On 19.3.1944, with the German occupation of Hungary, Yaakov received his mobilization orders for a forced labor unit. He enlisted and was sent to Budapest. He made contact with the leadership of the movement and arrived at the "Glass House". Since he knew Hebrew, Yaakov taught the language, songs and Zionism to the children who found shelter in children's houses in the responsibility of his movement. Friends who ran away from forced labor camps found refuge with Yaakov's help.
On October 15th, 1944, when the Arrow Cross Party took over the government in Hungary, Yaakov was caught by gendarmes but managed to escape. He joined the educational staff of the children's house on 90, Dob Street under the auspices of the International Red Cross and in

the responsibility of his movement. After the liberation of Budapest in January 1945, Ya'akov was caught by Russian guards and sent as a prisoner to Archangelsk on the North Sea coast. He was set free in June 1946 and returned to Budapest. From there Yaakov traveled to Germany to assist in the management of a children's house.

Yaakov made aliya in 1948 with a group of children within the framework of the "Ehad BeMay garin" and arrived in Kibbutz Ga'aton. He resides in Rehovot.

Hőnig Braha 'Bruhi'
Hőnig Borbála
Born in Carpatho-Ruthenia in 1928
Passed away
Member of "Hashomer Hatzair"

Braha arrived in Budapest in 1942 and joined the already outlawed "Hashomer Hatzair" movement. After the German invasion of Hungary on 19.3.1944, she equipped herself with forged Aryan documents and went underground. She was a liaison person among the members of the movement, passed on information about meetings and mainly about the departure of the tiyul. After the Arrow Cross Party formed the government on 15.10.1944, together with two of her friends who were her roommates, Braha safeguarded six suitcases, that contained the equipment of the forgery workshop, brought to them by David Gur. In 1945, after the liberation, Braha emigrated to France and studied at university in Paris. Braha had a tragic death.

Horn Yehuda
Horn Tibor
Born in Budapest on 14.7.1926
Member of "Hanoar Hatzioni"

On 19.3.1944, when the Germans invaded Hungary, Yehuda was studying in the Rabbinical Seminary which the Hungarian police turned into a prisoners' camp. The students were forced to work in the camp. Yehuda Horn made contact with the prisoners, passed on information to their relatives and to various authorities and revealed their location. Many detainees managed to escape thanks to this information. Horn himself served in a forced labor unit, escaped and returned to Budapest.

Yehuda made aliya in the 60's. He worked as an architect and resides in Jerusalem.

Hunwald Simha
Hunwald Sándor
Born in Kolozsvár (Cluj) in 1914
Murdered by the Fascists in January 1945
Member of "Hashomer Hatzair"

Simha was one of the leaders of the movement and among the most daring and talented underground activists. He came from an assimilated and well-to-do Jewish family. His father was a lawyer who died a sudden death in 1918. The family moved to Budapest in 1921 and suffered from poverty. In 1931 Simha joined "Hashomer Hatzair" and in 1936 was a member of the central leadership. The family apartment became one of the centers of the movement's activities. Simha's mother helped him by giving assistance to the refugees arriving to Budapest from Slovakia. In April 1942 fifteen activists from the movement were arrested and among them Simha Hunwald. They were imprisoned in the Garany detention camp. Due to his extraordinary organization skills Simha became the camp commander's chief assistant. Everything that happened inside the camp was his initiative, even the Hungarian soldiers' holiday roll. Simha made a kitchen garden, organized study courses and obtained permission for relatives to visit the prisoners. Because of an informer the commander of the camp was fired and the inmates were sent to the Ukraine front. From a unit of 243 Jews only five survived, including Simha Hunwald. He studied Russian, helped his fellow Jews a lot and succeeded in winning the trust of the Hungarian commanders who gave him various organizational roles. He even succeeded in sending regards to his family and comrades in Budapest.
In 1944 Simha escaped, walked hundreds of kilometers and managed to reach the Hungarian border where he was caught and returned to Ukraine. He escaped again and this time, in October 1944, he reached Budapest. Simha immediately reported at the "Glass House". Under the assumed name of Hans Kühne, a clerk at the Swiss legation, he joined the rescue activities with all his energy and skills. On 1.1.1945 Arthur Weiss, owner of the "Glass House" was kidnapped by the fascists from the gate of the house. Simha at once started to look for him. During this operation he was arrested while carrying 500 forged documents. Simha Hunwald was tortured and murdered, probably on 8.1.1945.

"Hashomer Hatzair" winter camp, Kóspallag, December 1943.
From left, standing: Berger Michael, Sharoni Tzivonit, Reichman Ezra, Netzer Miriam, Klein Moshe, Gur David, Ben-Dor Tova, [-], Kama Yirmiyahu, Ronen Avraham, Kilon Moshe, Fischer Avri, Epstein Sarah, Ronen Miriam, Epstein Yeshayahu, Lipkovics Tzvi. Sitting: Shlomi Judith, Schechter David.

"Bnei Akiva", 1943.
From left, top row: Braun Ya'acov, Lantos Yeshayahu, Wiesel Haim, Schneider.
Bottom: Friedman Malka, Johnny, Blum Pnina.

Members of "Dror", outing in the hills of Buda, 1943.

Izsák Hava
Izsák Éva
Born in Szatmárnémeti (Satu Mare) in 1925
Died in 1944
Member of "Hashomer Hatzair"

After the annexation of North Transylvania to Hungary in 1940, Hava took part in the communist, anti-fascist activities in her hometown. After the authorities discovered this activity, she fled to Nagyvárad and joined the Hungarian, Schwabs and Jews underground. However, she was not integrated and, in order to protect the group, they tried to force her to commit suicide. She then moved to Debrecen and ended her life by taking cyanide (these details are taken from the book written by her sister, Miriam Ziman [Izsák], "A Tombstone of Letters and Tears", 1989.)

Joszipovics Irén
Rosenberg Piri
Born in Nagyszőllős (Vinohragyiv) in 1918
Died in 1969
Member of "Hashomer Hatzair"

Irén's parents, Rudolf and Rosalie Rosenberg, had fifteen children. Her father was a cantor and a slaughterer. In 1939 she lived for a year in Prague, where she met Moshe Elefánt (Pil-Alpan).
In 1944, after the German occupation of Hungary, prior to the concentration of Jews in the Nagyszőllős ghetto, Irén escaped to Budapest, renewed contact with Moshe Alpan and started to work for "Hashomer Hatzair". She mainly dealt with the transfer of forged documents to the young Jews in forced labor units. After the liberation Irén returned to her hometown and married Shmuel Joszipovics. Later, she emigrated to France and from there she moved to the USA. She settled down in Los Angeles.

Jung Joseph
Jung József
Born in Munkács (Mukacsevo) in 1926
Died on 25.12.2002
Member of "Hashomer Hatzair"

After the Germans invaded Hungary on 19.3.1944, Joseph ran away from the Munkács ghetto, hid in the forest and later escaped equipped with forged documents he had received from the movement and arrived in Budapest. Joseph joined the "Hashomer Hatzair" underground activities. He went on daring missions and on one of them he was caught in the Gestapo headquarters on Schwabs Hill (Svábhegy). He was deported to Auschwitz.

After the liberation Joseph was involved in the B'riha. He made aliya in 1948 and joined Kibbutz Yassur. In 1960 he left the kibbutz and settled down in Bethlehem Haglilit. He passed away in 2002.

Prof. Kádár Iván
Born in Budapest on 27.10.1921
Died on 23.7.1995
Communist

Iván studied at the Jewish high school in Budapest and, despite the "Numerus Clausus", he completed his law and political science studies in the University of Budapest and got his diploma on 30.9.1944.

In 1944 he worked in the framework of the military committee of the Hungarian Communist Party: the László Sólyóm Group, György Pálffy, Lajos Fehér, the Maróti-Padányi Unit. Iván himself belonged to the auxiliary unit to the armed forces, Kiska-Kisegitő Karhatalom, with the rank of lieutenant. He was the liaison between the military committee and "Hashomer Hatzair" through David Gur. Kádár succeeded in housing the forgery workshop in the library building of the Student Union "Csaba". After the liberation Iván was active in the Communist Party until, as a result of the Rajk trial, he was expelled from the Party. Later he was also fired from his job at the university.

After the turnabout in Hungary in 1989 and the first free elections, Iván was elected to the parliament on the Sz.D.Sz. (The party of the Free Democrats) list. In 1990 his reputation was cleared.

Iván wrote books about the theories of numbers. Until his death in 1995 he was the chairman of the "Association for the Culture of Hungarian Jews" (Magyar Zsidók Kulturális Egyesülete).

Prof. Kadari Menahem Tzvi
Schwarcz Ernő
Born in Mezőkövesd in 1925
Member of "Bnei Akiva"

Menahem studied at high school in Miskolc and the Jewish high school in Ungvár. In 1943 and 1944 he was a member of the national leadership of "Bnei Akiva" and in charge of the educational and cultural activities. After the Germans invaded Hungary on 19.3.1944, Menahem was active in the Zionist underground and responsible for the tiyul operation within the framework of his movement. In 1945 and 1946 he completed his university studies in Budapest. He made aliya, studied at the Hebrew University in the Hebrew Language Department and in 1955 received his doctorate. Menahem is a professor at Bar-Ilan University. He was awarded the Israel Prize. He resides in Ramat-Gan.

Kadmon Eliezer
Kepes László
Born in Eperjeske in 1924
Member of "Hanoar Hatzioni"

Eliezer was brought up on a farm in the countryside. From the age of ten he studied at the Jewish high school in Debrecen, where he joined the "Hanoar Hatzioni" movement. At the time of the German invasion in March 1944, Eliezer was working in Budapest in an indispensable factory producing for the German army. Equipped with Aryan documents, he went under the name of László Koltai. Thanks to his Aryan appearance and his command of German, he took part in underground activities wearing the uniform of the Hungarian army with the rank of lieutenant. Eliezer was active within the framework of Department A of the International Red Cross, in the children's houses that were set up by the Zionist movements and in the Protected Houses where Jews were spared.

Within the framework of his activities Eliezer went to the foreigners' police, government offices and even the Gestapo headquarters on Schwabs Hill in Buda, the hilly part of the capital. He distributed Swiss Protection Documents and maintained contact with those serving in forced labor units in the city and its surroundings.
When the Death March was on its way to the Reich, Eliezer, driving a

truck and carrying Swiss Protection Documents, followed the marchers and managed to liberate many Jews.

During the final stage of the blockade on the capital he joined the auxiliary unit of the armed forces, "Kiska". Jews, among whom there were members of the Zionist movements, served in this unit. The commander of the unit was Lajos Gidófalvy who was killed in the battles for the city and who, years later, was recognized as a "Righteous Gentile". Eliezer represented the unit at the area's headquarters where the daily password was given which he passed on to the underground activists. Later the unit was dismantled by the fascists. Its members ran away and found a refuge until the liberation.
After the end of the war Eliezer was active in the B'riha. He made aliya. He is an economist and lives in Rosh Ha'ayin.

Kahani Meir Yehuda
Kahani Endre
Born in Gyöngyös on 28.5.1918
Died on 19.10.1969
Member of "Bnei Akiva"

Meir studied in a yeshiva and a commerce and industry school. In 1936 he stayed at a hahshara and was active in the "Hehalutz Hamizrahi" movement. In 1938 Meir was elected head of the "Bnei Akiva" leadership. He took part in the B'riha and Aliya Bet. He was caught by the police while in possession of documents and forbidden Zionist literature. Meir was released but continually harassed by the police. From 1942 he worked in the Eretz-Israel office (Pal-Mat) in Budapest, escorted people making aliya with Aliya Bet. Meir organized the escape of Jews from Poland and Slovakia and was active in the Relief and Rescue Committee as well as in the organization of Hehalutz.

In 1944 Meir made aliya with his wife, Miriam, joined the Hagana and started to work in the Aliya Department of the Jewish Agency. He held various high level positions in the Jewish Agency and government offices.

Kama Yirmiyahu
Kemény Jackie
Born in Nolcsó (Nolčovo) in 1924
Died on 7.5.1993
Member of "Hashomer Hatzair"

Yirmiyahu studied at high school in Eperjes (Prešov). In 1937 he joined the movement. In February 1943 Yirmiyahu ran away from Slovakia and moved to Budapest. After the German invasion of Hungary on 19.3.1944, he returned to Slovakia. In Bratislava Yirmiyahu worked in a shop where he was the coordinator of the "Hashomer Hatzair" underground.

He was caught in December 1944 but managed to escape in a daring operation. He was caught again and again escaped. Yirmiyahu joined the partisans under the leadership of Zhdanov, a Soviet. He worked in intelligence and sabotage.

After the war Yirmiyahu returned to Hungary on 1.4.1945 and took part in the revival of the movement. He was the instructor of a group of children in the movement's children's house in Békéscsaba.

Yirmiyahu was one of the founders of the "Ehad-BeMay" garin and of Kibbutz Ga'aton. He worked as a driver, a farmer, the kibbutz farm coordinator and a bookkeeper. He died in Kibbutz Ga'aton.

Karmi Tzvi
Weinberger János
Born in Kúnmadaras on 12.4.1924
Member of "Hanoar Hatzioni"

Tzvi's family moved to Budapest when he was thirteen and at the age of fifteen he joined the movement. He learned dental technology. After the Germans invaded Hungary on 19.3.1944, he was enlisted in a forced labor unit. Following the rise to power of the Arrow Cross Party in Hungary on 15.10.1944, Tzvi escaped from the forced labor camp and, together with Yeshayahu Rosenblum, took part in the establishment of a children's house on Budakeszi Street and provided it with food. Tzvi made aliya and worked as a bookkeeper.

Karmon Mordehai
Weingarten Martin
'Patyu'
Born in Gyertyánliget (Kobilecka Poljana) on 24.3.1924
Died on 20.7.2003
Member of "Dror Habonim"

In 1942 Mordehai arrived in Budapest in order to learn a profession. He learned tanning. He joined the movement in 1944. After the Germans invaded Hungary on 19.3.1944, Mordehai went underground and shared an apartment with Betzalel Adler. He took part in many rescue operations wearing a "Levente" and, later, a fascist Arrow Cross uniform. ("Levente" was a compulsory pre-military service for all youth; after the German occupation of Hungary on 19.3.1944 Jews were not allowed to take part in it.) Mordehai stood out for his courage. At the beginning of December 1944 he was caught in an ambush set up by the Hungarian secret police at the entrance to the house on 52, Baross Street, where the underground activists of "Dror Habonim" operated. Mordecahi was taken to the central military prison on Margit Boulevard and brutally tortured. He escaped, was caught again but managed to survive. Mordehai made aliya and lived in Bat-Yam.

Karni Avraham
Sugár György
Member of "Dror Habonim"

Avraham was an underground activist. In 1943 he traveled to Kolozsvár on a mission for the movement in order to warn the local Jews of what lay in store for them. In Kolozsvár he met with Ernő Marton, the editor of the Hungarian Jewish newspaper "Új Kelet", with the town's chief Rabbi, Weinberger, and with Ari Mendel and other members of the movement. Together they got organized and reached the conclusion that it was impossible to organize armed resistance and that they had to concentrate on rescue operations. From Kolozsvár Avraham traveled to Dés on a similar mission. He returned to Budapest and was enlisted in a forced labor unit where he served until October 1944. From that date he integrated his movement's underground activities.
Avraham made aliya. He resides in Ramat-Gan.

Karni Klári
Elfer Klári
Born in Kassa (Košice) in 1928
Member of "Hashomer Hatzair"

Klári arrived in Budapest in 1944 and at once integrated the underground activities. She made contact with the non-Jewish anti-fascist movement. Her underground name was Niederfűhrer Anna Mária. She was the liaison between the "Glass House" and the members operating in the underground and also transferred forged Swiss Protection Documents. After the liberation she took part in various activities for the movement.
Klári made aliya in 1947 and took part in the defense of Kibbutz Ma'anit. As a member of the "Ehad BeMay" garin she was among the founders of Kibbutz Yassur. She married Baruh Karni and moved to Kibbutz Hama'apil.

Dr. Kasztner Israel
Kazstner Rezső Rudolf
Born in Kolozsvár (Cluj) in 1906
Murdered in Israel in 1957
Member of "Ihud Mapai"

Israel studied at the Jewish high school and at university in the Department of Law in his hometown. He joined the "Barissia" Zionist youth movement. Israel started working as a journalist in the "Új Kelet" (New East) Jewish newspaper. In 1937 he married Elizabeth (Bogyó) Fischer. In September 1940 Transylvania was divided between Romania and Hungary. The city of Kolozsvár was given to Hungary. Anti-Jewish measures started and the "Új Kelet" newspaper was closed down. Kasztner moved to Budapest and became one of the prominent activists of the Zionist movement, "Ihud Mapai" and of the Relief and Rescue Committee.
Immediately after the Germans invaded Hungary on 19.3.1944, hard measures were imposed on the Jews and soon the deportations and exterminations started. On 5.4.1944 Joel Brand and Kasztner met for the first time with Dieter Wisliceny, an officer in Eichmann's headquarters, and this was the beginning of negotiations with the Germans in order to save Hungarian Jewry. These negotiations were later called by the name of "Goods for Blood". Since Brand had gone to Istanbul, Kasztner, as the representative of the Relief and Rescue Committee, led the negotiations

with Kurt Becher, an officer in Eichmann's headquarters, for a train transport from Hungary to Switzerland. This train did actually leave during the night between June 30 and July 1, 1944 with 1,685 Jews among whom leaders of the Jewish community, rabbis, wealthy people and members of the Zionist youth movements and, after hardships and delays, its passengers arrived in Switzerland.

After the war Kasztner and his family lived in Geneva, Switzerland. In 1947 he was invited to give testimony in the Nuremberg trials and gave a declaration in support of Becher.

In December 1947 Kasztner made aliya, started his public work, was "Mapai's" candidate for the Knesset and worked as a high official in the Ministry of Trade and Industry.

In 1952 Malkiel Grünwald, a Jerusalem resident born in Hungary, published a mimeographed leaflet containing serious accusations against Kasztner and his connections with the Germans during the Holocaust and even called for his extermination.

On 1.1.1954 Grünwald was put on trial on charges of slander against a government official. The trial turned from an accusation against Grünwald into an accusation against Kasztner. Judge Benjamin Halevi found Grünwald guilty on a sub-clause and gave him a one Lira fine. In spite of this, in his argumentation for the sentence, the judge accused Kasztner of "selling his soul to the devil". An appeal against the sentence was filed and a new trial opened. However, before the end of the trial, Kasztner was shot dead by a ex-member of "Lehi". After Kasztner's death the trial came to an end and his name was cleared.

Katic Mirkó
Born in Szabadka (Subotica) in 1918
Died in 1943
Member of "Hashomer Hatzair"

Mirkó was a member of the ken in Újvidék (Novi Sad). After the Hungarians conquered the area in 1941, he took part in anti-fascist activities. He was caught by Hungarian gendarmes and on 3.1.1942 the military court sentenced him to forced labor. He was sent with a forced labor punishment unit to Ukraine.

In 1943 he succeeded in crossing to the Russian side. He died in a prisoners' camp.

Katz Imre

Born in Nyiregyháza on 17.12.1919
Died in Israel in 1973
Member of "Hanoar Hatzioni"

Imre graduated from high school in Nyiregyháza. He learned to be a tailor. Prior to the German occupation, he moved to Budapest. Imre obtained forged documents and joined "Kiska", an auxiliary unit within the Hungarian army. He saved Jews from the ghetto. Imre was an expert in obtaining documents from the office of the Pope's representative. He once gave his comrades in the movement, who operated in the underground, sixty such documents. After the liberation Imre worked with the B'riha.

Katz Moshe

Katz József
Born in Csenger in 1923
Died on 2.12.2004 in Israel
Member of "Hanoar Hatzioni"

In 1939 Moshe joined the movement, graduated the Jewish high school in Debrecen and in 1943 he moved to Budapest. Upon the German occupation of Hungary on 19.3.1944, Moshe was enlisted in a forced labor unit. In July he escaped thanks to forged documents provided by the movement and arrived at the Jewish community house in Budapest. In October Moshe stayed in a bunker in Zugló, a suburb of Budapest, and underwent weapons training. The bunker was discovered and the occupants, among them Moshe Katz, were caught by Arrow Cross men. He was taken to the Gestapo center in Buda but released thanks to Protection Documents of the Swiss legation. Moshe arrived at the "Glass House" on Vadász Street and later at the branch of the Swiss consulate on Wekerle Street. He worked in the food storeroom from which food was delivered to the ghetto and children's houses under the auspices of the Zionist youth movements.
In 1946 Moshe made aliya. He stayed at Mivtahim and Kibbutz Tze'elim. Later he settled down in Petah-Tikva.

Katz Oszkár
Member of the "Shimoni Group"

Keshet Rahel 'Rahelka'
Schwartz Vera
Born in Budapest in 1928
Died in 2002
Member of "Maccabi Hatzair"

Rahel took care of Jewish children who were gathered in children's houses under the protection of the International Red Cross. She ran various errands such as the delivery of forged documents. About two weeks after the liberation, in February 1945, she left Hungary with her husband Tzvi Keshet to Romania on her way to Eretz Israel (Palestine). She was among the settlers of Tze'elim and moved to Kfar Hahoresh with the other members of the garin.

Keshet Tzvi
Bogen Pál
Born in Budapest in 1923
Member of "Maccabi Hatzair"

After the Germans invaded Hungary on 19.3.1944, Tzvi took part in his movement's organization of underground activities: setting up bunkers, forging documents and obtaining money. He received his mobilization orders and enlisted in a forced labor unit. At the end of June Tzvi received forged documents from members of the movement and intended to desert but gave up his plan for fear of his fellow inmates being punished. At the end of September 1944, nevertheless, Tzvi decided to escape and arrived in the "Glass House" on 29, Vadász Street. Operating under the name of Bokros Pál, he engaged in the forgery and distribution of documents. In February 1945, about two weeks after the liberation, he left for Romania on his way to Eretz Israel (Palestine). He was among the settlers of Kibbutz Tze'elim and moved to Kfar Hahoresh.

Kilon Moshe
Klein Tibor
Born in Budapest on 1.4.1925
Died on 23.3.1993
Member of "Hashomer Hatzair"

Moshe joined "Hashomer Hatzair" in the late 1930's. During the war he was an underground activist and distributed forged documents. He went on missions to the country towns. During such a mission Moshe was caught and deported to Auschwitz. After the liberation he returned to Hungary and was among the founders of Kibbutz "Ehad BeMay". In 1946 Moshe made aliya with his wife, Tova, and was one of the founders of Kibbutz Yassur. Moshe was a musician.

Klein Anna
Csech Anna
Born in Budapest on 28.7.1926
Member of "Hashomer Hatzair"

At the age of fifteen Anna joined the movement where she met her future husband, Uri Herman, whom she married in April 1944 in a small, intimate, family wedding. She obtained authentic documents from the Population Registry in Budapest, distributed them and took part in other underground activities. On 28.5.1944 Anna, her husband and other comrades were arrested and taken to the Gestapo headquarters on Schwabs Hill (Svábhegy). Anna was interrogated and tortured but did not reveal any information. After about three weeks she was transferred to other detention places and eventually taken to the Sárvár ghetto. From there she was deported to Auschwitz. Anna saw her husband for the last time on the ramp at Auschwitz. Anna was liberated by the Americans and returned to Budapest. She integrated the movement's activities and mainly took care of teenagers, orphaned children and families in need of help. In 1946, within the framework of Aliya Bet, she got on her way to Eretz Israel (Palestine) but the ship "Knesset Israel", that had 4,000 immigrants on board, was intercepted by the British and all the passengers were deported to Cyprus. They arrived in Eretz Israel (Palestine) only a year later.

In Eretz Israel Anna married her second husband, Dov and lived on Kibbutz Ga'aton for about six years. Anna is a social worker, the mother of two and has two grandchildren. She resides in Kfar Saba.

Klein Dávid 'Dudu'

Born in Nagyszőllős (Vinohragyiv) in 1923
Disappeared/murdered in 1944
Member of "Hashomer Hatzair"

David was enlisted to forced labor, escaped, arrived in Budapest and joined the staff of the International Red Cross. He escorted supply carts to the ghetto and the children's houses in Budapest. During one of his missions in December 1944, he disappeared and was murdered.

Klein Joli

Mansworth Joli
Member of "Maccabi Hatzair"

Joli was a member of "Maccabi Hatzair" in Pozsony (Bratislava). After the deportation of Jews in March 1942, she fled to Hungary. Thanks to her command of Hungarian, Joli engaged in helping the refugees arriving to Hungary from Slovakia. She obtained suitable documents and found accommodation for them. After the German invasion of Hungary on 19.3.1944, Joli joined the underground activities. She obtained authentic documents from the Population Registry offices. She escorted groups within the framework of the tiyul to the Romanian border. After 15.10.1944, when the fascist Arrow Cross Party rose to power, she engaged in looking for Jewish children and taking them to children's houses which were under the protection of the International Red Cross. Joli herself was appointed to the staff of carers in those children's houses. After the war she made aliya. Joli resides in Nahariya.

"Bnei Akiva", Hanukah 1943.

"Hanoar Hatzioni" at the Balatonboglár winter camp, December 1943.
From Left, top row: Spitzer Lili, Broshi Dov, Kirschner Shoshana, Gross Metuka, Ben-Yitzhak Eli, Even Hava, Keller Edit, Grünwald David 'Coca', Rosenblum Yeshayahu, Arbel Yitzhak 'Bukszi', Löwenheim Shmuel. Sitting: Braun Yitzhak (first from the left), Gera Shula (fifth from the left).

Klein Menahem 'Meno'
Klein Elemér
Born in Szakolca (Skalica) on 18.1.1917
Perished in Auschwitz in 1944
Member of "Maccabi Hatzair"

In 1943 and 1944 Menahem obtained documents. He made contact with a printing house whose owner was willing to print documents for use by the underground members. In June 1944 Menahem was caught, interrogated, tortured and deported to Auschwitz.

Klein Moshe 'Koshe'
Klein György
Born in Apagy on 15.1.1926
Died on 23.1.1987
Member of "Hashomer Hatzair"

At the age of seventeen Moshe moved to Budapest and was active in the movement. After the Arrow Cross Party rose to power on 15.10.1944, he stayed at the "Glass House" on 29, Vadász Street. Moshe distributed forged documents to Jews while donning the fascist Arrow Cross uniform. He was caught by Arrow Cross men but managed to rescue himself. He was arrested once more by the Gestapo but again he succeeded in escaping with his friends' help. After the liberation Moshe was the leader of an agricultural hahshara. In 1947 he was on his way to Eretz Israel (Palestine) but was deported to Cyprus. Eventually he made aliya in 1948.
Moshe was a member of Kibbutz Ga'aton. In the last years of his life, he resided in Nahariya.

Klein Shlomo
Klein Slomo
Born in Érsekújvár (Nové Zámky) in 1923
Probably perished in Auschwitz in 1944
Member of "Hashomer Hatzair"

Shlomo joined the movement in adolescence. In 1943 he moved to Budapest. After the Germans invaded Hungary on 19.3.1944, he joined the underground activities of his movement under a false name. Shlomo travelled to his hometown to visit his parents and convince them to escape to Budapest and avoid being deported. He was caught on the train and deported to Auschwitz. His traces were lost.

Klein Shoshanna-Shosha
Born in Nagyszőllős (Vinohragyiv) in 1923
Died in 1988
Member of "Bnei Akiva"

Shosha stayed in Budapest in 1944. She took part in the Death March towards Austria. Shosha was saved thanks to Swiss Protection Documents she was given near the border. She returned to Budapest and arrived at the "Glass House" on Vadász Street. She was an underground activist until the liberation on 18.1.1945.
Shosha made aliya. She resided in Petah-Tikva where her only son still lives.

Kleinman Haya
Klein Heléna
Born in Nagykapos (Vel'ké Kapušany) in 1923
Member of "Bnei Akiva"

Haya lived in Budapest from 1941. In 1944 she joined the underground. Thanks to Aryan documents she received from "Bnei Akiva", she maintained contact between the members of the leadership in the "Glass House" and comrades in hiding all around the city, some with Aryan documents and others without any documents. She stayed at the "Glass House" on Vadász Street from where she went on many missions. Haya distributed Swiss Protection Documents and made contact with activists from the movement who also operated with Aryan documents. Haya rescued Jews from the Death March. After the liberation of Hungary she collected Jewish children and educated them. She made aliya in 1947 as an instructor with a group of children on a long journey that took two years via Austria, Germany, France and Cyprus. From the day she arrived in Eretz Israel (Palestine), she continued to do educational work. Haya, a retired teacher, resides in Jerusalem.

Knapp Menahem
Knapp Béla
Born in Érsekújvár (Nové Zámky) on 2.7.1924
Member of "Hashomer Hatzair"

Menahem came from a religious Jewish family, studied at high school and in a yeshiva. In April 1944, about a month after the Germans invaded Hungary, he was enlisted in a forced labor camp where Anti Livni and Yitzhak Steiner were also serving. Menahem received forged documents from "Hashomer Hatzair" members so that he could escape when ready to. On his way from the forced labor camp to another one he got on a tramway with forged documents in his pocket. On the tram he was recognized by a man from his hometown who was wearing the fascist Arrow Cross party uniform and wanted to arrest him. Menahem managed to jump off the tramway and escape. He arrived in the "Glass House" on 29, Vadász Street and from there he was sent on various missions to distribute forged documents, obtain food and clothes. Many times he was about to be caught but thanks to his presence of mind and luck he always managed to avoid being arrested and continued his activities. A Hungarian officer from his former forced labor unit arrived in the "Glass House" and gave him Swiss Protection Documents for the whole unit thanks to which all the men were taken back to Budapest from the German border.
Menahem is a member of Kibbutz Yassur.

Kohavi Sarah
Miklós Zsuzsa
Born in Debrecen on 7.1.1922
Died on 24.12.1998
Member of "Hanoar Hatzioni"

In 1941 and 1942 Sarah was a member of the leadership of the outlawed ken in Debrecen. In January 1942 she went to a hahshara in Budapest. Sarah helped with the absorption of refugees from Poland who were members of the movement. After the Germans entered Hungary on 19.3.1944, she became an underground activist. She obtained authentic Aryan documents and distributed them. Sarah traveled to many places to distribute documents and she tried to convince friends to escape from the forced labor camps and the ghettos. She found apartments for the fugitives and was active in the tiyul to Romania. Sarah herself made aliya within the framework of the tiyul. On 15.8.1944 she arrived in Eretz Israel (Palestine). She was a member of Kibbutz Metzuba and worked as a biology, chemistry and agriculture teacher.

Cohen Eliezer 'Eli'
Kohn Karl
Born in Vienna in 1918
Member of "Maccabi Hatzair"

Eli's family moved to Slovakia. With the worsening of the situation and the increasing danger coming from the Germans, Eli set up an agricultural hahshara for the members of the movement next to the Hungarian border. Upon the beginning of the deportations of Jews from Slovakia, in three days he smuggled 28 members of the hahshara into Hungary by crossing the Vág River. In the same way another twenty comrades crossed the border with his help. Eli was a member of the movement's leadership and was in charge of the refugees, members of the "Gordoniya movement" that arrived from Poland to Slovakia. Eli himself escaped to Hungary after the German invasion on 19.3.1944 and took part in rescue operations. He left Hungary on the Relief and Rescue Committee train.

After the war he made aliya. He lives in Jerusalem. Eli's wife, Iluci (born in Bratislava in 1922), accompanied him and cooperated with him in all his underground activities.

Cohen Lea
Gaszner Lea
Born in 1924
Member of "Dror Habonim"

Lea was active in "Dror Habonim" from 1943. She was sent to the forced labor camps where members of the movement were serving and brought them forged documents in order to help them escape. She did this for about two and a half months until she was caught, sent to the ghetto and deported to Auschwitz.

After the liberation Lea made aliya and is a member of Kibbutz Parod.

Cohen Shlomo
Kohn Imre
Born in Ipolyság (Šahy) in 11.7.1921
Member of "Maccabi Hatzair"
Died on 13.3.1993

Shlomo helped obtain documents, food and money for the refugees from Slovakia. In 1943 he was drafted to a forced labor camp from which he escaped in July 1944. Shlomo arrived at the "Glass House" on 29, Vadász Street. He was one of the diggers of the bunker in Érdliget. He moved escapees from labor units and children from the ghetto to the Protected Houses under the auspices of the International Red Cross. From November 1944 he transported food from the warehouse on Wekerle Street to Jews hiding in various places and to the children's houses. Shlomo made aliya and joined Kibbutz Metzuba where he died.

Cohen Shlomo
Kohn Salamon
Born on 30.11.1921
Member of "Dror Habonim"

In 1937 Shlomo joined "Hehalutz Hatzair" and later "Dror". In 1939 he was sent by the movement to a hahshara in Budapest. In 1942 he was enlisted in a forced labor unit. In March 1944 Shlomo escaped and returned to Budapest. He was sent by Tzvi Goldfarb to Carpatho-Ruthenia to warn and save Jews. From June 1944 he worked with the tiyul. On one of the trips to the border, Shlomo felt he was being followed and decided not to return to Budapest but to cross the border into Romania. Shlomo made aliya. He is a member of Kibbutz Parod.

Kom Milan
Born in Újvidék (Novi Sad) in 1923
Died in 1941
Member of "Hashomer Hatzair"

Milan was a member of the local ken. He took part in the organization of a resistance movement in the area of Bački Petrovac (Petrőc). After he was caught by Hungarian gendarmes, he killed one of them and wounded another. Then he shot himself.

Komoly Ottó Nathan Ze'ev
Born in Budapest on 26.3.1882
Murdered in January 1945
Member of "Hatzionim Haclali'im"

Komoly was one of the most prominent figures of Hungarian Jewry during the Holocaust. In his adolescence he was active in the "Ivriya" movement and later in the Student Union "Maccabea".
He studied engineering and was a railway engineer. In WW I he served in the Hungarian army as a lieutenant and was given decorations for excellence. Later he was upgraded to the rank of captain.
Komoly translated Herzl's book "Altneuland" from German and called it "Ősi föld új hon". He wrote the following books: "The Future of the Jewish People" (1919), "How Shall We Build My House?" (1933) and "A Zionist World View" (Cionista életszemlélet).

In 1940 Komoly was elected president of the Hungarian Zionist Association in Hungary and was the leader of the Relief and Rescue Committee. He supported Kasztner who made contact with the Germans in order to save Jews. Komoly also supported the underground activities of the Zionist youth movements. He had contacts with the Hungarian liberal circles, the Spanish and Swiss consulates, the Pope's representative and the Protestant clergy. He was in touch with the younger son of Horthy, the Hungarian ruler.

After the Germans invaded Hungary on 19.3.1944, Komoly worked with all his heart and strength in the rescue of Jews. He was active in setting up children's houses for Jewish children most of whom were orphans. Komoly was appointed to a high position in the International Red Cross and through this organization expanded his activities. With the rise to power of the Arrow Cross Party on 15.10.1944 he left his apartment together with his wife and moved to the Ritz Hotel where he handled the rescue issues. Komoly was taken from the hotel by Arrow Cross thugs in a devious way and his traces disappeared. In 1944 and until he disappeared, Komoly kept a diary where he described the efforts, of which he was a partner, made to save Hungarian Jewry

Dr. Kőnig Moshe
Kőnig Pál
Born in Budapest on 10.8.1912
Died on 9.6.1995
Member of "Hatzionim Haclali'im"

Moshe was a certified rabbi and had a doctorate. He joined the "Maccabea" movement and later "Barissia". He worked as a teacher at the Jewish high school in Budapest but was fired because of his Zionist activities.
After the Germans invaded Hungary on 19.3.1944, Moshe participated in various underground activities. He took part in setting up the bunker on Zöldmáli Street. He distributed Swiss Protection Documents. Moshe was the representative of "Hanoar Hatzioni" in the plan to print 7,800 certificates in cooperation with Moshe Krausz.
After the liberation of Budapest by the Red Army (18.1.1945), Moshe engaged in collecting Jewish children and taking care of them. From 1945 to 1949 he was active in the framework of "Hashomer Hatzair" as an educator and also as the manager of a children's house. He was in charge of the pedagogical section of the children's department of the Joint in Hungary.
Moshe made aliya illegally from Hungary. In 1950 he arrived in Israel with his wife Miriam and their two children. He stayed in Kibbutz Haogen for fourteen months. In Israel he was a teacher, an educator and a schoolmaster.

Kos Avraham 'Andi'
Kos Andor
Born in Szenc (Senec) in 1924
Member of "Maccabi Hatzair"

Avraham's family lived in Surányka (Šurianky). After the town was transferred from Slovakia to Hungary, he assisted refugees who strived to arrive in Budapest.
In May 1944 Avraham was enlisted in a forced labor unit, deserted with the help of documents he was given and joined the underground activities. He helped in the rescue of members of the movement from the forced labor camps and went on various missions. In November 1944 Avraham joined the bunker on Hungary Boulevard. The bunker was discovered and Andi and his friends were incarcerated in the prison on Margit Boulevard. He was liberated in a daring operation of the Zionist Youth

underground. After the liberation Avraham was active in the framework of the B'riha and the manager of a children's house in Budapest.

Avraham made aliya in 1948 with the recruitment aliya, served in the 4th battalion of the Palmah and took part in various operations. When he was discharged in 1950, he joined Kibbutz Kfar Hahoresh. He left the kibbutz and worked in "Mekorot" as an electrical engineer. He is retired and lives in the Protea pensioners' village.

Köves Péter
Member of the "Shimoni Group"

Kövesi Gizi
Friedman
Born in Halmaj in 1909
Died in Tel-Aviv in 1975
Member of "Mizrahi"

Gizi helped the refugees who were arriving to Hungary from Poland and Slovakia. Her house in Budapest served as a shelter and transit station for them. Gizi moved to the "Glass House" on 29, Vadász Street where she was liberated in January 1945. After the liberation she was elected as chairperson of the "Mizrahi" women. She made aliya in 1952 and continued with her public work.

Krausz Moshe
Krausz Miklós
Born in Mezőladány in 1908
Died in Israel in 1985
Member of "Mizrahi"

Moshe studied at Rabbi Austerlitz's yeshiva in Miskolc. In 1932 he was appointed as the general secretary of the "Mizrahi" and "Hapoel

Hamizrahi" organizations in Hungary. In 1934 he was the secretary of the Eretz-Israel Office in Budapest and from 1938 to 1946 its manager. In April 1944, a few weeks after the German invasion of Hungary, all the 7,800 certificates that were not used by Jews, who were deported or exterminated by the Germans all over Europe, arrived. Through the Swiss consul, Karl Lutz, Moshe applied to the Hungarian government and received the authorization to make use of these certificates. After Romania switched alliance to the Russians (23.8.1944) the way to Palestine was blocked. Consul Lutz obtained from the Hungarian government the authorization to issue Protection Documents for those in possession of a certificate and thus the "Schutzpass" was born. Krausz had connections with the representatives of the neutral countries in Budapest. In June 1944 he distributed the "Auschwitz Report", which was smuggled into Hungary and described the extermination of Jews in the camp, abroad. Moshe Krausz was in charge of the "Glass House" on 29, Vadász Street, which was a branch of the Swiss consulate where about three thousand Jews found a shelter. The Swiss Protection Documents were forged by members of the Zionist youth movements. Tens of thousands of copies were made and given to Jews. Krausz worked for the liberation of Jews in possession of Protection Documents who were being taken westwards on the Death March. He was a prominent figure in the rescue operations. After the liberation Moshe made aliya.

In Eretz Israel (Palestine) he was the manager of the "Swedish Village" and worked for the Ministry of Social Welfare until he retired.

Kupferstein Joseph 'Kupi"
Kupferstein József
Born in Kassa (Košice) in 1921
Perished in 1944
Member of "Bnei Akiva"

Joseph came from an ultra-orthodox Jewish environment in Kaszony. He moved to Budapest. Joseph was one of the prominent figures in his movement. After the Germans invaded Hungary on 19.3.1944, he became an underground activist. Joseph fell sick, had to have an operation and for a long time was bedridden. He was enlisted in a forced labor unit. Joseph perished in an unknown place.

Kopfstein Miriam
Hertschka Magda
Born on 25.8.1919
Died on 31.1.1996
Member of "Dror Habonim"

From April to July 1944 Miriam was detained in the Kistarcsa camp near Budapest. Thanks to her knowledge of German, she worked in the camp office. She forged the documents of 80 Jewish men and wrote that they had not yet reached the age of sixteen. Thanks to this forgery they were released and arrived in Budapest. The forgery was discovered and Miriam was interrogated. She admitted her crime and was sentenced to deportation to the death camps but luckily she remained in the Kistarcsa camp where she was released in September 1944.

Lack Shulamit
Gara Mária
Born in Budapest on 22.2.1924
Member of "Hanoar Hatzioni"

In 1944 Shulamit distributed forged documents in the Hungarian country towns. She turned her apartment in Budapest into a shelter for the refugees on their way to Romania within the framework of the tiyul. Shulamit herself tried to cross the border into Romania but was caught, incarcerated in the Nagyvárad prison and later deported to Auschwitz and other camps. Shulamit made aliya in 1945 and participated in the War of Independence. She was awarded with a medal of "Fighter aginst the Nazis". She was married to Dov Broshi. After her second marriage she moved to the United States where she now lives.

Langer Miklós 'Miki'
Born in Poprad in 1923
Murdered in 1944
Friend of "Hashomer Hatzair"

Miki worked as a draftsman-planner in Budapest. He forged documents. Miki came up with original inventions and was very resourceful. On 21.12.1944 he was staying with David Gur and "Feigi" (Feigenbaum Endre - Fábry Andrej) in the forgery laboratory in an apartment on the first floor of 13, Erzsébet Street in Budapest when it was discovered by chance by Hungarian detectives who were looking for Jews in hiding. The three men were taken to the fascist Arrow Cross district headquarters which were located nearby. The suitcases with the seals, the empty forms and the finished forged documents were also taken away. The prisoners managed to swallow the notes and documents with their addresses. Miki and his friends were interrogated, brutally tortured and cruelly beaten. Miki Langer could not put up with the torture and beatings and, the day after he was caught, on December 22nd, he died. His two friends were taken to the central military prison on Margit Boulevard and were set free in a daring operation by the Zionist youth movements underground.

Lantos Yeshayahu
Born on 14.2.1926
Member of "Bnei Akiva"

Yeshayahu was an underground activist. He was a prisoner in the Kistarcsa camp. He stayed and worked in the "Glass House". From 1945 Yeshayahu lived in Hungary and Transylvania.
He made aliya in 1946 and worked as a high school teacher.

Lapid Yitzhak
Lefkovits Zoltán
Born in Polyán (Polany) on 26.12.1917
Member of "Hashomer Hatzair"

From 1943 Yitzhak lived in Budapest and earned a living as a carpenter. After the Germans invaded Hungary on 19.3.1944, he went underground with documents provided by the movement. He took part in underground activities until the beginning of August when he joined the tiyul and crossed the border into Romania.
He sailed from Constanţa on the "Bulbul" and, at the end of 1944, he arrived in Eretz Israel (Palestine). Yitzhak is a member of Kibbutz Ein Dor.

Lavi David
Lisszer László
Born in Beszterce (Bistriţa) in 1921
Member of "Hashomer Hatzair"

When David was fourteen, his family moved to Nyiregyháza. After graduating from the Jewish high school, he learned engraving. In 1941 David moved to Budapest and integrated the underground activities helping refugees from Slovakia. He was arrested together with a group of comrades and sent to the Garany detention camp. Being a craftsman, he was enlisted in the Hungarian army. With the retreat of the Germans, he went on the Death March and arrived in Austria. After the war David returned to Hungary and joined the "Ehad BeMay" garin. In 1948 he made aliya. David was among the founders of Kibbutz Ga'aton, where he still lives.

Lavi Moshe
Löwinger Martin
Born in 1919 in Dunaszerdahely (Dunajská Streda)
Died on 26.3.1998
Member of "Hashomer Hatzair"

Moshe learned locksmith's work and engraving. In 1940 he was enlisted in a forced labor unit, escaped and, in October 1944, arrived in Budapest. He joined his movement's underground activities. He distributed food coupons to Jews hiding in the city and, wearing a fascist Arrow Cross uniform, he took Jewish families from their homes to a secure place. Moshe stayed at the "Glass House" on Vadász Street.
He made aliya in 1945 and joined Kibbutz Ha'ogen. Later, he left the kibbutz. He was a resident of Tivon. Moshe wrote an autobiography "My Life in those Days", published by "Maarechet" in 1994.

Lavi Yirmiyahu 'Yirmi'
Lőbel György
Born in Miskolc on 10.7.1926
Member of "Bnei Akiva"

Yirmi was an underground activist and carried forged documents. He served as the liaison person between the center of the movement, which was located in the "Glass House" on 29, Vadász Street, and comrades all over the city. Yirmi distributed forged documents, food and money to the needy refugees. He saved Jews, who were to be deported to extermination camps, from the train wagons. Yirmi was caught three times but managed to escape and resume his activities. In January 1945, the day the Red Army attacked the city, he was staying in one of the suburbs. He cooperated with communist anti-Nazi activists and attacked a German machine-gun position. He was wounded in the leg by a bullet and hospitalized in a Russian military hospital. In 1947 Yirmi made aliya. He was a major in the IDF. He is now an industrialist in Carmiel.

Leibovics Tzvi
Leibovics Hirsch
Born in Kökényes (Ternove) on 8.10.1923
Member of "Dror Habonim"

Tzvi was an underground activist for the movement. From 1943 he lived in Budapest, set up and equipped bunkers in the Máramaros County. In April 1944 one of the bunkers was discovered and some of the occupants were caught but under cover of darkness Tzvi succeeded in escaping. He enlisted in a forced labor unit where he served until the liberation. After the war he collected Jewish children and took them to children's houses. Tzvi arrived with 130 children in Germany where a kibbutz by the name of Hanna Szenes was set up.
He made aliya and resides in Bat Yam.

Leiner Giora
Leiner György
Born in Kassa (Košice) in 1924
Died in 1983
Member of "Hashomer Hatzair"

Giora joined the movement in the early 1930's. He moved to Budapest and stayed at the hostel for working youngsters on Zöldmáli Street. Later he worked as a nurse in a Jewish hospital. After the German invasion on 19.3.1944, as he knew some Slovak, Giora moved to Slovakia, joined the uprising in Banská Bystrica and fought as a partisan.
Giora made aliya and joined Kibbutz Ga'aton. He left the kibbutz. Giora died in a road accident.

Levavi Dina
Komlós Karolina
Born in Szatmárnémeti (Satu Mare) on 16.1.1921
Member of "Hashomer Hatzair"

Dina's father was a doctor and the manager of a hospital. In 1923 the family moved to Kassa. In 1931 Dina joined the movement. She studied at the kindergarten teachers' college in Budapest.

In 1939 she went to a hahshara in Izbég. From 1943 Dina lived in Budapest. After the Germans invaded Hungary on 19.3.1944, she equipped herself with Aryan documents. Her apartment in Budapest served as a meeting place and shelter for the underground activists.

Dina saved the two sons of the family, whom she worked for as a nanny, after the mother committed suicide. Dina left Hungary on the Relief and Rescue Committee train.

In September 1945 she arrived in Eretz Israel (Palestine) and joined Kibbutz Ma'anit. She married Moshe Levavi. They left the kibbutz in 1949. Their son, Amit, was killed in the Yom Kippur War. She accompanied her husband who was sent by the Jewish Agency on Zionist missions to Italy, Brazil and France. Dina lives in Jerusalem

Levi Ágnes
Nahman Ágnes
Born in Budapest on 15.11.1928
Died in 2004
Member of "Hanoar Hatzioni"

Ágnes' father was among the deportees to Kamenetz-Podolsk. She hid with her mother in Budapest and was active in the movement. Ágnes provided forged documents and helped find accommodation and food for those in need. At the end of 1944 she worked at the "Glass House". Ágnes made aliya.

Prof. Levi Arie
Löwi László
Born in Mád on 13.8.1923
Member of "Hanoar Hatzioni"
Died in 12.2.2006

Arie studied in a Yeshiva and a rabbinical seminary in Budapest. At the time of the Holocaust he was active in his movement's underground activities. He helped get forged papers for servicemen in the forced labor units and for Jews who refused to enter the ghetto. Arie supplied food to elderly Jews who resided in Yellow Star houses, and patrolled the streets of Budapest, dressed up as a priest.

He made aliya in 1949. Arie Levi was a Professor in education and recipient of the Israel Prize for his work in the field of educational research.

Levi Moshe
Löwi György
Born in Léva (Levice) in 1922
Died on 20.7.2003
Member of "Hashomer Hatzair"

Moshe was enlisted in a forced labor unit. In October 1944 he arrived at the "Glass House" on Vadász Street in Budapest. He underwent weapons training to prepare for fighting. Moshe distributed forged papers and was a liaison person with the ghetto. He made aliya. Moshe was a member of the "Ehad BeMay" garin that founded Kibbutz Ga'aton. Moshe was a member of Kibbutz Hagoshrim.

Levi Simha
Löwi Viktor
Born in Mád on 24.10.1925
Member of "Hanoar Hatzioni"

Simha served in a forced labor unit but escaped to Budapest where he hid thanks to forged documents. He helped his friends who escaped from labor units, provided them with suitable papers and helped them find accommodation. After the Arrow Cross rose to power in Hungary on 15.10.1944, Simha stayed at and worked from the "Glass House" on Vadász Street.

He made aliya. He is an educational psychologist.

Levi Simon
Löwi Simon
Born in 1926
Perished in Auschwitz in 1944
Member of "Hanoar Hatzioni"

Simon was one of the first members of the movement in Hungary. He was active in the hahsharot and was among the organizers of the movement's 1943 winter camp in Balatonboglár. Simon distributed forged documents and taught the youngsters how to work in underground and self-defense conditions. He also took part in the smuggling of Jews from Slovakia into Hungary via Losonc (Lučenec). Simon escorted the fugitives from Hungary to Romania within the framework of the tiyul. During one of his trips towards the town of Nagyvárad (Oradea), he was caught together with his friend Hanna Cohen. They were both taken to Auschwitz where they perished.

Levi Yehuda 'Pici'
Löwi Lajos
Born in Kolozsvár (Cluj) on 5.3.1925
Died on 27.9.2000
Member of "Hanoar Hatzioni"

After the Germans invaded Hungary on 19.3.1944, with the help of his movement, Yehuda arrived in Budapest equipped with forged Christian papers. He joined the underground activities and engaged in obtaining and distributing forged documents. From June 1944 Yehuda often escorted Jews on trains to Nagyvárad in the framework of the tiyul. Yehuda himself sometimes crossed the border in order to put the smuggled Jews into safe hands. On one of these occasions, on a street in Nagyvárad, he shot a policeman who was about to arrest Jews but managed to escape.
Yehuda entered the ghettos in order to take out Jews and save them from deportation to Auschwitz. He was caught by the Germans and a swastika cross was burnt into his chest with white-hot iron. In a critical condition Yehuda was saved by the Red Army.
In 1947 he made aliya. He lived on a kibbutz for some years. Yehuda worked as an educational instructor in Alonei Yitzhak and was the manager of a technology school in Sarafend. He was a professional soldier in the IDF and was discharged with the rank of lieutenant colonel.

"Bnei Akiva".
From left: Blum Pnina, Klein Shoshana,
Kleinman Haya.

Members of "Dror Habonim"
at a forced labor camp.
From left: Steinmetz Shmuel,
Leibovics Tzvi, Rosenfeld
Lejbus, Kafri Yitzhak
("Hashomer Hatzair").

Members of "Dror Habonim" ("Hehalutz Hatzair"), 1943.
Second from left: Baumgarten Menahem; first from the
right: Prizant Tzvi.

"Hashomer Hatzair" winter camp,
Kóspallag, 1943.
From left, top row: Sharoni Tzivonit,
Kraus-Burger Yaffa, [-], Fischer Avri,
Fast Tova, Shalev Eli, [-]. Bottom: Ben-
Dor Tova, Kama Yirmiyahu, Harari
Yisrael, Ronen Avraham, Berger Michael,
Schechter David.

Lindenfeld Moshe Yehuda
Lindenfeld Ervin
Born in Mád in 1923
Murdered in 1944
Member of "Bnei Akiva"

Moshe studied at various yeshivot and became a certified rabbi. He joined his movement in Ungvár. When his Zionist activities and membership of "Bnei Akiva" became known, he was expelled from the yeshiva. After the Germans invaded Hungary on 19.3.1944, he equipped himself with the forged Aryan documents of a Protestant Priest and thus avoided being enlisted in a forced labor unit. Moshe took part in his movement's underground activities. He stayed at the "Glass House". After the Arrow Cross rose to power on 15.10.1944, he left the "Glass House" and delivered forged documents all over the capital. In December, during a "work" meeting in a café, he was caught while in possession of forged documents and taken for interrogation at the Arrow Cross headquarters on 60, Andrássy Street. His comrades organized a search for him but lost his traces. He was probably shot dead on the banks of the Danube.

Lipkovics Tzvi
Lipkovics György
Born in Tokaj on 18.9.1924
Murdered in 1944
Member of "Hashomer Hatzair"

Tzvi joined the movement in 1938. From April 1944 he was sent by the movement on missions to country towns in order to warn the local Jews of what lay in store for them and to give them forged documents. On one of these missions he was sent with Hillel Hakohen, Yitzhak Rotman and Yehuda Alpár to the South Transylvania area to open a route to Romania via the town of Brašov. All four men were caught, put into a train wagon and deported to Auschwitz. When the train crossed Slovakia, Hillel Hakohen, Tzvi Lipkovics and Yehuda Alpár jumped off the wagon. Tzvi was shot and killed by "Hlinka Guard" people. Hillel Hakohen was saved and joined the underground activities.

Liszauer Avri

Liszauer Zoltán
Born in Budapest in 1923
Member of "Hashomer Hatzair"

Avri was a member of the movement's leadership from 1943. After the Germans invaded Hungary on 19.3.1944, he engaged in obtaining Aryan documents in the offices of the Hungarian Population Registry. Avri made an attempt to move to Yugoslavia to join the partisans but in a meeting in Budapest to prepare for the escape, he was caught, imprisoned, interrogated, tortured and taken to the Mauthausen concentration camp from which he was later liberated. In Budapest Avri edited "Hadereh", the "Borohov Circle" paper. He did literary-scientific work. Avri resides in Budapest.

Livni Dan 'Anti'

Weisz Antal
Born in Érsekújvár (Nové Zámky) on 15.11.1924
Killed in an accident in 1953
Member of "Hashomer Hatzair"

In April 1944 Dan was enlisted in a forced labor unit. In September he escaped with another eleven comrades with the help of documents provided by the movement and arrived in Budapest, where he found refuge. Dan joined the movement's underground activities. He ran various errands and delivered food to the "Glass House". After the war Dan was one of the leaders of "Hashomer Hatzair" in Hungary. He was an instructor for the children in the movement's children's house. He wrote poems and did translations from Hebrew and world literature.
 Dan made aliya in 1949 and joined Kibbutz Ga'aton. He lost his life in a tractor accident.

A collection of his poems and translations was published by the "Society for Research of the History of the Zionist Youth Movements in Hungary" in : "Happiness, Sorrow and Age" (2003).

Löwenheim Shmuel
Löwenheim Sándor
Born in Budapest on 11.9.1926
Member of "Hanoar Hatzioni"

From 1943 Shmuel gave assistance to refugees from Poland and Slovakia by finding them accommodation and hiding places, obtaining food for them and maintaining contact with them. He also smuggled Jews across the Hungarian border. During this period of time he operated under the name of Klement Zoltán.
After the Germans invaded Hungary on 19.3.1944, he volunteered to the firemen and, wearing the uniform, he was free to walk around the capital. Shmuel distributed forged documents and, in order to do so, he traveled to country towns. He brought some youngsters back with him to Budapest and arranged accommodation for them in his parents' house and other places.
Shmuel traveled to forced labor camps carrying forged documents, helped those who wanted to escape arrive in Budapest and gave them accommodation and hiding places.
After the Arrow Cross came to power on 15.10.1944, he liberated young men from the forced labor units that passed through the capital on their way to the east. Shmuel's underground activities are mentioned in the following books: "We are Witnesses", "In the Shadow of Death" and "Shmulik, the Anonymous". Samuel operated with Mordehai Ben David distributing food to the bunkers and children's houses.
He is a member of Kibbutz Nitzanim.

Lung David
Lung Dezső
Born in Miskolc on 21.9.1921
Killed in battle in 1944
Member of "Beitar"

David was active in his movement in Miskolc from an early age. He had many talents and was a central figure in his ken of the movement. In 1942 David was enlisted in a forced labor unit. In October 1944 he deserted and joined the military unit Kiska under the name of Lukács Dezső. Wearing a fascist Arrow Cross armband, he engaged with his friends in resistance and rescue operations such as attacks on Arrow

Cross patrols and giving assistance to Jews staying in Protected Houses. He succeeded in liberating his father from a forced labor unit and taking him to Budapest. When he felt that his Jewish identity was about to be discovered, together with his comrades, he left Kiska and joined a bunker in the Zugló area. Prior to that, his brother, Mordehai, met him in the "Glass House". That was the last time they met. Another brother, Yitzhak, who was also staying at the "Glass House", was sent on a mission from which he never returned. Rumors spread that David's bunker had been discovered by the fascists and that about ten comrades, most of whom were members of "Beitar" from the Miskolc area, fought a shooting battle until they died as heroes.

Maajan Lea
Mann Edit
Born in Miskolc in 1919
Member of "Hashomer Hatzair"

Lea learned sewing. In 1934 she joined the movement. In 1938 Lea moved to Budapest where she took part in the activities of the movement. After the German occupation of Hungary on 19.3.1944, Lea dealt with obtaining authentic documents for the offices of the Population Registry in Budapest. She tried to cross the border into Romania within the framework of the tiyul without success. She left Hungary with her brother, Haim, on the Relief and Rescue Committee train and at the end of 1944 she arrived in Switzerland. Lea made aliya in 1945 and joined Kibbutz Ein Dor.

Mahrer Nusi
Rózsa Nusi
Born in Budapest on 22.12.1918
Member of "Hashomer Hatzair"

Nusi worked in the office of the "Keren Kayemet" on Király Street where she met members of the Hungarian "Hashomer Hatzair" movement: Rafi Benshalom, Dan Zimmerman and Moshe Alpan. Under their influence Nusi joined the movement. She was an underground activist under the fictitious name of Varga Ilona. Nusi obtained Hungarian documents. She worked in a large workshop producing rubber seals. She stole seals and other materials for the forgery of documents and gave them to Dan

Zimmerman. Nusi made aliya in 1944 via Romania within the framework of the tiyul. Nusi has been a member of Kibbutz Ha'ogen since then.

Makai Judith
Ellenbogen Heléna
Born in Érsekújvár (Nové Zámky) in 1923
Member of "Maccabi Hatzair"

Judith's family was a Jewish orthodox one. Her father was active in the "Mizrahi" movement. In 1936 Judith joined "Maccabi Hatzair" with her twin sister, Anni. Her father died in 1942 while serving in a forced labor unit. On 19.3.1944, the day the Germans invaded Hungary, Judith arrived in Budapest for a sewing training course. Her comrades from the movement convinced her not to return to her hometown and to stay in the capital. With the help of forged documents she changed her identity to Elmér Julia. Within the framework of the underground Judith distributed forged documents around the city. In order to provide her comrades from the movement with forged papers, she travelled to Győr, Várpalota and Komárom.
Judith left Hungary within the quota allocated to her movement on the Relief and Rescue Committee train. She made aliya and stayed in Kfar Hamaccabi, Kibbutz Huliot and Kibbutz Metzuba. She was also in Kibbuz Tze'elim and Kfar Hahoresh. Judith resides in Ramat Gan.

Mann Tzipora
Mann Erika
Born in Budapest in 1925
Died in Budapest in 1945
Member of "Hanoar Hatzioni"

Tzipora joined "Hanoar Hatzioni" at the age of thirteen. At the end of 1943 she dealt with obtaining Aryan documents from various government offices. Tzipora assisted the organizers of the bunkers which she provided with equipment, food and medicines. She tried to leave Hungary within the framework of the tiyul but was caught in Békéscsaba, interrogated under torture and imprisoned in a detention camp. After the Arrow Cross rose to power on 15.10.1944, she was taken to Budapest and succeeded in escaping. She went to Mérleg Street, to Department A of the International Red Cross. With the help of Ottó Komoly, who was the head of the Relief and Rescue Committee, she moved to the children's house on Orsó Street, the "Glass House" and then Wekerle Street. As a result of the beatings, her kidneys were injured and Tzipora died in the winter of 1945.

Margalit Joseph
Markstein József
Born in Érsekújvár (Nové Zámky) on 23.12.1923
Died on 19.5.1992
Member of "Hashomer Hatzair"

As of 1942 Joseph gave assistance to Jewish refugees who fled from Slovakia to Hungary. The geographical location of Érsekújvár, about twelve kilometres from the border on the Hungarian side, put him and his comrades in a central position in the "slipping across the border" operation. Sometimes the refugees had to stay for a day or two in the town so they needed accommodation and all their needs had to be taken care of until they resumed their journey. The local Jewish community disapproved of this rescue operation out of fear of the authorities. Joseph was caught by the police, beaten, warned not to continue his activity and released. At the end of 1943 Joseph was sent to the town of Kolozsvár (Cluj) where he stayed for four months. During his stay there he opened the "Hashomer Hatzair" ken which had about thirty members. On 20.3.1944, one day after the Germans invaded Hungary, he was warned by an emissary from Budapest not to do any overt activity for the movement. Joseph decided to return to his parents in his hometown and he stayed there for a few weeks. He saw his parents being taken to the ghetto from which they were sent to an extermination camp. Joseph was enlisted in a forced labor unit but shortly afterwards he escaped with the help of an emissary of the movement who appeared in the camp with forged documents and money. Joseph arrived at the "Glass House" in Budapest where Rafi Friedl (Benshalom) met him. Already the day after he arrived in Budapest he received suitable papers and money from Moshe Pil (Alpan) who accompanied him to the railway station on his way to Nagyvárad (Oradea) on the Romanian border. Ten members of the movement, among whom Joseph, crossed the border and arrived in Bucharest. Joseph stayed there for three months until he made aliya in October 1944. He joined Kibbutz Ein Dor, the 6th Eretz-Israeli kibbutz.

Markbreit Mordehai
Markbreit Tibor
Born in Debrecen in 1923
Killed in 1944
Member of "Hanoar Hatzioni"

Mordehai studied at the Jewish high school in his hometown and excelled in mathematics and music. In 1943 he moved to Újpest. In the spring of 1944 he was enlisted in a forced labor unit and sent to the Bór camp where he was severely wounded but managed to survive. He arrived in Budapest and joined the underground activities. He stayed in the bunker on Teréz Boulevard. During the days of the blockade on the city the house where the bunker was located was directly hit by a cannonball and caught fire. The people hiding in the bunker had to go out and were discovered by the concierge who reported them to Arrow Cross men. These arrived on the site and started chasing the young Jews. Mordehai and all his friends were killed during this chase. Only one of them, Moshe Katz, survived to tell the story.

Meir Joseph
Mayer József
Born in Nagyilonda (Ileanda) on 27.10.1922
Died on 10.11.1991
Member of "Hashomer Hatzair"

Joseph joined the movement at the age of sixteen. He went on a hahshara in Kolozsvár (Cluj) and prepared for aliya but the plan was not carried out. In that town he worked in a metal factory and met young Hungarians, communists and socialists who worked for the underground. Joseph also joined the anti-fascist movement in 1941. He moved to Budapest and joined the "Hashomer Hatzair" activities. He maintained contact with the leftwing workers and engaged, among other things, in collecting clothes and food for the political detainees. In October 1943 Joseph was enlisted in a forced labor unit. While serving there, he was arrested and interrogated about his relations with the leftwing groups and his activities in "Hashomer Hatzair" but was released and taken back to the labor unit.
In October 1944 Joseph escaped with the help of the movement and joined its underground activities. He was ordered to maintain his contacts with the Hungarian communist and anti-fascist underground and he opened

a new channel of cooperation between the two parties. The "Hashomer Hatzair" people provided the Hungarian underground activists with forged documents, food and clothes while they mainly helped find hiding places. Joseph Meir operated in the suburbs of the capital, in Kőbánya and Újpest and organized the desertion of a group of Hungarian officers and soldiers who gave him various weapons. He saved both groups of Jews and single ones while wearing an Arrow Cross uniform.

After the liberation Joseph joined the Political Department of the Hungarian Ministry of the Interior where he localized Nazi criminals, Arrow Cross men and officers of the forced labor camps. Later Joseph was appointed commander of the Hagana that was set up under the communist regime to protect the Jews.

Joseph made aliya in 1948. He took part in the War of Independence within the framework of the Palmah and, when he was demobilized, he joined Kibbutz Ga'aton. Joseph held various positions in his kibbutz, in public institutions and in the Kibbutz Artzi.

Meir Shulamit
Nuszbaum Ágnes
Born in Budapest in 1927
Member of "Hanoar Hatzioni"

Ágnes joined the movement in 1942. In 1943 she assisted Polish refugees who arrived in Budapest. After the Germans invaded Hungary on 19.3.1944, she went into hiding with forged documents. On June 26th she went on a tiyul to the Romanian border with a group of comrades. She succeeded in crossing the border but was caught by Romanian policemen. Shulamit was sentenced to five years in prison but stayed only two months.

In November 1944 she arrived in Eretz Israel (Palestine) via Bulgaria. For two years Ágnes was in the framework of Aliyat Hanoar. She took part in the War of Independence and was the girls' commander in the "Kuzari" unit. Ágnes engaged in education and was an inspector for the Ministry of Education. She lives in Jerusalem.

Meron Ya'akov
Markovics Jenő
Born in Kiskunmajsa in 1922
Member of "Hashomer Hatzair"

Ya'akov came from a religious Jewish family. His parents had five children and were business people. Ya'akov joined the movement when he was attending the high school. After graduating, he arrived in Budapest and started learning to be an electrician. Ya'akov joined the "Sela" Organization that consisted of adult members of "Hashomer Hatzair". The members of the organization lived in a "Heim", rooms shared by a few members of the movement. In 1942 Ya'akov assisted refugees arriving in Hungary from Slovakia. He gave them documents, food coupons and found shelters for them. In 1943 he was enlisted in a forced labor unit within the framework of the Hungarian army. After the German occupation of Hungary on 19.3.1944, Ya'akov tried to escape with some comrades and with the help of members of the movement who gave him documents and money, but he failed. Only in October 1944 did he succeed in reaching Budapest and finding refuge in the "Glass House". At the beginning of December Ya'akov moved to Pestszentlőrinc, where he lived in a suburb with a family of workers and made contact with the cells of Communists from the Demény Group. Later he worked within the framework of the Megyeri Group, led by Jóska Mayer (Meir), which operated in the 10th district of the capital, Kőbánya. He was also active in the Kispest area. Carrying a gun, he transferred propaganda materials and weapons. After the liberation of Budapest in January 1945, Ya'akov was among the founders of the "Ehad BeMay" garin. In 1946 he took part in the B'riha organization. On 29.11.1947, the day the UN announced the establishment of a Jewish state, Ya'akov arrived in Eretz Israel (Palestine) thanks to a certificate. Ya'akov is a member of Kibbutz Ein Dor.

Mező István
Born in Debrecen in 1923
Murdered in 1944
Member of Hanoar Hatzioni

István came from a Zionist family. He studied at the Jewish high school in his hometown. His father was the assistant manager of the Keren Kayemet and the chairman of the Zionist Organization in his town. After

19.3.1944 István fled to Budapest and joined the underground activities. He was caught while distributing forged documents and killed in unclear circumstances.

Minervi Hanna
Wertheimer Edit
Born in Debrecen on 1.8.1927
Member of "Hashomer Hatzair"

Hanna joined the movement at the age of eleven following her brother and sister's example.

In May 1944, while she was living in the Debrecen ghetto, Hanna received from her movement forged documents which enabled her to escape only four hours before the ghetto gates closed. She arrived in Budapest and was active in the underground. Hanna was supposed to meet Pil (Moshe Alpan) in a public park and to recognize him by his stick and hat. She made a mistake and approached another man but, luckily, she was not taken to the police. At the end of June 1944 Hanna left Hungary on the Relief and Rescue Committee train. She made aliya and stayed in Kibbutz Eilon within the framework of Aliyat Hanoar. She resides in Jerusalem.

Morberger Ervin Moshe
Born in Újvidék (Novi Sad) in 1919
Perished in 1943
Member of "Hashomer Hatzair"

Moshe was a member of the "Hashomer Hatzair" ken in Újvidék. In 1941 he joined an anti-fascist organization. His underground nickname was Móric. He was enlisted in a forced labor unit and taken to Ukraine where he died.

Nadav Ephraim
Lőwinger Ferenc
Born in Budapest on 14.7.1923
Member of "Hashomer Hatzair"

Efraim was an only child. In 1939 he joined "Maccabi Hatzair" but a year later he became a member of "Hashomer Hatzair" with a group of friends. In 1941, after graduating from high school, he learned construction locksmith's work. After completing his studies he worked as a professional locksmith. In December 1943 Ephraim was enlisted in the movement's activities.

On 19.3.1944, the day the Germans invaded Hungary, he was staying in Budapest on sick leave. Following the instructions from the movement he went underground equipped with forged documents. He was sent on missions to the country towns of Debrecen, Nyirbátor, Nyíregyháza, Kisvárda, Miskolc and some others in order to deliver Aryan documents and money to the local Jews, give them instructions on how to escape and information on what was happening.

At the beginning of June 1944, following instructions from Moshe Alpan, Efraim crossed the border into Romania near the town of Nagyvárad (Oradea). He arrived in Eretz Israel (Palestine) with his wife Tzipora on 4.11.1944. He joined Kibbutz Negba and was one of the founders of Kibbutz Yehiam.

In 1959 he left the kibbutz, worked for the Ministry of Agriculture and later worked independently. He lives in Tel-Aviv. Efraim was among the active members of the Society for Research of the History of the Zionist Youth Movements in Hungary.

Nadav Tzipora
Streger Edit
Born in Debrecen on 1.2.1925
Member of "Hashomer Hatzair"

Tzipora joined the movement at the age of ten. She learned sewing. In 1943 she moved to Budapest, earned a living and became a member of a group of adults and among them Efra, her future husband. After the Germans occupied Hungary on 19.3.1944, she equipped herself with Aryan documents and, following instructions from the movement, went underground. She rented an apartment with Ephra passing for fugitives from country towns fearing the approach of the Red Army. Tzipora went on missions to the country towns carrying forged documents, money and instructions for escape. In June 1944 she crossed the border into Romania near the town of Nagyvárad (Oradea) with Ephra. On 4.11.1944 she arrived in Eretz Israel (Palestine). In 1959 she left Kibbutz Yehiam with her husband. She resides in Tel-Aviv.

Nadivi Tzvi
Reich Hirsch
Born in Vágújhely (Nové Mesto nad Váhom) in 1924
Died on 23.12.1982
Member of "Hanoar Hatzioni"

Tzvi ran away from a forced labor unit. He saved his comrades wearing a Hungarian soldier's and an Arrow Cross uniform. Thanks to his Aryan appearance, blue eyes and light hair, he succeeded in saving some of his friends from the Death March. Tzvi supplied equipment and forged documents to people hiding in bunkers. He was caught by the Gestapo, taken to the Majestic Hotel in Buda, interrogated and tortured but his comrades from the movement succeeded in liberating him. He resumed his underground activities until the Red Army conquered the town.
He made aliya, got an M.A. in history at the Tel-Aviv University and taught in high schools. He was the manager of the education department in the Netanya municipality.

Dr. Natan Alexander
Nátán Sándor
Born in Érsekújvár (Nové Zámky) on 20.11.1907
Died in 1971
Member of "Hatzionim Haclali'im"

Before the war broke out, Natan was an officer in the Hungarian army. He operated in the "Glass House" on 29, Vadász Street where many young Jews who had been discharged or had escaped from forced labor, found refuge. Some of them were armed. Natan and his friends broke down the common wall with the adjacent cellar that used to be the office of the Hungarian Football Association and moved some of the youngsters there. When the Hungarian fascists broke into the "Glass House" and took about 1,500 Jews who were staying there to the street in order to lead them to the banks of the Danube and shoot them, the armed youngsters were ready to break out and rescue them. Natan, who was their commander, restrained them and his decision was the right one as the Jews eventually returned to the House. Thanks to his decision bloodshed was averted.

After the liberation Natan was the manager of the Eretz-Israel Office in Budapest. He made aliya, lived in Jerusalem and held high positions in the Jewish Agency in Jerusalem.

Német Shabtai (Nünü)
Német István
Born in Kassa (Košice) on 1.2.1925
Member of "Beitar"

Upon the German occupation of Hungary on 19.3.1944, Shabtai escaped to Budapest with the help of forged documents he had received from comrades in the movement. He engaged in a variety of underground activities: preparing forged documents, setting up bunkers and bringing comrades from country towns to Budapest. In July 1944 an article was published in a Budapest newspaper with Shabtai's photo saying that he was engaged in the forgery of documents and that the police were looking for him. Shabtai lived in various bunkers and was in charge of providing supplies to their occupants. In December 1944 he moved to the "Glass House" on Vadász Street where he was liberated from.

Shabtai learned pharmacy at the Brno University. He made aliya in 1949 and enlisted in the IDF. He was discharged with the rank of captain. Shabtai married Frieda Azarovitz. He worked as a pharmacist and was the national pharmacy manager.

Neuwirth Lea
Spitzer Edit
Born in Nagymegyer (Veľký Meder) in 1923
Died in 2000
Member of "Maccabi Hatzair"

In 1939, with the area's annexation to Hungary, Lea moved to Budapest with her family. Shortly after the Germans invaded Hungary on 19.3.1944, she received forged documents from her movement. Lea distributed forged documents to comrades in Budapest and in forced labor camps around Hungary.

Lea made aliya in 1946. Until 1961 she was a member of Kfar Hahoresh and then moved to Kfar Vitkin.

Neuwirth Yehoshua
Neuwirth Sándor
Born in Nagymegyer (Veľ'ký Meder) in 1924
Member of "Maccabi Hatzair"

In 1943 Yehoshua joined the movement following his sister's, Hanna (Atsmon), steps. After the German invasion of Hungary on 19.3.1944, his sister's apartment in Budapest served as a meeting place for the members of the movement who operated in the underground and some of whom were refugees from Slovakia. The activities included the forgery of documents and their distribution.

In May 1944 Yehoshua was enlisted in a forced labor unit. He escaped with the help of forged documents and money he had received from a comrade who came to the camp where he was staying. Yehoshua stayed in a bunker in a suburb of Budapest. At the end of November the bunker was discovered and its occupants were caught and incarcerated in the central military prison on Margit Boulevard.

Yehoshua and a large group of friends were liberated in a daring rescue operation of the underground activists. He arrived at a Protected House on Wekerle Sándor Street from where he was liberated.

After the liberation he gathered Jewish children from hiding places and from the ghetto and took them to children's houses.

Yehoshua was active in the B'riha.

At the end of November he boarded a ship that was caught by the British and its passengers taken to Cyprus. Yehoshua stayed in Cyprus for about a year, then he made aliya and joined the garin in Kfar Hahoresh. Nowadays he lives in Protea, a pensioneers' village.

Növe Mordehai
Mannheim
Born in 1929
Died in 1995
Member of "Bnei Akiva"

Mordehai's family lived in the town of Losonc (Lučenec). His mother sent him to a "Bnei Akiva" hahshara in Budapest where many youngsters found refuge from their persecutors. Mordehai dealt with the delivery of food to the needy in the Yellow Star Houses on a tricycle and carrying forged documents. His family was sent to extermination camps but in August 1944 Mordehai crossed the border into Romania with the help of comrades from the movement.

Mordehai made aliya and stayed within the framework of Aliyat Hanoar.

Növe Tova
Singer Mannheim
Born in 1932
Member of "Bnei Akiva"

Although she was only twelve years old, Tova engaged in taking orphaned children out of the ghetto and putting them in institutions under the protection of the International Red Cross in the Aryan section of Budapest. Carrying forged Christian documents and thanks to her Aryan appearance, Tova ran various errands from the "Glass House".

Tova made aliya and married Mordehai Növe. She resides in Jerusalem.

Offenbach Shalom
Offenbach Sándor
Born in Lodz, in 1899
Died in 1958
Member of "Ihud Mapai"

Shalom arrived in Budapest in the 1920's and worked in the textile business. Being an active Zionist, he was elected as the treasurer of the Relief and Rescue Committee, following Shmuel Springman's aliya on 18.1.1944.

On 27.5.1944 he was captured by the Hungarian counter-espionage, together with Hansi Brand and Israel Kastner but they were all released a short while thereafter.

Together with others, Shalom compiled the list of Jews who were to board a train from Hungary to Switzerland organized by the Relief and Rescue Committee. When "Department A", headed by Ottó Komoly, was established in the offices of the International Red Cross on 4, Mérleg Street, Shalom was in charge, among others, of obtaining funds for setting up and equipping children's homes. As the recipient of funds transferred from Istanbul and Switzerland, he allocated them to the Zionist youth movements for their rescue operations.

After the liberation Shalom continued his work in the textile business, until its nationalization by the communist government in Hungary.

He moved to Vienna in 1950 and to Germany in 1957.

Offner Róbert 'Fifi'
Born in Kassa (Košice) in 1925
Member of "Beitar"
Died in July 2006, Israel

Robert joined the movement at the age of thirteen. After the German occupation of Hungary on 19.3.1944, he was moved to a ghetto, together with other Jews of his town and its vicinity. Thanks to forged documents forwarded to him and his friend Shabtai Német, they escaped and arrived in Budapest.

He produced and distributed forged documents and traveled to the ghetto in Sopron. In Budapest, he hid in a bunker located at the Institute of Technology in Budapest. In August he was caught and tortured by the Hungarian police who wanted to get the names of his comrades. He survived the torture and did not reveal anything. Robert was transferred to the Kistarcsa detention camp, from which he later escaped. He returned to the underground in Budapest, and stayed at a bunker on Hungary Boulevard.

Together with Tommy Freiman, another member of the movement, he reported at the fascist "Arrow Cross" headquarters, and joined its ranks. He obtained authentic documents, which were instrumental in rescuing Jews from Protected Houses. He also took part in setting up the bunker at Laci-köz.

On 7.12.1944 he was captured again and detained at the main military prison on Margit Boulevard in Budapest. From there he was transferred to a jail in Sopronkőhida. By the end of January 1945 Róbert was sent to Szombathely and assigned to disassembling bomb duds. From there he fled to Yugoslavia. In 1948 he was recruited to the Czechoslovak army and began his technical academic studies in Prague.

In April 1949 Róbert made aliya. Between 1951 and 1961 he served in the engineering corps of the IDF, and was demobilized with the rank of major. He worked abroad as an agent for Solel Boneh from 1962 to 1970 and for ORS International from 1971 to 1990.

He lives in Haifa with his wife, Tzipora, nee Bieberstein.

Oren Hanna
Aczél Marika
Born in Székesfehérvár in 1927
Member of "Hanoar Hatzioni"

Hanna was active with obtaining Aryan documents mainly from the offices of the Population Registry. Her appearance helped her in distributing these documents and in special missions. She went on mission to country towns in order to warn the Jews of their fate.
In the summer of 1944 she moved to Romania by way of the tiyul.
She resides in Jerusalem.

Orosz György
Born in Budapest in 1920
Died on 14.12.1978
Member of "Hanoar Hatzioni"

György was a member of "Hanoar Hatzioni" from 1938. In 1942 he was called up to a forced labor unit, released in 1943 but recalled. In 1944, in behalf of "Omzsa", he was in charge of the supply of clothing to the Jews enlisted in the forced labor units. He also dealt with the supply of clothing to the refugees from Slovakia and Poland. He contacted officers of the Hungarian army serving in the Buda fortress, who dealt with the organization of the resistance movements, and, thanks to these connections, he obtained Christian identity cards which he gave to Slovak refugees. He, personally, also used such a document. From the Hungarian officers he obtained various weapons which he then passed on to his comrades in the underground.

György settled in the "Omzsa" offices in Bethlen Square. Together with his friends, he turned the synagogue in the square into a hospital and established a central kitchen that provided food for the Jews in the ghetto. He succeeded in rescuing his mother and his younger brother, Peter, by transferring them to "Omzsa" dwellings.

He took part in patrols in the streets of Budapest while armed and wearing an Arrow Cross uniform and in this way he managed to rescue many Jews. In December 1944 he saved the life of a young Jewish man who was shot, wounded and thrown into the waters of the Danube River but succeeded to reach the bank.

Orosz had connections with Joel Brand, Otto Komoly and Raoul Wallenberg.

He made aliya and died in Israel.

Palgi Joel
Nussbecher Emil
Born in Kolozsvár (Cluj) in 1918
Died in 1978
Paratrooper

In 1939 Joel made aliya and arrived in Kibbutz Afikim. In 1942 he enlisted in the Palmah and in 1943 volunteered for the mission of the paratroopers in German occupied Europe. He did the training and, on 15.4.1944, with Peretz Goldstein and two British soldiers he parachuted on Yugoslav territory. He arrived at the headquarters of the 6th Corps of the partisans in the Papok Mountains. On 19.6.1944 with Peretz he crossed the Drava River and arrived in Hungary. From the day they crossed the border they were followed by Hungarian counter-espionage men. Joel and Peretz arrived in Budapest within one day and first met with Dr. Israel Kasztner one of the leaders of the Relief and Rescue Committee and then members of the underground Zionist youth movement.

Joel was arrested by the Hungarian counter-espionage on June 27 and Peretz on July 1st. The Germans demanded that the Hungarians hand over the two paratroopers to them. Joel was taken to the Gestapo prison on Fő Street and from there both Joel and Peretz were moved to the central Hungarian military prison on Margit Boulevard where Hanna Szenes was already imprisoned. Joel was interrogated and tortured but did not reveal his secrets or the goal of his mission. As the Red Army approached the Hungarian capital, Joel and Peretz were transferred to the prison in Komárom.

On 8.12.1944 both paratroopers were put on a train wagon and were on their way to Germany. Joel managed to jump off the train and to return to Budapest where he found refuge with members of the Zionist underground. Peretz was taken to Germany and perished there.

After the war Joel returned to Eretz Israel (Palestine) and enlisted in the Israeli Air Force. He served as the managing-director of "El-Al" and as the Israeli ambassador in Tanzania.

In his book "Into the Inferno", published in 1948, he described his life during the war (2nd publication: 1977). English edition: Rutgers University Press, New Brunswick, New Jersey and London, 2003.

Paul Ernst
Pál Ernő 'Jancsi'
Born in Beregújfalu (Beregujfalu) on 14.1.1928
Member of "Dror Habonim"

Ernst arrived in Budapest in 1941 and, that same year, he joined the movement in the Újpest suburb of the capital. In 1943 he met Neshka Goldfarb and later, Tzvi Goldfarb, Vili Eisikovics and other comrades. Under a false name and with forged documents he started working for the underground. He went on missions to the forced labor camps in order to smuggle comrades into Budapest. He walked around the city wearing the uniform of a lieutenant of the pre-army "Levente" and, according to a list he had, Ernst took Jews out of the ghetto. Riding a motorcycle he maintained contact with the bunkers and supplied food and equipment for them. Ernst was arrested by fascist Arrow Cross men and taken to their headquarters on 60, Andrássy Street. Afterwards he was taken for further interrogation to the Gestapo headquarters in Buda. When he was being taken with a group of Jews to the banks of the Danube where the fascists intended to shoot them, Ernst succeeded to escape and arrive in one of the bunkers in Buda. However, he found out that the bunker had already been discovered by the Hungarian police. In a park in the vicinity of the Eastern Railway Station he met with Vili Eisikovics who led him to a nearby different bunker of the movement. Two days later that bunker too was discovered and its occupants were taken to the prison on Margit Boulevard. He underwent cruel interrogation and eventually was liberated by a daring operation of the underground Zionist Youth Movement and taken to one of the Protected Houses where he was liberated by the Red Army.
Ernst made aliya. Nowadays he lives in the USA.

Pesti Dov
Pesti Alfréd
Born in Budapest in 1929
Member of "Hanoar Hatzioni"

Dov came from a bourgeois family. When he was ten, he lost his father and the family lost their possessions. Dov was sent to a Budapest orphanage for orphans from Hungary, Ukraine and Poland and stayed there until 1944. He received forged Aryan documents with which he lived under a false identity.

At the end of 1944 he showed up at the offices of the International Red Cross and was sent to the children's house on Magdolna Street where he survived.

After the liberation he worked as a messenger boy for the Eretz-Israel delegation.

In July 1946 he was on his way to Eretz Israel (Palestine). He stayed in Cyprus for some time and in December 1947 he arrived in the Atlit camp (Palestine). He lived in Kibbutz Kfar Giladi, left and worked as a carpenter and instructor in carpentry. He resides in Netanya.

Péter Simha
Péter Sándor
Born on 22.5.1925
Member of "Hanoar Hatzioni"

After the Germans invaded Hungary on 19.3.1944, Simha engaged in underground activities. He obtained authentic Aryan documents from the offices of the Population Registry in Budapest. He stayed in a bunker, in a cave in the hills of Buda. The bunker, whose entrance was through a deep hole, was discovered and the rope down the hole was severed. Simha and another three comrades were trapped in the bunker for one month. Eventually he managed to get out and hid in a forest. He returned to Budapest and was caught by the fascists. Simha was taken to the Gestapo headquarters in the Majestic Hotel, tortured and moved to a prison. He was liberated thanks to a Swiss Protection Document. Simha stayed at the "Glass House" on 29, Vadász Street. After the liberation he collected Jewish children and sent them to Eretz Israel (Palestine).

Simha made aliya in 1949. He is a member of Kibbutz Shomrat.

Porat Dov
Fried Béla
Born in Párkány (Štúrovo) in 1921
Died in 2003
Member of "Maccabi Hatzair"

In 1942, according to the movement's decision, Dov moved from Slovakia to Budapest. His and his friends' mission was to obtain forged documents, find hiding places and obtain food coupons and money for the members of the movement. He was active in smuggling comrades from the movement from Slovakia into Hungary and absorbing them. Dov was caught on one of the bridges across the Danube but managed to escape. He was imprisoned together with Joseph Scheffer and Tzvi Amad in the Garany detention camp.

Dov made aliya in 1948. He worked as a teacher in Tiberias and Haifa.

Porgesz Judith
Born in Liptószentmiklós (Liptovský Mikuláš) in 1921
Member of "Maccabi Hatzair"

Judith was active in the B'riha from Slovakia to Hungary. In April 1944 she arrived in Budapest and distributed forged documents, found apartments for the refugees and was a liaison between the comrades. Judith was arrested in mid-June and deported to Auschwitz with Menahem-Meno Klein.

Prizant Tzvi
Prizant Herman
Born in Toronya (Toruny) on 12.4.1923
Member of "Dror Habonim"

Tzvi studied at a Hebrew elementary school in Toronya and high school in Munkács. In 1933 he joined the "Hehalutz Hatzair" movement which later became "Dror Habonim". In 1941 Tzvi moved to Budapest. He engaged in the planning and execution of rescue and resistance operations. After the German invasion of Hungary on 19.3.1944, he was sent by the movement to Huszt in order to organize the local underground and to meet his family who was living there. He carried a gun. Tzvi returned to Budapest but with the establishment of the ghetto in Huszt he was sent there again, with Menahem Baumgarten, in order to convince the Jews to escape. As a result eleven people fled.

On his way back to Budapest by train, Tzvi was caught and returned to Huszt and interrogated by the Hungarian counter-espionage. He ran away and joined his family in the ghetto. At the time of the organization of the deportations, Tzvi and his young brother, Albert, hid with a Gentile acquaintance. Tzvi's brother could not stand the stress of hiding and joined the Jews who were being sent to Auschwitz. Tzvi waited in hiding and, when a group of Jewish forced labor workers passed in the vicinity, he joined them and arrived in Budapest. Tzvi arrived in Dés with the forced labor unit.

In August members of his movement tried to liberate him and a group of his comrades with the help of money and forged documents delivered to them by Pál Ernő. Tzvi and his friends decided to stay where they were because of the approach of the Red Army and, hopefully, their liberation. They were caught by Romanian soldiers and transferred to the Russians. Eventually they were liberated by the Jews of Gyulafehérvár (Alba-Julia).

Tzvi and his parents arrived in Bucharest where they set up a hahshara. Tzvi returned to Hungary and was active within the framework of the B'riha.

In 1946 Tzvi arrived in Italy, was enlisted in the Palmah and underwent military training. He was sent to the Zionist Congress in Basel with a group of comrades and worked there as an usher wearing the uniform of the "Jewish Brigade". In 1947 he made aliya and was a member of Kibbutz Givat Brenner for about seven years. Tzvi resides in Ramat Hasharon.

Raab Tzadok
'Cicus'
Born in Nagymegyer (Vel'ký Meder) in 1922
Member of "Bnei Akiva"
Died in 19.10.2005

Tzadok's parents were religious Zionist Jews and related to the Raab family who were among the founders of Petah-Tikva.

Tzadok joined "Bnei Akiva" at the age of fifteen. From 1939 he worked as an instructor in Budapest and was among the founders of garin A of Bnei Akiva in Hungary and within that framework went on a hahshara. From 1942 he gave assistance to refugees from Poland and Slovakia.

After the Germans invaded Hungary on 19.3.1944, Tzadok dealt with the forgery and distribution of documents. He traveled to the towns of Nagyvárad and Kolozsvár in order to give forged documents to the local Jews and persuade them to escape from the deportations to the east. He was expelled from most of the places by the Jews themselves who accused him of diffusing tragic news.

When Tzadok returned to Budapest, he became active in the framework of the tiyul. Even after his partners in this activity, David Friedman and David Asael, were arrested by the fascists, Tzadok continued with his underground activities.

Tzadok was among the compilers of the list of members of the movement who were to leave Hungary on the train of the Relief and Rescue Committee. Tzadok himself left Hungary on this train. On the journey that lasted about six months, he took care of the education of children passengers.

At the beginning of 1945 Tzadok arrived in Eretz Israel (Palestine) where he stayed at Kibbutz Masuot Yitzhak in Gush Etzion. He fought in the War of Independence and fell prisoner to the Jordan Legion. He stayed in captivity for ten months.

After Tzadok returned from captivity, he settled down in Haifa with his wife, Shoshana. He was a forest ranger for the Keren Kayemet Le'Israel for 36 years.

He resided in Moshav Atzmona.

Reichman Ezra
Reichman Ernő
Born in Kunágota in February 1926
Fell in the War of Independence in the battle for the Castel
Member of "Hashomer Hatzair"

Ezra attended elementary school in his hometown and then studied at the Jewish high school in Budapest. After the Germans invaded Hungary on 19.3.1944, he went underground. Ezra engaged in obtaining authentic documents from the offices of the Population Registry in the capital. He engaged in transferring equipment for the forgery of documents and in hiding it. In May 1944 he traveled to Vésztő in order to give forged Christian papers to David Gur-Grosz' sister, Miriam (nowadays Reshef), and help her escape to Budapest. His mission did not go off very well due to the family's opposition. In June 1944 Ezra fled from Hungary in the framework of the tiyul and that same year he arrived in Eretz Israel (Palestine). He stayed for some time in Kibbutz Ramat Hashofet in the framework of a garin. Ezra moved to Jerusalem and studied biology at university. In November 1947 he married Aczél Marika, now Hanna Oren. During the War of Independence Ezra volunteered for service in the students' unit. He fought in the battles for the conquest of the Castel and fell there. Ezra's parents perished in Auschwitz.

Reisman Joseph
Reisman Joszke
Born in Kisvárda on 26.2.1923
Died on 30.8.1989 in Israel
Member of "Dror Habonim"

In April 1944, in Kisvárda, Joseph was enlisted in a forced labor unit and sent to Kassa. He ran away from the service thanks to forged documents he had received from Efra and Tzippi Agmon. He arrived in the "Glass House" on Vadász Street in Budapest and became a liaison person under a fictitious identity. He moved around the city riding a motorbike and took food and documents to the people who needed them. He was sent by Simha Hunwald to release five comrades who were being deported and already inside a wagon. With great courage he succeeded in setting them free and taking them to the "Glass House". Joseph joined the ranks of the fascist unit, "Skulls of the Dead", and within this framework he saved Jews. When the city was liberated, Joseph was caught by Russian soldiers while he was wearing a Hungarian officer's uniform. He managed to escape and arrived in Kisvárda where the Russians were already in control. He served as the liaison officer between the Russians and the Hungarians. He succeeded in bringing about the arrest of more than one fascist. Joseph left Kisvárda and joined the "Dror Habonim" movement in Budapest. He was active within the framework of the B'riha. From 1948 he worked for the Eretz-Israel Office in Budapest.
At the beginning of 1949 Joseph made aliya with his wife, Miriam. He worked as the manager of the supply and food services in El-Al.

Reshef Viktor 'Viki'
Fischer Viktor
Born in Vágújhely (Nové Mesto nad Váhom) in 1919
Member of "Maccabi Hatzair"

After graduating from high school Viktor studied at the Institute of Technology in Prague. In 1942 he arrived illegally in Budapest. For about a year he worked as a clerk and was active in the movement. According to the movement's demand, Viktor quit his job and became the movement's treasurer a job he kept until the Germans invaded Hungary on 19.3.1944. Viktor organized a workshop for the forgery of documents. He was considered to be the first forger of his movement. In the laboratory he dealt primarily with the technical aspect of duplicating documents. Viktor specialized in the collection of relevant materials for forgery such as the list of churches in Hungary, policemen's notepads with the list of streets etc. In addition, he kept track of the new regulations and instructions in the daily papers so that the forged documents would match the changing requirements. Viktor took care of the distribution of the forged documents. After the fascist Arrow Cross Party rose to power, he took part in additional rescue operations. Viktor made aliya. For years he worked for the Ministry of Foreign Affairs. He resides in Jerusalem.

Reuveni Sarah
Beer Sári
Born in Budapest in 1928
Member of "Hashomer Hatzair"

Sarah came from a traditional Jewish family. There were three children in the family: Menahem, the eldest, Sari and Hava, the youngest. After the Germans invaded Hungary on 19.3.1944, Sarah lived in a Yellow Star House and was employed with other Jewish women in the removal of rubble. She had contact for the first time with the Zionist underground after the Arrow Cross Party rose to power on 15.10.1944. She received forged papers from underground activists and she, herself, began forging documents by modifying old documents for the Jews living under false names. Sarah engaged in taking children out of the ghetto to the children's houses which were under the protection of the International Red Cross. After the liberation in January 1945 Sarah worked in a children's house for Jewish orphans. In 1948 she made aliya. She worked at Yad Vashem and did research on Hungarian Jewry. Sarah published books and many articles about the Holocaust and anti-Semitism. She deals with the "Righteous Gentiles", rescuers of Hungarian Jews. Sarah resides in Jerusalem.

Révész Márta
Weisz Márta
Born in Budapest on 23.8.1928
Member of "Hanoar Hatzioni"

Márta was active in the Zionist underground. She engaged in obtaining authentic Aryan documents from the offices of the Population Registry in Budapest. She maintained contact with members of the movement who were serving in forced labor units, helped them escape and reach Budapest. Under a false name Márta and one of her friends succeeded in finding accommodation in a girls' hostel belonging to the fascist Arrow Cross Party and to steal documents and forms from there. As their real identity was discovered, Márta and her friend escaped to the "Glass House" where they stayed until the liberation of the city. Márta moved to Romania where she married Gabby Révész. She returned to Hungary with her husband and tried to cross the border again but this time into Yugoslavia. In Yugoslavia Márta was caught by the police but managed to get free and arrive in Italy where she gave birth to her son. She returned to Hungary with her husband to complete her studies. Marta made aliya in 1956. She lives in Rishon LeTzion.

Révész Noemi 'Nonika'
Feder Róza Ráhel
Born in Nyitrabánya (Handlová) on 1.12.1919
Member of "Maccabi Hatzair"

Noemi's family was from Nagytapolcsány (Topolčany) in Slovakia. She operated in the underground by the side of her husband Peretz, one of the leaders of the Zionist underground. Noemi moved to Budapest with him and they arrived at the house of Hansi and Joel Brand. Noemi operated with forged documents and showed much wisdom. She frequently faced danger. She worked in Budapest as a children's nanny and also took care of Hansi and Joel's children, Miki and Danny. In June 1944, after being followed, she was almost arrested but managed to convince the detective to let her go. After the liberation she continued her diverse activities.
On 26.5.1949 Noemi made aliya with Peretz and their two children. Noemi is a member of Kibbutz Kfar Hamaccabi.

Révész Peretz
Révész László
Born in Holics (Holič) in 1916
Member of "Maccabi Hatzair"

Peretz was among the prominent figures of the Zionist underground. He came from an educated Jewish family. His father was a lawyer. Peretz studied medicine but, in 1938, before he could finish his studies in the University of Bratislava, he had to interrupt them. He was an excellent sportsman and the Slovak champion in the 100 meter race.

Peretz joined the "Gordonia Maccabi Hatzair" movements and in 1941 became a member of the leadership. When the deportations of Jews from Slovakia started in 1942, he assisted in the escape to Hungary of members of the movement. Peretz himself was caught, managed to escape and, with his wife, Noemi-Nonika, slipped across the border into Hungary and arrived in Budapest. Equipped with letters from the Slovak Zionist institutions asking for help for the refugees, Peretz applied to the Jewish institutions in Budapest but his request was denied. He made contact with comrades from his movement, especially Joel Brand, and worked for the Relief and Rescue Committee.

In 1943 he became a member of the tiyul committee that dealt with the smuggling of Jews from Poland. After the Germans invaded Hungary on 19.3.1944, the Zionist Youth underground was even more active and Peretz was one of its leaders. He established connections with the heads of the neutral states' organizations, initiated and took part in rescue operations.

After the liberation Peretz continued with his diverse activities for the movement as well as his public work amidst his comrades and the remaining refugees. He took care of Jewish children and sent them to Eretz Israel (Palestine). He was active in the B'riha.

In May 1949 Peretz made aliya. He founded and managed an educational institute. He is a member of Kibbutz Kfar Hamaccabi. In his book "Facing Evil Waves" (Maarehet Kibbutz Dalia Publishing House, 2002) he describes his life story and actions.

Révész Yirmiyahu

Révész István
Born in Budapest in 1926
Perished in 1944
Member of "Hashomer Hatzair"

Yirmiyahu studied at the Jewish high school in Budapest and joined the movement. When the activities of the Zionist youth movements restarted at the beginning of 1944, he was sent to Kassa to coordinate the ken there. After the Germans invaded Hungary on 19.3.1944, Yirmiyahu returned to Budapest and joined the underground activities. Due to an informer he was caught in his apartment, where he lived under a false Aryan name, deported to Auschwitz and perished there.

The "Help and Rescue Committee" - "Hehalutz", 1944.
From right: Goldfarb Tzvi, Révész Peretz, Kasztner Israel, Brand Hansi, Komoly Nathan.

"Hanoar Hatzioni" at the Balatonboglár winter camp, December 1943.
From left, standing: Rosenzweig Haim, Klein, Gatmon Alex, Rosenblum Yeshayahu, Berko. Sitting: Löwenheim Shmuel, Levi Simon.

Rip Imre
Born in Újvidék (Novi Sad) in 1919
Perished in 1943
Member of "Hashomer Hatzair"

Imre was a member of the local ken. In 1941, after the invasion of the area by the Hungarians, he fled to Budapest. He took part in the underground activities of the Yugoslav anti-fascist committee. Imre was caught and sent to do forced labor in Ukraine, where he perished.

Robicsek Avraham 'Avri'
Robicsek Ottó
Born in Budapest in 1925
Member of "Maccabi Hatzair"

At the age of fourteen Avraham learned carpentry and joined the movement. After the Germans invaded Hungary on 19.3.1944, he engaged in the collection of documents and photos for further use. While traveling on a Budapest tramway, Avraham was caught with other Jews. Thanks to his profession he was sent to the Kistarcsa detention camp while the other Jews were deported to Auschwitz. His movement decided to transfer Avraham to Romania within the framework of the tiyul. Two attempts to slip across the border failed and on his second attempt he was caught and deported to Auschwitz-Birkenau. Avraham made aliya and became a member of Kfar Hahoresh. After he left the kibbutz, he taught carpentry. Avraham lives in Nahariya.

Robinson Baruh
Robinson Béla
Born in Eperjes (Prešov) on 15.8.1918
Member of "Maccabi Hatzair"
Died in 19.3.2002

From 1942 to 1944 Baruh organized the escape across the border between Slovakia and Hungary. In the summer of 1944 he was also active on the Hungarian-Romanian border in smuggling members of his movement. After 15.10.1944, when the fascist Arrow Cross Party rose to power, Baruh operated wearing the uniform of that party and rescued Jews. After the liberation he made aliya.

Ron Ya'akov
Reisz Jakov 'Jaksi'
Born in Dunaszerdahely (Dunajská Streda) in 1924
Member of "Hashomer Hatzair"

Ya'akov joined the movement in 1938. In 1941 he dealt with the smuggling of Jewish refugees from Slovakia to Budapest. One of the smuggled Jews was caught. As a result Ya'akov was incarcerated in the Mosonyi prison and later sent to the Garany detention camp. From Garany he was transferred to Komárom, from there to Sárvár and then to Auschwitz. After the liberation Ya'akov returned to Budapest and joined the Ehad BeMay garin. He made aliya and was one of the founders of Kibbutz Ga'aton, where he is still a member.

Ronald Anton
Rosenberg Tuli
Born in Nagyszőllős (Vinohragyiv) in 1919
Member of "Hashomer Hatzair"

Anton's parents were Rudolf and Rosalia Rosenberg. His father was a cantor and slaughterer. Tuli was the youngest of fifteen children. On 15.3.1939 his hometown was annexed to Hungary. At the time Tuli was living in Prague and from there he returned to his family. In 1942 Anton received his mobilization orders to a forced labor unit but managed to avoid being enlisted. In 1943 he was forced to enlist and at the beginning of 1944 he arrived in Budapest. After the Germans invaded Hungary on 19.3.1944, Anton escaped and, with help from his sister, Piri, who was also living in Budapest, he joined the underground activities within the framework of "Hashomer Hatzair". At the beginning of April 1944 Anton traveled to Nagyszőllős in order to give the Jews forged documents and take them out of the ghetto but he did not succeed. At the beginning of June while he was staying with his family in Nagyszőllős, prior to the last deportation to the death camps, Anton and three friends decided to hide in a wine cellar behind a wall that was especially built to hide them. When they came out, after hiding for a couple of weeks, they were caught and imprisoned. They were transferred to different prisons until they arrived in Budapest. Anton's three friends were released but he was sent to a penalty camp. With help from the movement he managed to get free. At the end of October 1944 Anton made contact with Joseph-Jóska Meir and took part in operations carried out together with the communist underground, especially the "Demény Group". In 1945, after the liberation, Anton arrived in France and in 1953 he emigrated to the USA. He lives in Los Angeles.

Ronel Aliza 'Lulu'
Barmat Aliza
Born in Érsekújvár (Nové Zámky) on 6.2.1922
Member of "Hashomer Hatzair"

Aliza joined the movement under the influence of her older sister, Violet. She was active in the local ken. In 1939 she stayed at a hahshara in Izbék. From 1942 to 1944 Aliza gave assistance to the refugees arriving to Budapest from Slovakia. At the end of June she left Hungary on the Relief and Rescue Committee train.
In 1945 Aliza made aliya and joined Kibbutz Ein Dor. She left the kibbutz and lives in Holon.

Ronen Amikam
Reichman Amikam
Born in Tel Aviv on 20.12.1927
Died on 16.1.1999 in Israel
Member of "Hanoar Hatzioni"

Amikam was born in Eretz Israel (Palestine) but happened to be in Hungary with his mother on the eve of WW II. His father was a dentist who worked in Angola and wanted his son to have a European education. In Eretz Israel (Palestine) he lived with his grandparents in Kfar Saba. When the Germans invaded Hungary on 19.3.1944, he was a twelfth grade student at the Jewish high school and among the activists of "Hanoar Hatzioni" who operated in the underground. Amikam dealt mainly with the tiyul. He was caught and arrested by the Gestapo and incarcerated in the prison where the paratroopers from Eretz Israel (Palestine), Hanna Szenes, Joel Palgi and Peretz Goldstein, were being held. Amikam shared a cell with Peretz Goldstein. He was liberated in a daring operation of the Zionist underground on 25.12.1944. Amikam resumed his underground activities and dealt mainly with the release of prisoners, the distribution of forged documents and the establishment of children's houses under the protection of the International Red Cross. After the liberation Amikam returned to Eretz Israel (Palestine), studied economics, held professional and public positions, served in the IDF, in the artillery and in the general headquarters as the head of the data center in the Operations Department. He was discharged with the rank of colonel. Amikam lived in Ramat Hasharon.

Ronen Avraham 'Bunyu'
Landesmann Árpád
Born in Kassa (Košice) in 1924
Member of "Hashomer Hatzair"

Avraham joined the movement in 1938. He learned to be a tailor. In 1941 he moved to Budapest and was an instructor in the hostel for apprentices on Zöldmáli Street where he helped Dan Zimmerman to forge documents. After the Germans invaded Hungary on 19.3.1944, Avraham moved to Bratislava, Slovakia (re-tiyul). He made contact with Egon Roth, the leader of underground "Hashomer Hatzair". Avraham took part in the Slovak uprising and left for Banská Bystrica. He fought in various places. In Bukovec he served in a unit under the command of Bielov, the Russian. The fighters passed through the Carpatho-Ruthenia region villages where hiding Jews joined them and eventually the unit counted 70 people. They collected information about the Germans and were sent to blow up railroad tracks and an ammunition factory. Bunyu was the commander of a patrol. At the end of the war Avraham returned to Budapest (1..4.1945) and was one of the founders of the Ehad BeMay garin. He made aliya in 1945 on the "Knesset Israel" ship. Avraham was among the settlers of Kibbutz Ga'aton. He was a cost accountant, manager of a factory, the kibbutz farm coordinator and head of the Regional Council.

Ronen Ya'akov 'Benito'
Rosenberg Tibor
Born in Eperjes (Prešov) in 1917
Member of "Hashomer Hatzair"

Ya'akov joined the movement at the age of fifteen. From 1938 he was a member of the council and secretary of the movement. He dealt with the smuggling of refugees from Poland and Slovakia, their absorption and equipping them with Aryan documents.
In 1942 Ya'akov moved illegally to Budapest and continued with his

underground activities. At the beginning of 1943 his friend, Ruth Loránd, was arrested and then Ya'akov too was caught. After interrogation he faced a dilemma: he could either be sent back to Slovakia or to a forced labor camp in Hungary. Unaware of the then temporary cessation of deportations from Slovakia to Poland, he chose to be sent to a penalty unit of forced labor. He deserted, crossed the border into Slovakia and joined his movement's underground activities.

Ya'akov participated in the International Council of "Hashomer Hatzair" that took place on 31.12.1943 in Vágújhely (Nové Mesto nad Váhom). According to the decision of the council, in 1944 prior to the German invasion, Ya'akov made aliya with Yoshko Baumer, via Hungary, using an authentic certificate. He joined Kibbutz Ha'ogen. Ya'akov married Haika Klinger, a member of the movement and a refugee from Poland. Ya'akov left the kibbutz. He resides in Moshav Sde Nitzan.

Rosenbaum Moshe
Rosenbaum Mose
Born in Kökényes (Ternove) in 1924
Died in 1984 in Israel
Member of "Dror Habonim"

In 1942 Moshe moved to Budapest and joined "Hehalutz Hatzair" which later became "Dror Habonim". In January and February 1944 he shared an apartment with his brother, Shmuel, and other comrades. Together they planned resistance and rescue operations. After the Germans invaded Hungary on 19.3.1944, Moshe was sent to the Carpatho-Ruthenia region to rescue comrades with the help of forged documents. When he returned to Budapest, Moshe became active in the underground. He left Hungary on the train of the Relief and Rescue Committee. He made aliya and worked in the Israel Military Industries.

Rabbi Dr. Rosenbaum Pinhas
Rosenbaum Tibor
Born in Kisvárda in 1923
Died in Geneva in 1985
Member of "Bnei Akiva"

Pinhas was the offspring of an outstanding family of rabbis. His father was the last rabbi in his town. His whole family perished in Auschwitz. Pinhas studied in a yeshiva in Ungvár (Uzshorod) and in other places. He studied at universities in Austria and Germany and got a doctorate in political science and law. Pinhas was a member of the Zionist executive committee on behalf of "Hapoel Hamizrahi". In 1943 he joined the "Bnei Akiva" movement. He was enlisted in a forced labor unit, ran away and arrived in Budapest. After the German invasion on 19.3.1944, Pinhas became one of the leaders of the"Bnei Akiva" movement. He operated in the "Glass House" on Vadász Street. Donning the Hungarian fascist Arrow Cross uniform he liberated Jews from the Yellow Star Houses and the Death March. After the liberation Pinhas served for some time as rabbi in Kisvárda. He was active in the revival of his movement, a member of the national leadership of "Bnei Akiva" and active within the framework of the Joint and UNRRA. Pinhas participated in the 22nd Zionist Congress in Basel. He married Sarah Stern, a Holocaust survivor who left Hungary on the train of the Relief and Rescue Committee. He was appointed as the manager of the Eretz-Israel Office in Geneva. In Switzerland he founded finance companies as well as a bank. Pinhas held a senior position in the high institutions of the Zionist movement.

Rosenbaum Shmuel

Rosenbaum Smuel
Born in Kökényes (Ternove) on 25.2.1926
Member of "Dror Habonim"

Shmuel studied in a Czech and a Hungarian school. In 1943 he moved to Budapest and joined "Hehalutz Hatzair", the future "Dror Habonim". He learned knitting and earned a living from various jobs. In January-February 1944 Shmuel shared an apartment with his brother, Moshe, and Tzvi Prizant. Together they planned rescue and resistance operations. After the Germans invaded Hungary on 19.3.1944, Shmuel went underground with forged documents. In June he was enlisted in a forced labor unit and served in Dés. In August Shmuel and a group of comrades had the opportunity to escape and reach Budapest with forged documents brought to them by a member of the movement, Pál Ernő. However, the group decided not to run away because the Red Army was approaching and they hoped to be liberated. Shmuel was taken prisoner by Romanian soldiers, taken to Alba-Julia (Gyulafehérvár) but liberated with his friends by the local Jews. He arrived in Italy, enlisted in the Palmah and did military training.
In 1947 Shmuel made aliya and joined Kibbutz Givat Brenner. He resides in Ramat-Gan.

Rosenberg Moshe

Born in Csenger on 26.11.1889
Died on 14.6.1972 in Israel
Member of the "Gordon Circle"

Moshe was the manager of Keren Hayesod and commander of the "Hagana Headquarters" of the Zionist youth movements. Within the framework of the Jewish Council in Budapest he worked in the department of country towns (Vidéki-Osztály) to where he sent emissaries (Efra Agmon, Efra Nadav) in order to help the isolated ghettos with Aryan documents, money and information. Moshe was a member of the Relief and Rescue Committee. He got on the train to Bergen-Belsen. He made aliya via Switzerland. In Israel he was the owner of the engineering company "Rosenberg & Luriya" in Ramat-Gan.

Rosenberg Saul 'Sheli"

Born in Kassa (Košice) in 1924
Member of "Bnei Akiva"

In 1944 Saul operated together with Menahem Tzvi Kadari in the framework of the tiyul. He himself crossed the border and arrived in Eretz Israel (Palestine) in 1944. He served in the independent Czech army. Saul resides in the USA.

Rosenberger Raphael

Rosenberger Rezső
Born in Meggyeshegy (Mediaş-Vii), Romania on 14.5.1922
Died in Israel in 1986
Member of "Hanoar Hatzioni"

Raphael was a member of the movement from childhood. He was a prominent activist in the Zionist underground in Romania and a member of the central council of "Hanoar Hatzioni". In the summer of 1944 Raphael operated in Arad, a border town on the Romanian side of the border where he met and took care of the Jewish refugees who crossed the border from Hungary. Raphael himself crossed the border into Hungary many times in order to organize the smuggling of Jews. He helped the refugees to reach the city so they would not fall into the hands of the authorities and not be returned to Hungary. Thanks to his personality Raphael made connections with the Romanian authorities so that the absorption of the refugees would be carried out as planned and he encouraged the Jews of Arad to help the fugitives. Thanks to the escape operation thousands of Jews arrived in Romania and from there they continued their journey to Eretz Israel (Palestine). After the war Raphael engaged in giving assistance to the remains of the Jewish communities in Transylvania. In 1945 and 1946 he lived in Hungary and again helped refugees to reach Eretz Israel (Palestine).

Raphael made aliya in 1947. He lived in Bnei Brak.

Rosenblum Lea
Révész Márta
Born in Petroşani, Romania in 1929
Member of "Hanoar Hatzioni"

When Lea was one year old, her family moved to Budapest. In 1943 she joined the movement. After the Germans invaded Hungary on 19.3.1944, Lea operated under a false name within the framework of the Zionist underground. She engaged in obtaining authentic Aryan documents from the offices of the Population Registry in Budapest. With Márta Révész (Weisz) she managed to find accommodation in a hostel for girls who were members of the Arrow Cross Party and to steal documents from there. Their identity was discovered but they managed to escape. Lea stayed at the "Glass House" on 29, Vadász Street. After the liberation she completed her matriculation examinations. In 1949 Lea made aliya. She joined Kibbutz Mavki'im and married Yeshayahu-Sajó Rosenblum. In 1951 they left the kibbutz. Lea worked as a teacher. She resides in Tel-Aviv.

Rosenblum Yeshayahu 'Sajó'
Rosenblum Sándor
Born in Putnok in 1924
Member of "Hanoar Hatzioni"

Yeshayahu's parents came from Poland. In 1933 the family moved to Budapest. In 1938 Yeshayahu joined the movement. He engaged in obtaining forged Aryan documents, the planning of bunkers and getting hold of army uniforms. In the first month of 1944 He travelled to

Northern Hungary in order to warn the local Jews of what lay in store for them from the fascists and to recruit the young Jews to his movement. He was a liaison person for the underground activists.

In May 1944 Yeshayahu enlisted in a forced labor unit and took advantage of his holiday passes to distribute forged documents. A few days after the 15th of October 1944 he ran away from his unit and hid as a Hungarian soldier. At the end of October, following Dr. Bilitzer's suggestion, Yeshayahu founded a children's house under the protection of the International Red Cross on 65, Budakeszi Road where 220 children and about 70 adults found refuge. This children's house, located in Buda, the hilly part of the capital, was liberated on December 25, 1944 by the Red Army. On that day Yeshayahu was already in the "Glass House" on 29, Vadász Street. He moved to the house next door, where the Hungarian Football Association used to have their office, and was made in charge of one of the resistance groups. He was wounded by a bullet and taken to an Aryan hospital.

After the liberation of Budapest (18.1.1945) Yeshayahu moved to Szeged where he set up a city hahshara and a children's house.

In 1945 he left Hungary within the framework of Aliya Bet (B'riha) as the instructor in charge of 90 teenagers on their way to Eretz Israel (Palestine). He made aliya and was a kibbutz member for five years. He worked as a teacher, schoolmaster, inspector and researcher in education, and editor of text books published by the Ministry of Education. He resides in Tel Aviv..

Rosenfeld Lejbus
Member of "Dror Habonim"

Rosenfeld Yitzhak 'Izsu'
Born in Ungvár (Uzshorod) in 1922
Member of "Bnei Akiva"

In 1942 Yitzhak was enlisted in a forced labor unit but escaped and joined the underground work in the "Glass House" on Vadász Street. He mainly dealt with distributing Swiss Protection Documents (Schutzpass). Yitzhak made aliya and reached the rank of senior officer in the Israeli Police Force.

Rosenzweig Haim 'Imka'
Born in Budapest in 1926
Died in Australia
Member of "Hanoar Hatzioni"

Haim's father was Jewish and his mother was Christian. He joined "Hanoar Hatzioni" at an early age. He read many books about Judaism and Zionism. After the Germans invaded Hungary on 19.3.1944, Haim equipped himself with forged documents and became an underground activist. Haim traveled to country towns to distributed documents and money to the members of his movement so that they could escape from the camps and ghettos. He operated in a daring and determined way. After the war Haim emigrated to Australia.

Roth Miriam
Feldman Mirjam
Born in Kassa (Košice) in 1920
Member of "Bnei Akiva"

Miriam joined the movement at the age of twelve. In 1939, when the area was annexed to Hungary, she was forced to escape because she was wanted by the police for her Zionist activities. Miriam arrived in Prešov and Bratislava in Slovakia where she worked for the national leadership of "Bnei Akiva". When it became known that Jewish girls risked being deported from Slovakia (1942), Miriam fled to Hungary and arrived in Budapest. She joined the "Bnei Akiva" national leadership and took part in the underground activities which included the forging and distributing of forged documents, finding hiding places for the refugees, food and equipment for those in hiding and smuggling Jews over the Romanian border and from there to Eretz Israel (Palestine). Miriam herself failed in her attempt to cross the border and she joined the train of the Relief and Rescue Committee whose destination was Switzerland. After she arrived in Switzerland Miriam agreed to the movement's request that she remain in Europe for some time as an educator for orphans who were Holocaust survivors.

In 1945 Miriam made aliya with a group of children. She worked as a nurse in the agricultural school "Mikveh Israel". She married Yitzhak Roth and they built a large family.

Dr. Roth Stephen
Roth Siegfried Stephan
Born in Gyöngyös in 1915
Died in 1995 in England
Member of "Hanoar Hatzioni"

In 1938 Stephen received his doctorate in law. From 1941 he was active in giving assistance especially to refugees from Poland. From 1942 he was the representative of "Hatzionim Haclali'im" at the Relief and Rescue Committee. After 19.3.1944, he became the leader of "Hanoar Hatzioni". Stephen was among the organizers of the tiyul and, as a result, was arrested, incarcerated in the prison on Fő Street and later in the Kistarcsa detention camp. He was liberated thanks to Ottó Komoly, the president of the Hugarian Zionist Association. After the Arrow Cross Party rose to power on 15.10.1944 Stephen was active in the branches of the Swiss consulate on Wekerle and Vadász Streets. After the liberation he was the manager of the information center on the persecution of Jews in Hungary on behalf of the World Jewish Congress. Stephen arrived in London and worked with Dr. Nahum Goldman. For four years he was the president of the British Zionist Organization.

Roth Yitzhak
Roth Izsák
Born in Nyitra (Nitra) in 1915
Died in 1994 in Israel
Member of "Bnei Akiva"

Yitzhak studied in a yeshiva. He joined "Tze'irei Hamizrahi" and the "Bnei Akiva" movement. In 1939 he was elected to the national leadership of "Bnei Akiva" and engaged in the establishment of new kenim of the movement in Slovakia. In 1942, after the proclamation of an independent Slovakia, Yitzhak served in the Sered labor camp. In 1943 he fled to Budapest and joined comrades of the movement working for the underground. Yitzhak worked in the Eretz-Israel Office in Budapest in the Youth Department and organized aliya to Eretz Israel (Palestine). He helped rescue his comrades who had remained in Slovakia. Yitzhak participated in the proceedings of the Eretz Israel Office managed by Moshe Krausz.

In 1944 Yitzhak left Hungary with a certificate and was on his way to Eretz Israel (Palestine). He was delayed in Ankara and took part in the deliberations of the Relief and Rescue Committee that was working for the recruitment of European Jews for the rescue of the remaining refugees.

When Yitzhak arrived in Eretz Israel (Palestine), he met with the leaders of "Hapoel Hamizrahi" in order to convince them to take part in the rescue of European Jewry. He fought as a private soldier in the War of Independence. He worked for many years as a printer.

Rothbart Pál
Member of the "Shimoni Group"

Rottman Yitzhak
Győri Gyuri
Born in Budapest on 12.12.1924
Member of "Hashomer Hatzair"

Yitzhak grew up in Dombrád where he attended primary and high school. He took his matriculation examinations in Nyiregyháza where he also joined the "Hashomer Hatzair" movement. In 1942 Yitzhak moved to Budapest and started publishing short stories and articles in the movement's newspaper. He took part in underground activities and, in the summer of 1944, he was sent by the movement, together with three comrades, Tzvi Lipkovics, Hillel Hacohen and Yehuda Alpár, to South Transylvania in order to open a new route for the tiyul in the direction of the town of Braşov. However, they were soon discovered, caught and deported to Auschwitz (Yehuda Alpár was saved). Tzvi Lipkovics and Hillel Hacohen jumped from the deportation train on Slovak land. Tzvi was shot but Hillel succeeded in reaching the partisans.

Yitzhak was deported to Auschwitz and Mauthausen. He was able to finish his university studies in Hungary only in 1960 because of the restrictions imposed at the time on Jews in the institutions of higher education. He worked as a locksmith, librarian, teacher and journalist and mainly wrote on pedagogical issues. He published books in Hungarian among which are: "My Escapes" and "Memoirs".

He resides in Budapest.

Sadeh Shlomo
Szabó Tamás
Born in Budapest on 21.6.1924
Died on 19.11.2003 in Israel
Member of "Hashomer Hatzair"

Shlomo was a member first of "Dror Habonim" and later of "Maccabi Hatzair". He was enlisted in a forced labor unit, deserted with other members of the movement and arrived in the bunker in Hüvösvölgy. At the beginning of December 1944 the bunker was discovered by the fascists and all the dwellers were transferred to the military prison on Margit Boulevard. Shlomo was liberated by a daring operation of the Zionist underground on 25.12.1944 and arrived in Wekerle Street. After the liberation he was among the founders of the "Ehad BeMay" garin. In October 1948, Shlomo made aliya and joined Kibbutz Yassur. In 1950 he left the kibbutz. He was an English teacher.

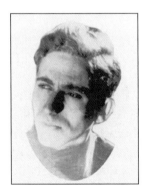

Sagi Eliyahu 'Eli'
Schwartz László
Born in Budapest in 1924
Died on 18.5.1984
Member of "Hashomer Hatzair"

Eliyahu joined "Hashomer Hatzair" in 1939. In 1942 he graduated from the Jewish high school in the capital. At this time he earned a living as a worker and a private teacher of Jewish children. Within the framework of the movement he helped refugees from Slovakia find a shelter in Budapest. After the Germans invaded Hungary on 19.3.1944, Eliyahu was enlisted in a forced labor unit but, after the fascist Arrow Cross Party rose to power on 15.10.1944, he ran away from the service with a group of friends and joined his movement's underground activities. Eliyahu mainly distributed Swiss Protection Documents. He enlisted in a Hungarian armored military unit, "Hunyadi László", which served within the framework of the SS, so that, when necessary, he would be able to help his comrades as a Hungarian soldier. During the registration to the unit he managed to avoid the physical check up but eight of his comrades were discovered as Jews and shot on the spot.

Eliyahu was a member of Kibbutz Ga'aton. In his last years he taught history and Bible in the regional school in Kibbutz Evron.

Sajó Eli
Sajó Péter
Born in Pöstyén (Piešťany) on 31.1.1920
Perished in 1944
Member of "Maccabi Hatzair"

Eli was one of the most prominent figures of the Zionist movements in Hungary. In 1943 he arrived in Budapest, joined the underground and was the representative of his movement in various Zionist institutions. He coordinated the movement's organization for underground activity after the Germans invaded Hungary on 19.3.1944. Eli had connections with the Jewish representatives in Switzerland and Turkey. He was caught at the Romanian border and deported to Auschwitz where he perished.

Shalmon Yitzhak
Salamon Ignác
Born in Felsőárad (Siroke) in 2.9.1924
Member of "Bnei Akiva"

Yitzhak moved to Budapest and in 1942 joined the "Bnei Akiva" movement. In February 1944 he was enlisted in a forced labor unit. During his service he maintained contact with members of the movement, equipped himself with forged documents and procured Aryan documents for some of his friends. The commander of the unit, Farkas, suggested that the men serving in the unit convert to Christianity in order to receive Protection Documents from the Vatican and in fact 70% of the men did convert. After the Arrow Cross Party formed the government, the unit was transferred to the Sopron area and the men dug anti-tank tunnels. Yitzhak escaped and returned to Budapest. In December 1944 he was caught by Arrow Cross men, tortured and moved to the Gestapo headquarters on Schwabs Hill (Svábhegy). He cut the prison bars and escaped. After the liberation he worked as an interpreter in Russian for the Red Army. Yitzhak resumed his activities for the movement: he obtained food for the children's houses and helped smuggle people across the border. In 1947 he made aliya. In 1948 he was drafted to the army and took part in the capture of Beit Shean. He resides in Petah-Tikva.

Salomon Hava
Barmat Éva
Born in Érsekújvár (Nové Zámky) on 3.11.1926
Member of "Hashomer Hatzair"

Hava came from a religious Jewish family. At the age of ten, following her sisters' steps, she joined the "Hashomer Hatzair" movement. After the Germans invaded Hungary on 19.3.1944, in order to escape to Budapest she received forged documents from Nesher Adler, who was sent to her by the movement. She was arrested at the railway station by a local policeman who knew her and allowed her to get on the train. In Budapest she found work with a family who supported the fascist Arrow Cross Party. Hava met her comrades from the movement in public gardens. She was engaged in the distribution of forged documents and food coupons. At the end of December 1944 she stayed in an apartment in Kőbánya, a Budapest suburb. David Gur brought her six suitcases containing equipment for the forging of documents and forged documents. Hava hid them under her bed.
Hava made aliya after the liberation and joined Kibbutz Ein Dor.

Salomon Menahem Mendel
Salamon Mihály
Born in Zilah (Zalău) in 1897
Died in 1991 in Israel
Member of "Mizrahi"

Menahem was a prominent figure in "Mizrahi", held senior positions in the central institutions of the movement and represented it in various forums. In 1941 he was elected as the chairman of the Eretz-Israel Office and in 1943 he held the position of chairman of the "Mizrahi" executive committee. During the Holocaust Menahem took part in rescue activities and was among the leaders of the "Glass House" on 29, Vadász Street. After the liberation Menahem was elected as president of the Hungarian Zionist Association and participated in the 22nd Zionist Congress in Basel.
In 1948 he made aliya and continued with his public work. Menahem was among his movement's candidates for the Knesset. He wrote a book: "I Was a Christian in Europe" (Keresztény voltam Európában, Tel-Aviv, 1955).
Menahem was one of the editors of the Új Kelet daily paper in Tel-Aviv.

Sandak Sarah
Kertész Sári
Born in Budapest on 18.12.1920
Died on 4.1.2005
Member of "Hashomer Hatzair"

In 1939, together with her brother, Shimon, Sarah joined the hahshara in Izbék. Her brother died in a work accident in the nearby quarry. Sarah helped refugees, members of her movement that arrived in Budapest. She provided food and food coupons for them and even accommodated some of them in her house. She obtained authentic documents from the Population Registry.
Sarah made aliya after the liberation of Hungary and joined Kibbutz Yassur. Later she left the kibbutz and lived in Ra'anana.

Sas Dov
Born in Kassa (Košice) in 1922
Fell in 1944
Member of "Hashomer Hatzair"

Dov was a member of the ken's leadership in his hometown. He was enlisted in a forced labor unit and sent to Ukraine. He managed to cross the enemy lines and joined the Red Army. He fell in battle in 1944.

Schamschula Katalin
Herzfeld Rut
Born in Budapest on 29.3.1926
Died in 2003 in Australia
Member of "Hanoar Hatzioni"

In 1938 Katalin joined the "Hanoar Hatzioni" movement. Her family gave assistance to the first refugees from Poland. After the Germans invaded Hungary on 19.3.1944, Katalin was taken to Tattersaal (Todt Lager). In Dinnyés Borgonpuszta, rescued by members of her movement and arrived at the "Glass House" on Vadász Street. Under the name of Horváth Katalin, Katalin distributed forged documents around the city. After the liberation she intended to make aliya and arrived in Romania but, due to an illness, she was forced to return to Budapest. In 1949 Katalin left Hungary. She lived in Sydney, Australia where she died.

Schechter David
Born in Técső (Tyacsiv) in 1924
Killed in 1944
Member of "Hashomer Hatzair"

David studied at a yeshiva and learned carpentry. He was among the founders and activists of the "Hashomer Hatzair" ken in his hometown. In April 1944 he was enlisted in a forced labor unit. In July 1944 his sister, Tzippi, was sent to him and brought him and his friends forged documents, money as well as instructions for escape. In August David arrived in Budapest and joined the underground. He crossed the border into Romania within the framework of the tiyul. When he passed through the city of Arad, on his way to Bucharest, the train was attacked by German planes. David was hit and died. The attack was the result of Romania's decision to break its alliance with Germany. David was buried in the Jewish cemetery in Arad.

Prof. Scheffer Joseph
Schaeffer József
Born in Budapest on 5.5.1922
Died in 1984
Member of "Maccabi Hatzair"

Joseph was a member of the movement's leadership. In 1942 he dealt with the absorption of refugees, members of "Maccabi Hatzair" from Slovakia and equipped them with documents and money. Due to his activities Joseph was arrested and sent to the Garany detention camp. After about eleven months he was transferred to a forced labor camp. On 15.10.1944 Jopseph escaped, arrived in Budapest and joined the underground activities. After the fascist Arrow Cross Party rose to power on 15.10.1944, he worked with Ottó Komoly in Department A within the framework of the International Red Cross and dealt mainly with the organization of children's houses. After the liberation Joseph made aliya and joined Kibbutz Kfar Hahoresh. He held a number of central positions in his kibbutz. Joseph completed his doctorate in sociology. He was one of the prominent figures of the "Institute for Kibbutz Research". Joseph was a professor at Haifa University.

Schlesinger Joseph
Born in 1900
Died in 1981 in Israel
Member of "Mizrahi"

Joseph was a member of the Hungarian Zionist Association and "Mizrahi" leaderships. In 1943 he was a member of the Relief and Rescue Committee and the Eretz-Israel Committee (Pal-Amt). Joseph left Hungary in 1944 on the train of the Relief and Rescue Committee. He made aliya in 1945 with his wife, Ruhama and their two daughters. He worked as an accountant in the taxation office of the Income Tax.

Schlesinger Nurit
Fleischer Hédy
Born in Pozsony (Bratislava) in 1927
Member of "Maccabi Hatzair"

Nurit joined the movement in her hometown, Bratislava, in 1939. One of her first instructors was Peretz Révész. She moved to Budapest with her family. Nurit was an underground activist for her movement. Nurit's sister, Trudi, was caught by the Hungarian police but, with help from Peretz Révész, Nurit managed to set her free. Nurit left Hungary at the end of June 1944 on the Relief and Rescue Committee train. In September 1945 she made aliya. She was a member of Kfar Hahoresh. Nowadays Nurit lives in Kalmaniya.

Schlesinger Ruhama
Weisz Rózsi
Born in 1905
Died in 1988 in Israel
Member of "Mizrahi"

Ruhama cooperated with her husband, Joseph Schlesinger. She was active within the framework of the "Mizrahi" women. In 1944 she left Hungary on the train of the Relief and Rescue Committee. Ruhama made aliya in 1945 with her husband and two daughters.

Schlesinger Yaffe Gabriel
Born in 1896
Died in 1979 in Israel
Member of "Mizrahi"

In 1919 Yaffe founded the "Young Mizrahi" in Hungary and from 1920 to 1922 he was its chairman. In 1943 he was vice-chairman of the Keren Kayemet LeIsrael. He held the position of finance comptroller for the Relief and Rescue Committee and was a member of the Eretz-Israel Committee (Pal-Amt) that helped Jewish refugees arriving in Hungary. Yaffe left Hungary in June 1944 on the train of the Relief and Rescue Committee and made aliya in 1945 with his wife, Ziszl, and their daughter Tova. In 1952 Yaffe was the chief secretary of the rabbinical tribunal in Tel-Aviv/Jaffa.

Schlesinger Ziszl
Herskovits Eugénia
Born in 1896
Died in 1975 in Israel
Member of "Mizrahi"

Ziszl took part in her husband's, Schlesinger Yaffe Gabriel, activities. She was active with the "Mizrahi" women. She left Hungary in June 1944 on the train of the Relief and Rescue Committee and made aliya.

Schönwald Benjamin Haim
Born in Sátoraljaújhely on 15.10.1922
Member of "Hashomer Hatzair"

Benjamin's family was religious. In 1943 he was enlisted in a forced labor unit. He escaped and hid at his older bother's house in the village of Nagymuzsaj (Muzsijeve) in the Carpatho-Ruthenia region Mountains. In April 1944 Benjamin was discovered by Hungarian gendarmes, arrested but, eventually, managed to escape and arrive to Budapest by train.
After meeting Rafi Benshalom and Efra Agmon, who were members of "Hashomer Hatzair", Benjamin joined the members of the movement staying at the "Glass House" on 29, Vadász Street and soon integrated the underground activities. He walked the streets of the city wearing an Arrow Cross armband and took Jews out of places where they were at risk to the "Glass House". After the liberation (18.1.1945) Benjamin obtained food for Jewish orphans. He made aliya. Benjamin resides in Nataniya.

Schultz Shlomo
Born in Dunaszerdahely (Dunajská Streda)
Murdered in 1944
Member of "Beitar"

Shlomo lived in Budapest from 1944. He was an underground activist. Equipped with forged documents he joined the fascist Arrow Cross Party. Shlomo escorted the Jews to the gathering places and succeeded in liberating many of them. Eventually his Jewish identity was discovered. He was taken to the bank of the Danube and shot dead.

Schwartz Amikam
Born in Pozsony (Bratislava)
Member of "Dror Habonim"

Amikam arrived in Budapest with his sister, Herta, as a refugee. After the Germans invaded Hungary on 19.3.1944, he stayed in one of the bunkers which was taken by the fascists and was imprisoned. Amikam was rescued on 25.12.194a by comrades of the movement. He resides in Australia.

Schwartz György
Murdered in 1944
Member of "Beitar"

In 1944 György hid in a bunker in Laci köz. The bunker was discovered and he, and his friends, were killed.

Schwartz Shaye
Schwartz Frigyes
Born in Kassa (Košice) on 31.7.1927
Murdered in 1944
Member of "Beitar"

Shaye arrived in Budapest in 1944 thanks to forged documents given to him by members of the movement. He helped set up bunkers. He traveled to the town of Munkács in order to distribute forged documents. Shaye stayed in a bunker in Laci köz that was attacked by brutal Arrow Cross troopers and the gendarmes. Shaye and his friends tried to break out and were killed in an exchange of fire with the attackers. Together with Shaye, Sándor Guttmann, György Schwartz and another seven friends from Miskolc, whose names are unknown, were killed.

Schwartz Shmuel Arie

Schwartz Samu
Born in Szikszó in 1894
Died in Tel-Aviv in 1953
Member of "Mizrahi"

Shmuel was drafted to the Hungarian army and fought as an officer in
WW I. He stayed in an Italian prisoners' camp for a year and a half.
After he returned from the war, he became a dedicated Zionist. In 1944
Shmuel gave assistance to Jewish refugees who arrived in Budapest from
Slovakia. In May to June 1944, the tiyul to Romania for the "Bnei Akiva"
movement was planned from his house. He used forged Aryan documents.
Shmuel was among the 24 official employees of the "Glass House" on 29,
Vadász Street in Budapest and took part in the underground activities.
After the liberation he was active in the B'riha. At the Zionist Congress
in 1946 he participated as an observer on behalf of his movement. In
1949 Shmuel made aliya. He died four years later.

Schweitzer Shoshanna

Schweitzer Oszkárné
Born in 1902
Died in Israel in 1978
Member of "Mizrahi"

When Shoshanna was 6 years old her family moved to Budapest. She was
active in "Mizrahi" from an early age. Shoshanna was among the principal
assistants to refugees arriving to Budapest from Poland. Her house was
open to them and she got the nickname of 'the good heart'. Endangering
her own life, Shoshanna worked hard for the refugees in the Hungarian
government offices. After the liberation (1945) she was the leader of the
"Mizrahi" women and the chairwoman at the first national congress in
1947.
In 1948 Shoshanna made aliya and continued with her public work. Her
son, Yitzhak, fell in the Negev during the War of Independence. Her
second son, Avraham, was an editor for the "Ha'aretz" newspaper until
his death.

Seidenfeld Tzvi 'Sidi'
Born in Ungvár (Užhorod) in 1923
Passed away
Member of "Bnei Akiva"

In 1944 Tzvi hid in Budapest thanks to Aryan documents. He was engaged in maintaining contact with the movement's members and operated within the framework of the "Glass House" on Vadász Street. Tzvi was arrested and tortured then smuggled out of prison. He was appointed to the young leadership of "Bnei Akiva" and played a central role when David Friedman and David Asael (Auszlaender) were arrested. After the war Tzvi was among the members who worked for the revival of the movement in Hungary. He made aliya.

Shaanan Haim
Stern Heni
Born in Érsekújvár (Nové Zámky) in 1922
Member of "Maccabi Hatzair"

Haim took part in his movement's hahshara. In September 1943 he was enlisted in a forced labor unit, ran away and arrived in the movement's bunker in Hüvösvölgy, in the hilly part of Budapest. Haim was caught due to an informer, incarcerated in the military prison on Margit Boulevard, interrogated and tortured. He was liberated on 25.12.1944 in a daring operation of the Zionist underground and arrived at the branch of the Swiss consulate on Wekerle Street and from there he moved to Vadász Street. Haim made aliya. He is a member of Kfar Hahoresh.

Shahar Lea
Weisz Lya
Born in Kolozsvár (Cluj) in 1927
Member of "Dror Habonim"

Lea prepared documents for the refugees who arrived in her town. As she spoke Romanian, she helped the Jews in the framework of the tiyul. Lea herself crossed the border and arrived in Eretz Israel (Palestine). She is a member of Kibbutz Dovrat.

Shahar Tzvi
Schechter Herrmann
Born in Tecső (Tyacsiv) on 10.1.1926
Member of "Hashomer Hatzair"

Tzvi came from an ultra-orthodox family and was one of seven siblings. He studied in several yeshivot. In the late 1930's he distanced himself from religion and joined the "Hashomer Hatzair" movement. In the summer of 1943 he arrived in Budapest at the Zöldmáli hostel for apprentices. He learned metal engraving. He ran various errands for the underground. At the end of April 1944 he received his mobilization orders for a forced labor unit. He was equipped with forged documents which he hid, when necessary, in a loaf of bread. In July, while on holiday, he escaped, lived under a false name and was active in the underground, and crossed the border to Romania.
In 1945 he made aliya. He was among the settlers of Kibbutz Gvulot. In 1961 he moved to Kibbutz Ha'ogen where he is still a member. About one hundred of his relatives perished in the Holocaust. His brother, Piri, and his sister, Tzippi (Efra Agmon's wife) made aliya and were members of Kibbutz Ha'ogen. Another sister, Esther Vardi, is also a member of Kibbutz Ha'ogen.

Shalev Eli
Slomovics Eli
Born in Aknaszlatina (Szolotvina) on 27.11.1922
Died on 10.12.1979
Member of "Dror Habonim"

Until the age of thirteen Eli studied at a yeshiva. He joined the "Hehalutz Hatzair" movement which was to become "Dror Habonim". He was a Zionist underground activist in Budapest. Eli was one of the initiators of the bunkers. He was the commander of the bunker on Hungary Boulevard that was captured by Arrow Cross men in a battle. Eli was arrested by the Arrow Cross and imprisoned. He was liberated on 2512.1944 by members of the Zionist underground. After the liberation Eli continued with his activities, especially finding Jewish children in Hungary and Germany and helping them make aliya. Eli made aliya in 1947 and joined the "Parod" garin staying in Kibbutz Ein Harod. With the garin he founded a new settlement. He held the position of head of the regional council "Merom HaGalil" for four terms, totaling 22 years. When he died, Eli left behind a widow, one daughter and three sons.

Shapira Moshe
Shapira Mór
Born in Nyirmegyes in 1920
Died in February 2004 in Israel
Member of "Hashomer Hatzair"

Moshe studied at a yeshiva. He joined the movement at an early age. In 1943 he was imprisoned with other comrades in the Garany detention camp because they had helped refugees from Slovakia, members of the movement, transferred them and absorbed them. Moshe escaped, in 1944 joined the underground of his movement, was caught and deported to Auschwitz. In May 1945 he returned to Hungary and resumed his activities in the movement. In October 1945 Moshe made aliya with the Ehad BeMay garin. Moshe was among the settlers of Kibbutz Yassur.

Sharoni Tzivonit
Weisz Rózsi
Born in Nagymegyer (Vel'ký Meder) on 2.1.1924
Died on 24.6.2000 in Israel
Member of "Hashomer Hatzair"

Tzivonit came from a religious Jewish family. After her hometown was annexed to Hungary, she was trapped in Bratislava and studied there. She smuggled across the border into Hungary and arrived in Budapest. Tzivonit joined the "Hashomer Hatzair" movement and, equipped with forged documents, she took part in the underground activities. She left Hungary on the train of the Relief and Rescue Committee. In September 1945 Tzivonit made aliya, and, after being detained in the Atlit camp, she was a member of the garin In Kibbutz Negba. She served in the Hagana. She lived in Kiryat Ono.

Shemer Rahel
Lőwy Olga
Born in Budapest on 6.9.1927
Member of "Hanoar Hatzioni"

After the Germans invaded Hungary, Rahel engaged in obtaining authentic documents at the offices of the Population Registry and distributed them to comrades in the underground. She stayed at the "Glass House" and, after the Arrow Cross Party rose to power, she was an instructor in the children's house on Orsó Street in Buda where fugitives from the forced labor units also found refuge. At the end of December 1944 Rahel returned to the "Glass House". She caught typhus but recovered. Rahel made aliya in June 1946. She resides in Kiriyat Bialik.

Shenhav Joseph
Weisz József
Born in Budapest in 1930
Member of "Dror Habonim"

In 1944 Joseph received the confirmation from the government office for refugees that he indeed was a refugee from North Hungary who had run away from the Russians. Equipped with his new documents, Joseph applied to the local branch of the fascist Arrow Cross in Budapest and received a member's documentation and uniform. Joseph transferred Swiss Protection Documents and ran various errands for the underground. In 1947 he left for Eretz Israel (Palestine) on the "Lanegev" ship from France. The ship was intercepted and Joseph stayed for about six months in Cyprus until he made aliya. Joseph stayed for half a year in Kibbutz Heftziba and then enlisted in the Palmah. He resides in Jerusalem.

Shimoni Dov
Schwartz Ervin
Born in Budapest on 19.2.1919
Member of the "Shimoni Group"

In 1940, according to his conscription year, he was enlisted in the regular Hungarian military service and later transferred to forced labor. When the Germans invaded Hungary on 19.3.1944, he was on sick leave. The central Jewish hospital was taken over by the S.S. Shimoni, who was a German speaker, served as the assistant of the hospital director, Dr. Lajos Levi, and maintained daily contact with the S.S. officers. When the hospital was evacuated, Dov organized the smuggling of the operation room equipment to the new Jewish hospital on 44, Wesselényi Street. Shimoni had to return to his unit but deserted, returned to Budapest and continued to work in that hospital and in another hospital that he founded on 14, Rákóczi Street, outside the ghetto. The medical staff in this hospital came from Wesselényi but the auxiliary staff was enlisted by Shimoni from among his friends of the forced labor camp and other units where foreigners served. In the hospital on Rákóczi Street, many Jews, patients and staff members, were saved. After the liberation of Hungary in 1945, Dov was among the founders of the "Oved" movement, national secretary of "Ha'ihud" and among the leaders of the Joint. He left Hungary in 1948 within the framework of the "Recruitment aliya". He made aliya in 1949 and held management positions in various hospitals. He resides in Tel-Aviv.

Singer Joseph
Singer József
Born in Volóc (Volovec) on 19.5.1923
Died on 19.7.1997
Member of "Dror Habonim"

Joseph learned carpentry. He moved to Budapest, where he met Joseph Gárdos, Neshka and Tzvi Goldfarb and other "Dror" members. After the Germans entered Hungary on 19.3.1944, Joseph tried to cross into Romania by way of the tiyul, was caught and incarcerated in various prisons. At the end of August 1944 members of his movement succeeded in setting him free. Joseph Singer returned to Budapest and served as a carpenter in setting up his movement's bunkers on Hungary Boulevard and in Hűvösvölgy. After the Arrow Cross seized the power on 15.10.1944, Joseph was among those in charge of the supply of food and equipment to the bunkers. Both bunkers were discovered by the fascists. Joseph Singer was in the bunker on Hungary Boulevard and among those who had to surrender to the fascists. He was taken to various prisons, tortured, interrogated but, eventually, he was released in a daring operation by the Zionist youth movements. Together with a group of friends from the military prison on Margit Boulevard he was taken to the branch of the Swiss consulate on Wekerle Street.
Joseph made aliya. He resided in Moshav Beit Zayit.

Solti György Róbert
Born in Budapest in 1926
Murdered in Budapest in January 1945
Member of "Hanoar Hatzioni"

György joined the movement when he was in grade 7 at the Jewish high school. Shortly after the Germans invaded Hungary on 19.3.1944, he was enlisted in a forced labor unit. When his unit was about to be sent westwards, György escaped and returned to Budapest where he joined the underground activities of his movement. He engaged in distributing forged documents, taking Jewish children to the children's houses in the care of the Zionist youth movements and in other activities. György stayed in one of the bunkers, was caught and murdered along with another eight comrades.

Sólyóm Rahel
Grünberger Zsuzsanna
Born in Kolozsvár (Cluj) on 9.9.1925
Member of "Hanoar Hatzioni"

Rahel obtained Aryan documents from the office of the Population Registry, i.e. she found a fictitious name, copied real names from the population register and issued authentic documents. Rahel also distributed those documents. At the beginning of June she left Budapest in order to escape across the border near Nagyvárad into Romania. On the train with her, were comrades from the movement, Hanna Cohen and Simeon Levi who were caught during an inspection of the train. Rahel managed to reach Romania. In November 1944 she left Bucharest on her way to Eretz Israel (Palestine). She arrived in Haifa, was transferred to the Atlit camp where she stayed for three weeks. Later, with a group of friends, Rahel joined Kibbutz Nitzanim. She now lives in the USA.

Somló Sándor 'Uncle Somló'
'Somló bácsi'
Born in 1880
Member of the "Gordon Circle"

Sándor was one of the prominent figures of the Jewish community and the underground during the Holocaust. He was one of the big food traders in Budapest. He came from a poor orthodox Jewish family. From the late 1930's until the early 1940's Sándor helped Jewish refugees arriving from Slovakia cross the border into Yugoslavia and Romania. He was caught and imprisoned in a detention camp. His wardens soon discovered his skills for obtaining food, which they needed, and appointed him as the man in charge of supplies. Even after his release from the detention camp, the commander still used his advice.
After the Germans invaded Hungary on 19.3.1944, the head of the Jewish

community in Budapest appointed Sándor as the person responsible for the supplies, a position he filled with talent and success. Thanks to his many connections, Sándor obtained food for the Jews serving in forced labor camps and, later, for the ghetto Jews. In some cases he managed to reach the wagons in which Jews were being taken to Auschwitz and give them food. Sándor made a point of obtaining food, supplies, clothing and heating materials for the Jewish children who were concentrated in tens of children's houses under the protection of the International Red Cross and administered by the Zionist youth movements.

'Uncle Somló' was remarkable for his great courage, outstanding persuasion skills and he often put his own life at risk. He held negotiations with Hungarian and German authorities in order to obtain food. His identifying sign was his green scarf that he always wrapped around his neck. He kept precise notes of the details of the deals he signed.

Sándor's cooperation with the Zionist Youth underground is worth mentioning. 'Uncle Somló' did deliberately not see any difference among the various youth movements and worked with all of them. The products he obtained were mainly milk, cheeses, oil, rice, and beans. Heating materials, clothing, bed linen were also included in his line of work. He bought and obtained thousands of kilograms of all these items. He did not interrupt his activities even when the city was bombarded and shelled or when his private apartment was completely destroyed. After the liberation in 1945 Sándor continued with his activities and especially helped in obtaining food and other necessary supplies for Jewish orphans who were gathered in children's houses. In 1973, after he passed away, people who honoured his memory planted a small forest in his name on the Carmel Mountain near the university.

Sonnenberg Lev
Sonnenberg Lév
Born in Újvidék (Novi Sad)
Member of "Hashomer Hatzair"

Lev was caught by the Hungarian gendarmerie because of his participation in the anti-fascist movement. He was sentenced to forced labor and sent to Ukraine where he perished.

Spiegel Sándor 'Sanyi'
Member of "Bnei Akiva"

Sándor was a member of his movement's ken in Ungvár (Uzshorod). In 1942 he was enlisted in a forced labor camp. In 1944 he hid in Budapest. Sándor was an underground activist. After the war he took part in the revival of the movement.

Somló László
Spitzer László
Born in Budapest in 1922
Member of the "Shimoni Group"

In 1943 László was enlisted in a forced labor unit which was transferred to Germany, but he managed to desert and arrived in the hospital organized by Dov Shimoni under the auspices of the International Red Cross on 14, Rákóczi Street in Budapest. A staff of eight people, including László, dealt with fulfilling all the hospital needs and many Jews were saved there.
After the liberation László worked in the Jewish Hospital in Budapest.

Stark Moshe
Stark László
Born in Nyirbátor in 1923
Member of "Hashomer Hatzair"

Moshe was a member of the movement in his hometown. In 1943 he moved to Budapest and worked in construction. In April 1943 Moshe enlisted in a forced labor unit in Tata, received forged documents and money from Efra Agmon, a member of his movement, and, together with two friends, he escaped and arrived in Budapest. He was an underground activist for the movement. Moshe was caught and imprisoned in the Sárvár detention camp where he worked as an electrician. It was only thanks to luck that he was not caught and deported to Auschwitz. He escaped from the detention camp and moved to Romania within the framework of the tiyul and from there Moshe made it to Eretz Israel (Palestine). He joined Kibbutz Ein Dor which, later on, he left. In Israel Moshe worked in construction as a maintenance and storage worker. He resides in Haifa.

Steiner Miriam
Bernson
Born in 1928
Died in 2001
Member of "Maccabi Hatzair"

In 1942, when she was fourteen years old, Miriam joined "Maccabi Hatzair". After the Germans invaded Hungary on 19.3.1944, she hid in Budapest thanks to forged documents by the name of Burza Klára she received from the movement. Together with her friends she stayed for about one month in a country town where she did agricultural work. Miriam returned to Budapest in order to join the Relief and Rescue Committee train but arrived too late. She took part in the underground operations. With help from the movement she succeeded in crossing the border into Romania. In November 1944 Miriam made aliya and joined an Aliyat Hanoar group in Kfar Rupin.

Steiner Tzvi 'Bébi'
Steiner Hermann
Born in 1922
Died on 29.7.2005
Member of "Hashomer Hatzair"

Tzvi grew up in a traditional Jewish family in Érsekújvár (Nové Zámky) in Czechoslovakia. He joined the "Hashomer Hatzair" movement at an early age. In 1942 Tzvi was enlisted in a forced labor unit and sent to Ukraine. Because he fell sick with typhus, he was sent back to Győr in Hungary. In the fall of 1944 an emissary of the Zionist underground arrived in Győr with a bag full of forged documents for members of "Hashomer Hatzair", "Dror" and "Maccabi Hatzair" who were serving in the camp. Tzvi ran away from the camp and, together with his friend, Anti (Dan Livni) arrived in Budapest. Both of them joined the underground activities. As a member of the staff of the International Red Cross, Tzvi went to the Protected Houses and the ghetto to help the Jews by giving them Swiss

Protection Documents and food. Tzvi also escorted the 'Rudi Bácsi' carts. While in hiding on Wekerle Sándor Street, he forged seals. After the liberation he took part in the organization of children's houses. Tzvi was sent to Romania in order to set up transit stations for olim. For two and a half years he worked in Transylvania as the movement's secretary. In July 1948 Tzvi arrived in Israel, joined the garin in Kibbutz Dan and later, in the framework of hashlama, he moved to Kibbutz Megiddo. Tzvi was a member of Kibbutz Usha.

Steiner Yitzhak 'Itzki'
Steiner László
Born in Érsekújvár (Nové Zámky) in 1925
Member of "Maccabi Hatzair"
Died on 4.4.2006 in Israel

Yitzhak joined the movement at the age of thirteen. After the German invaded Hungary on 19.3.1944, he was enlisted in forced labor unit. Thanks to forged documents from the movement he managed to escape. Miraculously he was not caught and reached Budapest. Yitzhak was sent by the movement to a bunker in a farm courtyard close to Budapest and later arrived in the "Glass House" on 29, Vadász Street where he was liberated in January 1945. After the liberation Yitzhak collected Jewish orphans. He made aliya in June 1949. He was a member of Kfar Hahoresh. Nowadays he lives in the Protea pensioner's village.

Steinmetz Shmuel
Born in Kökényes (Ternove) on 15.10.1923
Died on 18.9.1999
Member of "Dror Habonim"

Foreseeing the fate of the Jews Shmuel and his friends prepared two bunkers in Máramaros County even before the Germans invaded Hungary on 19.3.1944. Shmuel was enlisted in a forced labor unit. He was liberated by the partisans in Yugoslavia and remained with them until the end of the war. After the liberation he was a Hebrew and geography teacher of a group of children staying in Germany on their way to Eretz Israel (Palestine). Shmuel made aliya on the "Exodus" ship and was detained in Cyprus. On 1.5.1948 he arrived in Eretz Israel (Palestine) and joined Kibbutz Afek. Later he left the kibbutz.

Stern David 'Duda'
Born in Kassa (Košice) in 1915
Murdered in 1945
Member of "Hashomer Hatzair"

David studied at an agricultural school in preparation for life in a kibbutz in Eretz Israel (Palestine). He was the manager of the "Hehalutz" center in Bratislava. In 1942 David moved to Budapest where he remained until April 1944. He gave assistance to refugees from Slovakia. David returned to Slovakia within the framework of the re-tiyul and worked in an arms factory as a German with Aryan documents. He was in charge of the distribution of the Joint funds. David was caught and deported to the extermination camps in Poland. He was shot during the evacuation march from the camp one day before the liberation.

Stern Eva
Friedl Stern Éva
Born in Arad in 1913
Died in 1944
Friend of "Hashomer Hatzair"

Eva was Rafi Friedl Benshalom's sister. She and her husband were friends of the movement and gave assistance to members who arrived in Arad (Romania) from Hungary. In 1944 Eva, her husband, Imre, and their son Freddie, made illegal aliya on the 'Mafkura' ship that sank in the Black Sea after hitting a floating mine. She and her husband and son drowned with all the other passengers.

Stern Yitzhak 'Igi'
Stern Ignác
Born in Érsekújvár (Nové Zámky) on 19.12.1924
Member of "Hashomer Hatzair"

From 1943 Yitzhak lived in Budapest and worked as a car painter. In April 1944 he was enlisted in a forced labor unit. In September 1944 Yitzhak escaped from the camp and arrived in the "Glass House" on Vadász Street in Budapest. He equipped himself with forged documents and ran various errands for his movement, such as the transfer of documents, distribution of food and deliveries. After the liberation of Budapest Yitzhak was caught by Russian soldiers and, although he claimed to be Jewish, he was incarcerated in the prisoners' camp for Hungarian and German soldiers. He managed to escape and arrived in a hahshara. In 1946 Yitzhak made aliya and joined Kibbutz Yassur. He left the kibbutz and moved to Kiriyat Tivon.

Sternberg Yonatan Zvulon
Born in 1880
Died in 1945 in Switzerland
Member of "Mizrahi"

Yonatan was among the founders and leaders of his movement. In 1935 he made aliya, stayed in Eretz Israel (Palestine) for fourteen months. Due to the events he lost his capital and returned to Hungary. During the war Yonatan supported the underground activities. The Belz Rabbi, Aharon Rokah, and his assistants, were smuggled out of the ghetto near Cracov in Poland and, at the end of 1943, to Hungary by Hungarian officers. Moshe Shapira, head of the aliya department in the Jewish Agency (and the representative of "Mizrahi") in Jerusalem ordered Moshe Krausz, head of the Eretz-Israel Office in Budapest, to add the Belz Rabbi and his assistants to the list of olim as part of the quota for 'senior Zionists'. And indeed the rabbi left Hungary on 18.1.1944 with a legal group of olim with a certificate in place of Yonatan Zvulon Sternberg and his family who were at the top of the list of senior Zionists. In June 1944 Yonatan left Hungary on the train of the Relief and Rescue Committee but died upon his arrival in Switzerland.

Sternberg Margit Gitl
Born in 1888
Died in 1975 in Israel
Member of "Mizrahi"

Margit was active in the movement from 1908 and was among the founders of the "Mizrahi" women in Hungary. In 1923 and 1939 she visited Eretz Israel (Palestine) in order to prepare her family's aliya but the war put an end to the plans. Margit took part in the activities of her husband, Yonatan Zvulon Sternberg. She left Hungary on the train of the Relief and Rescue Committee. Her husband died upon their arrival in Switzerland. Margit made aliya and settled down in Jerusalem.

Steuer Ágnes
Arnstein Lajla
Born in Budapest in 1922
Member of "Dror Habonim"

Ágnes was the daughter of a wealthy modern orthodox Jewish family in Budapest. She studied at the Jewish high school and joined "Dror Habonim". In the underground Ágnes dealt with finding accommodation for the refugees from Poland and Slovakia. She operated under the name of Horváth Éva and obtained from the Population Registry authentic birth certificates that were then modified to match the data of the people who needed them. A local detective suspected her of being Jewish and she was arrested but managed to escape. Ágnes resumed her underground activities on 52 Baross Street and in the offices of the International Red Cross.
She travelled to the Slovakian border carrying in her bag 36 Swiss Protection Documents that she gave to young men serving in a forced labor camp among whom was her future husband, Miki. She learned how to use a weapon from Vili Eisikovics. Ágnes was caught by Arrow Cross men, taken for interrogation but again she managed to escape. After the liberation in 1945 she engaged in locating Jewish children and youngsters and sending them to Eretz Israel (Palestine). Ágnes herself tried to leave Hungary for her aliya in 1949 but was caught. She was detained for six months. Again she tried to cross the border with her husband Miki and this time she succeeded. She made aliya in 1952.

Stevens E. Andrew
Steinberger Endre
Born in Budapest on 5.3.1928
Independent , did not belong to any movement

Andrew studied at the Jewish elementary school on Wesselényi Street, the high school on Dob Street and at a teachers' seminary next to the Rabbinical Seminary for one year. After the Germans invaded Hungary on 19.3.1944, he was enlisted in a forced labor unit and worked in the building of a railway near Zirc and in removing debris in Budapest. Two days after the Arrow Cross rose to power (15.10.1944), he escaped. He equipped himself with forged documents by the name of Sólyom Endre that he received from one of his comrades. He engaged in the forgery of documents and posed as an injured soldier returning from the Russian front. He was arrested in his apartment by two armed Arrow Cross men, led in the direction of the district headquarters on Teréz Boulevard, escaped from imprisonment, was shot in his ankle but still managed to run away. He was active in the building of the International Red Cross on 4, Mérleg Street and mainly dealt with the forging of documents. In October 1944 Andrew's father was enlisted in a forced labor unit, made to march to the Mauthausen extermination camp but succeeded in surviving. At the end of November he saved a young girl by the name of Jaeger Piroska and hid her in his apartment. Andrew's mother managed to escape from the Death March and she hid thanks to forged documents she received from her son. After the war Andrew arrived in Germany, worked as a journalist for the Útunk (Our Way) newspaper in Hungarian and studied chemical engineering in Munich for two and a half years. In 1949 Andrew emigrated to the US and his parents also followed him there. He is an independent real-estate agent. He received the Golden Cross from the Hungarian Government.

Szabó Israel
Szabó Jisráel "Rebe"
Born in Bustyaháza (Bustina) on 6.2.1918
Died in 2003
Member of "Maccabi Hatzair"

Israel was one of the prominent figures in his movement. He was a spiritual leader and an underground activist. In 1944 Israel was sent to Romania where he dealt with the absorption of the fugitives from Hungary, gave them accommodation and helped them move forward on their way to Eretz Israel (Palestine). After the liberation Israel returned to Hungary. He made aliya and joined Kibbutz Kfar Hamaccabi. Later he lived in Haifa.

Prof. Szamosi Ya'akov
Szamosi Géza
Born in Budapest on 23.3.1922
Member of "Hanoar Hatzioni"

Ya'akov was a member of the movement from 1938 to 1946. He was the head of a group, member of the ken leadership and of the national committee. Ya'akov was sent by his movement on trips to distribute the Zionist shekel throughout Hungary. During the Holocaust he was engaged in the distribution of forged documents. In September 1944 he was arrested by the Gestapo and incarcerated for three months in the Svábhegy prison. Ya'akov was set free by the Hungarian Zionist Association's lawyer, Dr. Beregi. After the liberation he studied at university in Budapest. He made aliya. Ya'akov did research. He emigrated to Canada and got a worldwide reputation as an atom researcher. At the age of 80 he retired as Professor at Concordia University. He resides in Toronto, Canada.

Szántó Hedva
Müller Hedvig
Born in 1923
Member of "Hehalutz Hatzair" and "Dror"

From an early age Hedva was a member of "Hehalutz Hatzair" in Visk (Viskove) where her family lived. In 1939 she arrived in Budapest and joined the "Dror" movement. In order to be accepted in the movement's hahshara, she exchanged name with her sister as she was two years older. Hedva took part in the underground activities from 1942. She and her friends gave assistance to refugees from Poland and Slovakia. After the German invasion of Hungary on 19.3.1944, Hedva distributed forged documents. When the Arrow Cross Party rose to power, she helped Jews escape from the ghetto and the Yellow Star Houses in Budapest. She traveled to the Mohács labor camp and gave the comrades imprisoned there documents, clothes and money. In Pécs Hedva managed to save one of the Jews. She underwent weapons training on the hills of Buda under the instructions of Asher Arni and Vili Eisikovics. She worked as a dental assistant in one of the hospitals where she stole medicines and various medical supplies for the underground. Hedva served as a liaison person between the underground storerooms and the bunkers that were set up in Budapest. She witnessed the arrest of Asher Arni and managed to warn the other comrades. She stayed in one of the bunkers, was arrested and incarcerated in the central military prison on Margit Boulevard. Hedva was brutally interrogated and tortured but was eventually released together with other friends in a daring operation of the Zionist underground activists. She lives in Rishon LeTzion.

Szántó Shmuel
Szántó Andor Miklós
Born in Budapest on 20.12.1922
Member of "Dror Habonim"

Shmuel learned precision mechanics. In 1942 he joined the Zionist activities in whose framework he met his wife, Hedvig (Hedva) Müller. In October 1943 he was enlisted in a forced labor unit. In August 1944 Shmuel was wounded and hospitalized in Pécs. His wife, who visited him, brought him forged documents. After the Arrow Cross Party rose to power on 15.10.1944, Shmuel escaped, arrived in Budapest and joined the underground activities. His role was to take care of the cultural life in the bunkers that were set up by his movement. He was the editor of the movement's underground newspaper. His wife distributed the paper around the city. In December 1944 Shmuel was caught, taken to the prison on Margit Boulevard, interrogated and tortured. He was liberated by members of the movement.
Shmuel resides in Rishon LeTzion.

Székely Ernő 'Marci'
Born in Budapest in 1923
Murdered in 1944
Member of "Maccabi Hatzair"

From 17.4.1944 to 20.9.1944 Marci served in a forced labor camp with Tzvi Bogen (Keshet). He was among the comrades who found refuge in the bunker on Hungary Boulevard in Budapest. When the bunker was attacked by the fascists, he was standing outside on guard. He shot at the fascists who returned fire and killed him. He died as a hero.

Szendrő Hava
Szendrő (Bruck) Ilona Éva
Born in Budapest in 1925
Member of "Hashomer Hatzair"

Hava hid with another twenty Jews in a stalactite cave in Buda on Szépvölgyi Street in Rózsadomb but they were discovered and she was arrested. At first she was taken to Radeczki Laktanya (military camp) and then to the central military prison on Margit Boulevard. She stayed there at the same time as Hanna Szenes. Hava was liberated by underground activists but caught again by Arrow Cross men and taken to the district headquarters in Városmajor where she was tortured and transferred to the Gestapo. As the Russians approached the capital, she was moved with other prisoners from Buda to Pest. Some of the prisoners were shot on the banks of the Danube but others, among whom Hava and her mother, succeeded in reaching the ghetto where they were liberated by the Red Army.

After the liberation Hava studied at the Business Academy in Budapest and continued with her activities for the movement until she made aliya in 1949. Hava married Dr. Szendrő Károly. In Israel she worked as a nurse in a hospital and did volunteering work. Hava resides in Jerusalem.

Dr. Szendrő Károly
Born in Ballasagyarmat in 1913
Died in July 1985
Member of the "Gordon" and "Borohov" Circles

Károly completed his law studies in Budapest. From 1938 he was an active Zionist within the framework of the Hungarian Zionist Association and a member of the national leadership of the "Gordon Circle" which was connected with "Hashomer Hatzair". From 1942 until the end of 1943 Károly served in a forced labor unit. In 1944 he was active in the "Glass House" and a member of the management until the city was liberated by the Red Army (18.1.1945).

From 1945 to 1948 Károly was a member of the executive committee of the Hungarian Zionist Association for the "Borohov Circle" and served as its representative in the B'riha operation. He held the position of head of the personnel department in the Hungarian Joint. In 1949 Károly made aliya illegally from Hungary. In Israel he worked for many years in the Settlement Department of the Jewish Agency until he retired in 1978.

Szenes Hanna
Szenes Anikó
Born in Budapest in 1921
Executed on 7.11.1944 in Budapest
Paratrooper

Hanna was the daughter of an assimilated family of writers, poets and musicians. Her father, Béla Szenes, was a well-known writer in Hungary. Hanna was an excellent student and her literary talent was discovered while she was still a child. She wrote poems and a diary. Hanna became an enthusiastic Zionist and in September 1939 she made aliya. She studied for two years at the agricultural school in Nahalal and in 1941 she joined Kibbutz Sdot Yam. In November 1943 she volunteered to parachute over German occupied Europe. She underwent the necessary training in the framework of the British army and, on 14.3.1944, five days before the Germans invaded Hungary, she jumped over Yugoslavia and stayed with the partisans. On 9.6.1944 Hanna crossed the border into Hungary and was immediately caught by the Hungarians while still in possession of her radio and other suspicion casting equipment. She was taken to the prison in Szombathely, interrogated and tortured. In spite of the threats to her and her mother's life (her mother lived in Hungary) Hanna did not reveal the transmission code or the goals of her mission. She was taken to Budapest, to the central prison of the Hungarian army on Margit Boulevard. During her interrogation she was allowed to meet her mother. Hanna was tried by a military court, convicted and sentenced to death on charges of treason. She refused to ask for a pardon and on 7.11.1944 she was executed. Before she went on her mission, Hanna wrote in her diary: "I am going happily, out of my free will and fully aware of the difficulties. I see this mission as a right and also a duty."
In her poem "On the Way", she wrote: "A voice called me and I went/ I went because the voice called."

Szilágyi Tzvi
Szilágyi Ernő
Born in Kaposvár in 1898
Died in Budapest in 1973
Member of "Hashomer Hatzair" and the "Gordon Circle"

Tzvi was one of the prominent figures in his movement. He was a scholar and graduated from several universities. He was an active Zionist.

From 1937 to 1940 Tzvi was the head of the Keren Kayemet LeIsrael in Budapest. In 1939 he represented his movement in the Eretz-Israel Office. He worked with Ottó Komoly and Mihály Salomon. From 1943 he took part in the activities of the Relief and Rescue Committee and was the vice-president of the Hungarian Zionist Association. Tzvi also took part in the debates about the rescue of Jews held by Joel Brand and Israel Kasztner. He assisted in the selection of the passengers who left Hungary on 30.6.1944 on the Relief and Rescue Committee train. Tzvi was involved in the attempt to rescue Jews in Szeged by applying to the SS officer. As a result, part of the Jews who were taken to the Strasshof camp were from Szeged. Szilágyi himself left Hungary on the Relief and Rescue Committee train. After the war Tzvi returned to Hungary but did not take part in Zionist activities. He worked as a bookkeeper in one of the institutes of higher education and in 1958 he retired. In 1970 Tzvi intended to make aliya and a suitable apartment was even made ready for him in Kibbutz Ein Dor with the help of Arie Ya'ari. However, in the end he changed his mind.

Szirtes Lev
Szirtes Lajos
Born in Bácskatopolya in 1920
Died in 1943
Member of "Hashomer Hatzair"

Lev was a member of the Újvidék (Novi Sad) ken. At the beginning of the Hungarian invasion in 1941 he took part in the anti-fascist movement. He was enlisted in a forced labor unit. His death place is unknown.

Tov Esther
Scheer Erzsébet
Born in Nyiregyháza in 1920
Member of "Hashomer Hatzair"

Esther's family moved to Debrecen. She learned cutting and sewing. In 1937 she joined the movement and stayed at an agricultural hahshara in Izbég. During the war she lived under several identities and often moved house. Esther took care of the elderly. She gave them food and medicines and, thanks to her, they survived. Esther made aliya in 1945.

Tzahor Baruh
Weisz Béla
Born in Terebesfejérpatak (Gyilove) in 1922
Member of "Dror Habonim"

When he was a child Baruh was a member of "Beitar" and later of "Hehalutz Hatzair". As soon as 1941, he helped refugees from German occupied areas arrive in Budapest. In 1943 he was enlisted in a forced labor unit and within that framework he took part in underground activities. With help from liaison people, members of the Zionist youth movements, he distributed forged documents to the people in the unit in order to help them escape. He deserted and joined a unit of partisans, named after the Hungarian poet "Sándor Petőfi", which was set up after the failure of the Slovak uprising. Baruh received the "Uprising Decoration" from the Slovak government. He is a member of Moshav Tzofit.

Tzahor Dov
Weisz Berthold
Born in Kökényes (Ternove) on 13.4.1917
Died in 1995
Member of "Bnei Akiva"

Dov was a central figure of "Hapoel Hamizrahi" in Slovakia from the 1930's. As a representative of the movement Dov was a member of the delegation to the Zionist Congress in Basel held prior to the outbreak of WW II. In 1943, together with his wife Miriam, he moved to Hungary and in Budapest he became a member of the "Bnei Akiva" leadership. He mainly took care of the Jewish refugees arriving from Slovakia. Dov was a member of the Relief and Rescue Committee on behalf of "Bnei Akiva" and as a representative of the refugees. He corresponded with the members of the Eretz-Israel delegation in Istanbul.
Dove made aliya on 7.3.1944. He was active in the institutions of "Hapoel Hamizrahi" and the manager of the Mashhav construction enterprise. He died in Israel.

Tzahor Miriam
Weisz Eisenberg Mirjam
Born in Kassa (Košice)
Member of "Bnei Akiva"

In 1943 Miriam and her husband Dov moved to Hungary. She took part
in the underground activities. Miriam returned to Slovakia to visit her
parents, was caught and sent back to Hungary.
She made aliya. She worked as a nurse.

Tzur Haim
Burger Endre
Born in Nagymihályi (Michalovce) on 8.11.1923
Member of "Hashomer Hatzair"

Haim arrived in Budapest in 1941. He gave assistance to refugees
arriving from Slovakia. He was caught and deported back to Slovakia
but succeeded in returning to Budapest.
After the Germans invaded Hungary on 19.3.1944, Haim was caught
again and imprisoned in the detention camp in Kistarcsa. He escaped
and, in June 1944, managed to cross the border into Romania within
the framework of the tiyul together with a group of friends. In Romania
Haim was caught again but managed to get free.
In November 1944 he arrived in Eretz Israel (Palestine). He was a member
of the garin of the hahshara in Kibbutz Negba and from 1946 to 1960
was a member of Kibbutz Yehiam.
He is married to Lea Tzur and lives in Givatayim.

Tzur Lea
Wertheimer Olga
Born in Hajdúsámson on 19.10.1925
Member of "Hashomer Hatzair"

Lea joined the movement in 1939. After the Germans invaded Hungary
on 19.3.1944, she was rescued from Debrecen by Haim Golan (Fettmann),
an emissary from the movement, together with another four girls. She
took part in rescue operations equipped with forged documents. She
traveled mainly between Debrecen and Budapest and moved house in

order to avoid being arrested. On 30.6.1944 she left Hungary on the train of the Relief and Rescue Committee. On 2.9.1945 Lea arrived in Eretz Israel (Palestine). She was a member of the hahshara garin in Kibbutz Negba and, from 1946 until 1960, a member of Kibbutz Yehiam. She is married to Haim Tzur and resides in Givatayim.

Ungár Meir Béla, Dr.
Born in Nagytétény in 1899
Died in 1974 in Israel
Member of "Mizrahi"

Meir was the son of the chief orthodox rabbi. He was the founder of the "Hahashmona'im" association and a member, secretary and chairman of "Maccabea". In addition Meir was the leader of "Hakoah". He had a doctorate in law and was a public figure and publicist. He filled various positions in the Hungarian Zionist Association. After the Germans invaded Hungary on 19.3.1944, Meir took part in the rescue of Jews. He stayed at the "Glass House" and worked in the department that dealt with the production of Protection Documents. After the liberation in 1945 Meir held positions in the World Zionist Organization and in the Joint. He was also a legal consultant for the Israeli Legacy in Budapest. He made aliya in 1950. From 1957 to 1959 he served as the chairman of the "Hungarian Immigrants' Association" in Israel.

Vajda Simha
Vajda Zsigmond
Born in Budapest on 5.10.1908
Died on 2.2.2005 in Natanya
Member of "Dror Ha'oved"

Simha was the maintenance manager of the Jewish Hospital in Budapest on 3, Szabolcs Street. After Austria was annexed by Germany, many Jews who did not have Austrian citizenship were deported. Some of them were put on a ship that sailed on the Danube River in the direction of the international border of three countries. The refugees did not receive any food or water. 300 refugees came off the ship and found refuge in a hospital until the end of the war.
After the Germans invaded Slovakia many refugees were taken to the hospital out of concern for their welfare. Simha Vajda was in charge of

their employment and financial maintenance. He helped the refugees in all ways to enable them to survive the wartime years.

Simha Vajda made aliya. He worked for Solel Boneh. Later he lived in a home for the elderly in Natanya.

Vardi Esther
Sechter Edit
Born in Técső (Tyacsiv) in 1922
Member of "Hashomer Hatzair"

Esther came from a Jewish ultra-orthodox family. In 1942 she joined the movement and in March 1944 arrived in Budapest. After the German invasion of Hungary, Esther went underground and, thanks to her Aryan appearance, she ran errands, obtained authentic documents from government offices and distributed them. She was sent to Kisvárda carrying a bag of forged documents and money for the Jews in the ghetto so that they could escape. Esther was arrested by Hungarian gendarmes but, when she went to the toilet, she managed to conceal the forged documents. After a few days of interrogation, when she did not reveal anything about her mission, but admitted to being Jewish, she was sent to prison in Budapest and within three weeks was deported to Auschwitz and Bergen-Belsen. Esther was liberated on 19.4.1945. She returned to Budapest and in July she was on her way to Eretz Israel (Palestine). She stayed in camps in Cyprus and Atlit.

Esther is a member of Kibbutz Ha'ogen.

Vardi Rahel
Flohr Gabriella
Born in the village of Olaszliszka , Hungary in 1923
Member of "Maccabi Hatzair"

Rahel arrived in Budapest in 1941 and joined a hahshara. In 1942 she smuggled comrades from Slovakia into Hungary. Her roles were to find dwellings, food and forged documents as well as to move refugees to hiding places. After the German occupation of Hungary and the beginning of deportations, Rahel traveled with her sister to her village from where she was deported to Auschwitz.

After the liberation she stayed in Sweden in order to recover her health. Rahel made aliya in 1948 and joined Kibbutz Kfar Hahoresh where she is still a member. She held various positions in the kibbutz and in the movement.

Wagman Hans
Born in Vienna in 1924
Died in 1943
Member of "Hashomer Hatzair"

Hans was a member of the "Hashomer Hatzair" ken in Újvidék (Novi Sad). He was engaged in the anti-fascist movement. Hans was caught in February 1941, sentenced to forced labor and sent to a unit in Ukraine where he perished.

Weidman Zorzeta
Vajdman Zorzeta
Born in Újvidék (Novi Sad) in 1924
Murdered in 1942
Member of "Hashomer Hatzair"

Zorzeta was a member of the "Hashomer Hatzair" ken Újvidék. She took part in anti-fascist activities. Zorzeta was murdered by Hungarian soldiers in January 1942 during the Újvidék massacre.

Weil Sarah
Taub Éva
Born in Nyirbogdány on 18.4.1920
Member of "Hashomer Hatzair"

Sarah's father was a dentist and she practiced in his clinic. In 1941 she married Shraga Weil. When the deportations from Slovakia started in 1942, the couple fled to Budapest. In 1943 they were caught by the Hungarian police, imprisoned until 1944 and then under police supervision in Miskolc. Sarah was her husband's partner in his underground activities. She returned to Slovakia and was liberated in 1945. Sarah returned to Hungary and integrated the movement's activities mainly rescuing Jewish youngsters and helping them make aliya. In 1947 she herself made aliya and became a member of Kibbutz Ha'ogen.

Weil Shraga
Weil Ferenc Ferdinánd
Born in Nyitra (Nitra) on 24.9.1919
Member of "Hashomer Hatzair"

The family moved to Bratislava and Shraga joined the movement in 1931. He studied at an art school in Prague. In 1941 he married Sarah Taub. Shraga worked as a building draftsman. When the deportations from Slovakia started in 1942, the couple moved to Budapest. They were caught by the Hungarian police and imprisoned for about a year. After the German invasion of Hungary on 19.3.1944, Shraga engaged in forging documents with Dan Zimmerman and David Gur. He returned to Slovakia with Sarah and, in 1945, they were liberated by the Red Army.
Shraga returned to Hungary and integrated the movement's activities, mainly with the mission of helping young Jews to make aliya.
In 1947 Shraga and Sarah made aliya. Shraga is a member of Kibbutz Ha'ogen. He is a painter, a multi-faceted artist and one of the outstanding artists in Israel.

Weiner Magdalena
Apor-Weiner Magda
Died in Budapest in 2003
Member of the "Gordon Group"

In the years 1942 and 1943 Magdalena and her husband, Zoltán Weiner, assisted refugees, members of "Hashomer Hatzair", who arrived in Hungary from Slovakia.
In 1944 she was in contact with underground activists of the movement, Rafi Friedl-Benshalom, Ephra Teichman-Agmon, Moshe Pil-Alpan, Yehuda Weisz and Yitzhak Herbst-Mimish. Meetings with members of the Demény Group which belonged to the communist underground were held in her house. After 15.10.1944, when the Arrow Cross Party rose to power, Magda distributed Protection Documents. She escorted Jewish children to the children's houses that served as shelters. Magda was caught with a bagful of forged documents and taken to the Arrow

Cross headquarters on Szent István Boulevard. Luckily for her, the bag was not inspected and she was released.

After her husband's death, Magda remarried and adopted the name Apor.

Weiner Zoltán
Born in 1904
Died in 1962
Member of the "Gordon Circle"

In the years 1942 and 1943 Zoltán and his wife assisted refugees, members of "Hashomer Hatzair", who arrived in Hungary from Slovakia. In 1944 they made contact with underground activists of the movement, Rafi Friedl-Benshalom, Ephra Teichman-Agmon, Moshe Pil-Alpan, Yehuda Weisz and Yitzhak Herbst-Mimish.

Zoltán was active in the branch of the International Red Cross on Mérleg Street in the financial department and the children's department. He maintained contact with the communist underground, especially with the Demény Group which held meetings in his house.

After the liberation he worked for the Joint. Later he went into the fur business. During the communist regime he was the manager of the National Fur Factory (Pannónia).

Weiszkopf Moshe
Weiskopf Ernő
Born in Budapest in 1922
Died on 7.8.1986
Member of "Bnei Akiva"

After the German invasion of Hungary on 19.3.1944, Moshe equipped himself with Aryan documents under the name of Horák Pál. He himself forged documents. Moshe went to Miskolc in order to distribute documents among the Jews there. He returned to Budapest where he also distributed forged documents. He transferred grenades, ammunition, information and documents. He was active in "Department A", the children's department, on Wekerle Street under the auspices of the International Red Cross. He delivered food to the children's houses in a truck and gathered Jewish orphans mainly from the ghetto.

Part of the time he operated while wearing the uniform of the Arrow

Cross Party. During one of his missions he was caught but managed to escape in a cunning way.

After the liberation he obtained food for orphaned Jewish children.

In Israel he owned an office for the planning of electricity works.

Weiss Eliezer
Weiss László
Born in Miskolc on 16.11.1923
Member of "Bnei Akiva"

In April 1944 Eliezer was enlisted in a forced labor unit, escaped and joined the "Bnei Akiva" movement. He operated with false documents under the name of Vitéz József, ran errands and took part in the preparation of the bunkers. After the Arrow Cross rose to power on 15.10.1944, Eliezer distributed Protection Documents to the members of a battalion of forced labor units on its way to Germany. Together with two of his comrades wearing the Arrow Cross uniform, he saved a group of 140 Jews, who were headed for the banks of the Danube River where the fascists were going to shoot them, and took them to the ghetto. Eliezer saved the lives of Jewish patients in an Aryan hospital on Wesselényi Street and took them too to the ghetto. After the liberation he gathered Jewish orphans and took them to children's houses. In August 1946 he made aliya.

Eliezer worked in citrus plantations, construction, a textile factory in Petah-Tikva and later in the "Ata" factory as the manager of dye-works for 30 years. Then he retired. Eliezer is married, has one son and three grandchildren. He resides in Kiriyat Bialik.

Weisz Haya
Róth Ilona
Born in Budapest on 7.8.1923
Member of "Hashomer Hatzair"

Haya was an underground activist. In 1944 she worked for the International Red Cross, in Department A, with Ephra Teichman-Agmon.

She made aliya and resides in Givatayim.

Weisz Levi
Weisz Lévi 'Pupos'
Born in Dunaszerdahely (Dunajská Streda) in 1920
Perished in Auschwitz in 1944
Member of "Hashomer Hatzair"

In 1942 Levi was caught smuggling Jews from Slovakia into Hungary.
He was detained in the Garany forced labor camp. After his release he
returned to Dunaszerdahely and was deported with all the Jews from the
ghetto to Auschwitz where he was murdered.

Weisz Mordehai
Weisz György
Born in Budapest in 1918
Died in 1994
Member of "Hanoar Hatzioni"

Mordehai joined the movement at the age of fourteen. He was one of
the main underground activists. He obtained documents and distributed
them to Jews in the ghettos and other places. Mordehai also found hiding
places for Jews who were in imminent danger. He was one of the builders
of the Rózsa domb bunker. Mordehai saved the lives of women and young
girls on the Death March. He worked within the framework of the "Glass
House", mainly obtaining weapons in case of an attack by the fascists.
Mordehai was a member of the movement's leadership from 1941.
He made aliya in 1947.

Weisz Moshe
Weisz Mór
Born in Nagyszőllős (Vinohragyiv) on 30.10.1923
Member of "Hashomer Hatzair"

Moshe took part in the underground activities of his movement in the
"Glass House" on Vadász Street in Budapest. He was an instructor in
the children's house on 90, Dob Street which was established under the
auspices of the International Red Cross.
Moshe made aliya. He resides in Jerusalem.

Weisz Moshe
Born in Munkács (Mukacsevo) on 7.5.1922
Died in 1969
Member of "Dror Habonim"

Moshe came from a religious Jewish family and his parents opposed
his activities for a Zionist movement. He was enlisted in a forced labor
unit.
Moshe made aliya in 1946.

Weisz Rudolf
Born in 1893
Died in Israel
Member of the "Gordon" and "Borohov" Circles

Rudolf learned to be a printer. He served five years in the Hungarian
Navy during World War I. He was a member of the Hungarian Social-
democrat Party. In 1930, following his wife, Aranka Herceg, he joined the
Zionist activities. After the German invasion of Hungary on 19.3.1944,
he cooperated with the members of the Zionist youth movements,
was a consultant for the forgery of documents and helped obtain the
equipment for the laboratory. Rudolf was active within the framework
of the International Red Cross and in the "Glass House". He was also
responsible for the logistics of the delivery of goods. He delivered food
and heating materials to the starving ghetto. He was caught and taken to
the prison on Margit Boulevard and then to the Gestapo headquarters. He
was tortured and interrogated but managed to get released. Towards the
end of the war he stayed at the branch of the Swiss consulate on Wekerle
Street where members of the Zionist youth movements operated. After
the liberation he managed the transportation department of the Joint.
In 1950 he made aliya and worked as a printer.

Weisz Shmuel 'Koli'
Weisz Sándor
Born in Kassa (Košice) in 1926
Member of "Beitar"

Shmuel joined the movement at the age of ten. In 1941 he helped
refugees from Poland move to Budapest. In 1944, after the Germans

occupied his town and concentrated the Jews in the ghetto, Shmuel ran away to Budapest under a fictitious identity. In the Hungarian capital he became an underground activist and mainly forged and distributed documents. At the beginning of June 1944 Shmuel was turned in to the Gestapo by an informer, tortured and taken to the central military prison in Budapest. From there he was sent to the Sárvár concentration camp and then deported to Auschwitz. From Auschwitz he was transferred to Buchenwald and from there to the Magdeburg camp where he did forced labor for six months. He was returned to Buchenwald and later liberated by the American army.

He spent two months in hospital and, after he recovered, he went to Karlovy Vary to complete his studies. In 1946 he got on his way to Eretz Israel (Palestine) in the framework of Aliya Bet.

He stayed in Belgium for about nine months and in Cyprus for about a year. Shmuel worked for the IDF as a civilian for eight years. He opened an independent technical office and was a partner in many defense projects. He resides in Herzliya.

Weisz Vera
Weisz-Lefkovics Vera
Born in Budapest in 1927
Died in 1998
Member of "Maccabi Hatzair"

Vera was engaged in the forgery of documents. She operated on Perczel Mór and Mérleg Streets. On Perczel Mór Street Vera was responsible for 130 children and ten mothers who were hiding there. The escapees from detention places also found refuge in those locations.

Vera had contacts with Jews who were hiding on Kolombusz Street, was caught and taken to the Arrow Cross headquarters on 19, Teréz Boulevard. From there, Vera was taken with a group of Jews to the banks of the Danube for execution. Before they could shoot her, she jumped into the freezing waters of the river, managed to remain underwater and to get out near one of the bridges. While swimming in the river she was hurt in her neck by a sharp block of ice and was bleeding heavily. As she was walking to find a refuge, she was caught again by a soldiers' patrol that took pity on her, hid her and helped her escape to the branch of the Swiss consulate on Perczel Mór Street where she stayed until the liberation.

Vera made aliya. She passed away in 1998.

Weiss Yaakov

Weisz Imre
Born in Érsekújvár (Nové Zámky) on 15.7.1924
Executed by the British in 1947
Member of "Beitar"

Yaakov joined the "Beitar" movement during his studies in Munkács. In 1944 he moved to Budapest and was a prominent activist of his movement in the underground. He saved Jews from the gathering places for deportation by giving them forged documents. Under his influence and with his help, a group of comrades from the movement arrived in Budapest and joined the underground activities of "Beitar". Yaakov left Hungary in June 1944 on the train of the Relief and Rescue Committee. He made aliya in 1945 and took part in the armed operations against the British mandate in Palestine. He was caught and sentenced to death. He refused to sign an appeal for pardon and was executed in July 1947.

Weiss Yehoshua

Weisz Herrmann
Born in Nagymegyer (Veľký Meder) on 3.4.1922
Member of "Hashomer Hatzair"

Yehoshua came from an orthodox family. He arrived in Budapest in 1941, and operated within the framework of the underground as a member of the staff at the hostel for adolescents on Zöldmáli Street. From October 1943 to October 1944 he was enlisted in a forced labor unit. Yehoshua succeeded in escaping and reaching the "Glass House" on Vadász Street in Budapest. Later he was active on Wekerle Street. He prepared lists of people entitled to stay in Protected Houses. After the liberation of Budapest he engaged in rescuing children at Teleki Pál Street, and worked as an educator in the Polish orphanage on Szentkirály Street, as well as on Hungaria Boulevard.He took part in founding a hahshara on Ilosvai Street and Kibbutz Ehad Bemai. In 1945 Yehoshua made aliya by a legal certificate. He was a member of a group in Kibbutz Ruhama. In 1946 he was among the founders of Kibbutz "Hasela" in Kiriat Haim, and in 1947 of Kibbutz Yehiam.
He resides in Givatayim.

Weiss Yehuda
'Apus' Weisz Ernő
Born in Sopron in 1917
Died on 1.1.1982
Member of "Hashomer Hatzair"

In 1942 Yehuda arrived in Budapest, joined the activities of the movement and was engaged in preparing for the dangers Jews would be facing.

After the German invasion of Hungary on 19.3.1944, Yehuda engaged in underground activities within the framework of the movement. He left Hungary as a member of the "Hashomer Hatzair" group in the summer of 1944 on the train of the Relief and Rescue Committee.

After the liberation Yehuda returned to Czechoslovakia in order to rehabilitate the movement. He was elected president of the Zionist Organization in Czechoslovakia and represented it at the Zionist Congress in Basel in 1946.

In 1949 Yehuda made aliya and joined Kibbutz Ha'ogen. He worked in journalism.

In 1960 he settled down in New York, completed his studies and was appointed Professor of Judaica.

He died of a heart attack.

Weiss Yirmiyahu 'Yirmi'
Born in Tótsóvár (Solivar) in 1917
Died in 1944
Member of "Hashomer Hatzair"

Yirmi's family lived in Eperjes (Prešov) where he graduated from high school. In 1941 he was conscripted into the Slovak labor army and served in the 6th Battalion. Yirmi escaped from the army with the help of Egon Roth, from his hometown, and crossed the border into Hungary intending to continue traveling to Romania and from there to make aliya. During his stay in Hungary he took advantage of his knowledge of Hungarian and his Aryan appearance to take part in the underground activities. In the summer of 1944 he succeeded in crossing the border into Romania and reaching Bucharest. In the port of Constanţa he boarded the ship "Mafkora" that was sunk by an unidentified submarine and Yirmi drowned in the sea. His friend, Johanan Gárdos in Kibbutz Haogen, gave his eldest son the name of Yirmi in his memory.

Wettenstein Moshe

Wettenstein Miklós
Born in Munkács (Mukacsevo) on 17.12.1927
Died in 1970
Member of "Hanoar Hatzioni"

Moshe lived in a hostel for apprentices in Budapest. After the German invasion of Hungary on 19.3.1944, he was enlisted in a forced labor unit. Moshe ran away and arrived at the "Glass House" on Vadász Street. He returned to the hostel where a forgery laboratory was being organized. Arrow Cross men broke in, interrogated him, broke his nose and beat him until he became unconscious. When he regained consciousness, Moshe succeeded in escaping and reaching the movement's center.
He patrolled the town's streets wearing a uniform of the National Guard whose role it was to protect public buildings. More than once he and his friends were able to release Jews who had been arrested by the fascists or were being led to their death.
Moshe made aliya..

Wetzler Ora

Kohn Olga
Born in Vágsellye (Šal'a) in 1920
Member of "Maccabi Hatzair"

Ora moved to Budapest where she learned machine knitting. She helped refugees from Slovakia. Ora distributed forged documents and ran various errands. She left Hungary at the end of June 1944 on the train of the Relief and Rescue Committee. She made aliya in September 1945. She stayed in Kfar Hamaccabi and Kibbutz Metzuba. She was one of the founders of Kibbutz Tze'elim. Nowadays she is a member of Kfar Hahoresh.

Wetzler Michael 'Misho'

Born in Vágújhely (Nové Mesto nad Váhom) on 31.12.1913
Died in February 1970
Member of "Maccabi Hatzair"

In 1942 Misho was smuggled into Budapest as a refugee. After the Germans invaded Hungary in 1944, he was active in the return-tiyul. Later he worked with the team of forgers of documents on Rózsa Street

and was in charge of their distribution.
Misho made aliya in 1949.

Wetzler Shlomo
Wetzler András
Born in Léva (Levice) in 1921
Died in 1996
Member of "Maccabi Hatzair"

Shlomo learned to be a tailor. In 1938 he was engaged in organizational activities for the movement in Hungary. In 1939 he went to a hahshara. He was one of the main activists of his movement.
In 1942 Shlomo was enlisted in a forced labor unit and served there for 21 months. He was an underground activist. He distributed documents, transferred refugees and money to the border area in order to finance the B'riha operation. He left Hungary at the end of June 1944 on the train of the Relief and Rescue Committee.
Shlomo made aliya in September 1945. He was one of the founders of Kibbutz Tze'elim. He was a member of Kibbutz Kfar Hahoresh where he died.

Wiesel Haim
Wiesel Bernát
Born in Salgótarján on 16.12.1924
Member of "Bnei Akiva"

Haim studied at yehsivot in Galanta (Újpest) and learned the job of grave builder in Győr. He moved to Budapest and in 1942 he joined the movement. On the day the Germans invaded Hungary on 19.3.1944, Haim was staying in a hostel in MIKÉFE - Magyar Izraelita Kézműves és Földművelő Egyesület (Hungarian Jewish Artisan and Agricultural Association). In May 1944 he was enlisted in a forced labor unit. In autumn, equipped with forged Aryan documents, he arrived in Budapest. The movement gave him rescue missions. Haim operated under a fictitious name, Balogh Sándor, worked in an electronics workshop and received a certificate as an indispensable worker for the war effort. Haim travelled to forced labor camps and gave documents to comrades from the movement so they could escape. He also engaged in the transport of food to the children's houses. In December 1944 Haim arrived at the

"Glass House" and moved to the next-door building, which beforehand was used as the Football Association club, and was a member of the armed defense unit. After the liberation he arrived in Temesvár where, with his friends, he set up a hahshara for members of his movement. Six months later he returned to Budapest and continued with his activities, especially taking care of children and their aliya. In June 1948 Haim made aliya and, right off the ship, he was drafted to the Hagana. He did military training and took part in the conquest of Lod and Beer-Sheva. He was a member of Moshav Nir Etzion and later settled down in Petah-Tikva.

Yaar Shoshanna
Elefánt Zsuzsa
Born in Lazony (Ložin) on 5.1.1924
Member of "Hashomer Hatzair"

In 1944 Shoshanna moved to Hungary and joined the underground activities of the movement under the name of Ilona Jávor. She maintained contact with the members of the underground and transferred forged documents and papers to those in need. In the summer of 1944 Shoshanna worked as a German governess for the attaché of the Bulgarian embassy in Hungary. After the war she made aliya and lived in Yavniel. Shoshanna is Moshe Alpan's sister.

Yahin David
Kemény István
Born in Békéscsaba in 1919
Died in 1961
Member of "Hashomer Hatzair"

At the age of twelve David moved to Budapest with his family. In spite of the restrictions on the number of Jewish students, he was admitted to the department of electricity at university. In 1939 David joined the "Hashomer Hatzair" movement. In 1941 he had to abandon his studies, enlist in a forced labor unit and was sent to Ukraine. He managed to return to Budapest and at once joined the underground activities of his movement. After the Germans entered Hungary on 19.3.1944, David was again enlisted in a forced labor unit, but this time he was taken to the copper mines in Bor, Yugoslavia. He was rescued by Tito's partisans.

Prior to his second draft he had managed to complete his studies and received a diploma as an electrical engineer. David was a member of the movement's leadership.

He made aliya and joined Kibbutz Ein Dor. He left the kibbutz and settled down in Rishon Letzion. David was chief engineer in "Elco" factory.

Yahin-Kemény Sarah
Schwartz Sára
Born in Budapest on 27.9.1922
Died in October 2002
Member of "Hashomer Hatzair"

Sarah was a member of the "Sela" Organization. In 1944 she married David Yahin. Sarah gave a lot of assistance to the refugees who arrived to the Hungarian capital from Slovakia. After the Germans entered Hungary on 19.3.1944, she obtained authentic documents from the offices of the Population Registry in Budapest in order to deliver them, after some required changes, to those in need. Sarah worked as a clerk in the "Glass House" with Alexander Grossmann. Together with him she moved to Wekerle Sándor Street, another branch of the Swiss consulate. After the liberation Sarah made aliya with her husband and they joined Kibbutz Ein Dor. She left the kibbutz and lived in Rishon Letzion.

Dr. Yakobi Menahem
Jakubovics Emil
Born in Csap (Csop) on 30.11.1923
Member of "Bnei Akiva"

Menahem studied at the Jewish high school in Ungvár (Uzshorod). In 1944 he was one of the organizers of the "Bnei Akiva" underground. In May 1944 Menahem moved to Romania where he met and took care of the Jews smuggled from Hungary by way of the tiyul. In 1945 he returned to Hungary and was a member of the movement leadership. Between 1947 and 1949 he worked at the center of the movement in Paris. Later, he was in charge of Jewish education in Los Angeles until his retirement. Menahem lives in Los Angeles.

Dr. Yeshurun Eliyahu
Szabó Ödön
Born in Budapest on 7.10.1914
Died in 2003
Member of "Hanoar Hatzioni"

In 1938 Eliyahu did a doctorate in eastern languages and pre-history and was a certified neologue rabbi. He was active in the Jewish students' union, chairman of the "Maccabea" and member of the executive committee of the Hungarian Zionist Association. From January to April 1944 Eliyahu served in a forced labor unit. He escaped and joined the underground activities of "Hanoar Hatzioni". Eliyahu warned Jews of what lay in store for them. He transferred weapons, equipment and food to the bunker on Zöldmáli Street in Buda. After the bunker was discovered, he found refuge in the camp on Aréna Street where the candidates for leaving Hungary on the Relief and Rescue Committee train were concentrated. Eliyahu made aliya. He lived in Natanya.

Yitzhaki Yitzhak
Izsák István
Born in Debrecen on 21.6.1926
Died in 1982
Member of "Hanoar Hatzioni"

In 1943 Yitzhak was enlisted in a forced labor unit, escaped, arrived in Budapest and lived under a false name as a refugee from Carpatho-Ruthenia. After the Germans entered Hungary on 19.3.1944, he joined the underground activities of his movement. He delivered food and forged documents to the Jews living in Protected Houses. Yitzhak was caught a few times by Arrow Cross men but always managed to escape. During the German occupation he operated wearing the uniform of an officer of the Hungarian army. As member of the "Kiska" unit, Itzhak was in charge of the security of the movement's underground activities. In 1946 he made aliya. He died during a visit to Budapest.

Zarhi Judith
Schaeffer Judit
Born in Budapest in 1924
Member of "Maccabi Hatzair"

Judith lived in Budapest and distributed forged documents. She was active in the "Glass House" on Vadász Street. After the liberation she took care of children who had survived the Holocaust. She accompanied them to Marseille on their way to Eretz Israel (Palestine). Judith made aliya. She is a member of Kfar Hahoresh. She held positions in the education system of her kibbutz and at the Oranim Seminary.

Zimmerman Dan
Zimmerman György
Born in Cinkota on 17.4.1919
Member of "Hashomer Hatzair"

Shortly after he was born, Dan's family moved to Slovakia. He studied at German and Slovak schools. In 1939 he joined the "Hashomer Hatzair" movement. In 1942, with his wife Hanna, he moved to Hungary. He dealt with the forgery of documents. In June 1944 he moved to Romania, stayed for about two months in Arad in order to organize the reception of the tiyul fugitives from the other side of the border.
Dan made aliya in August 1944 and joined Kibbutz Ha'ogen. In 1949, while serving in the IDF, he became blind after an explosion that occurred during an experiment with explosives. Being blind, Dan studied chemistry in the USA. He was the manager of the laboratory in "Ha'ogenplast", a rubber factory in his kibbutz and served as the manager of the rubber institute of the Technion.
Dan resides in Ra'anana.

Zohar Kálmán
Sonnenschein Kálmán
Born in Budapest in 1926
Died in 1973
Member of "Hanoar Hatzioni"

Kálmán joined the movement at the age of fourteen. As an underground activist he obtained Aryan documents and distributed them. He was enlisted in a forced labor unit where he served until the liberation. After the liberation Kálmán was among the first to volunteer for work in the B'riha and helped many people who wanted to make aliya via Western Europe. He made aliya, enlisted in the IDF and reached the rank of lieutenant colonel. He was killed in a car accident.

Zsoldos Rahel

Zsoldos Fischer- Körner Rahel
Born in Nagyszombat (Trnava) on 21.6.1915
Died on 14.7.1999 in Toronto, Canada
Member of "Hashomer Hatzair"

After the Germans occupied Hungary, Rahel arrived in Budapest with her husband, Peter Fischel, and joined the Zionist Youth underground activities as a worker for the International Red Cross. As of September 1944 she dealt with the rescue of Jewish children, taking them out of the ghetto to safe places such as the children's house on Budafoki Street.

Zuckerman Aharon

Zuckerman Aron
Born in Budapest in 1926
Member of "Hashomer Hatzair"

In 1944 Aharon was enlisted in a forced labor unit. He escaped twice when the unit was about to march across the German border. He decided to follow the Jews who were forced to go on the Death March. Aharon received documents of the International Red Cross from Bumi and Klára Elfer (Karni), members of "Hashomer Hatzair", who operated in the "Glass House". On 15.11.1944 he set off on foot and on random lifts towards the border. He was arrested many times by the Hungarian gendarmes as well as German and Hungarian soldiers but managed to get free and to continue his journey. He obtained information about the necessary documents for the rescue of the Jews. He decided to return to Budapest in order to give this information to his comrades. He was identified by Hungarian soldiers as a Jew but he managed to escape and arrive in Budapest. As he got off the train he was arrested but again succeeded in getting free. He arrived in the "Glass House" and gave the information to Alexander Grossman who used it for further rescue operations.
Aharon made aliya. He resides in Jerusalem.

EPILOGUE

This book is dedicated to the memory of Tzvi Goldfarb, friend and leader, who passed away in 1977, about four years after his son, Uri, fell in battle in the Yom Kippur War.

Tzvi knew the horrors of the Holocaust in his fatherland, Poland. In 1942 he was sent by his movement, "Dror", to Hungary in order to warn the Jews of what lay in store for them from the Nazis and to prepare them for resistance and rescue. Tzvi stayed for almost one year in Slovakia and only then did he manage to reach Budapest. In the Hungarian capital he operated under a false name and immediately carried out his mission. He initiated the establishment of bunkers, was an active partner in the planning of the tiyul, the release of comrades from forced labor camps and many other activities. I had the chance to know Tzvi, to respect him, to work with him and under his instructions. Tzvi was a close friend and an exceptional person. On one of the missions, Tzvi, Neshka, his girlfriend (and future wife) and myself were caught by the fascists. We suffered brutal torture and were going to be executed. We were freed by a daring operation of the Zionist Youth underground. After the war too we worked together and were members of Kibbutz Parod. Neshka, who passed away in the year 2000, was his loyal partner.

The book of biographies of the underground activists is a memorial monument to Tzvi Goldfarb who was a courageous, determined and wise Jew with friends in the underground many of whom have passed away.

Ze'ev Eisikovics

GLOSSARY

Aliya Bet: A term denoting illegal emigration movement to Eretz Israel (Palestine) during the British mandate, which allowed immigration within a certain quota only (see: Certificate)

Aliya: Hebrew for ascent; a term commonly used to denote the emigration of Jews to Palestine (Israel).

Aliyat Hanoar: "Youth Aliya" - a special project of the Zionist movement for organized immigration of Jewish youth to Eretz Israel (Palestine) and Israel, and their education in the spirit of fulfillment of the Zionist idea.

Arrow Cross Party: The Hungarian Nazi Party headed by Ferenc Szálasi, who came to power in Hungary in October 1944.

B'riha: Hebrew for flight, an organized operation to rescue Jewish survivors of the Holocaust from various countries in Europe, on their way to Eretz Israel.

Certificate: A formal document, which permits the entry of Jews into Eretz Israel (Palestine) during the British mandate, issued by the British administration in Palestine.

Department A: A section within the International Red Cross in Hungary active in rescue and protection of Jewish children in Budapest.

Eretz Israel: In Hebrew The Land of Israel, synonymous to Palestine prior to the establishment of the State of Israel.

Forced Labor Service: Legally established companies in Hungary. Mainly Jews served in these companies in lieu of compulsory military service.

Glass House: A house on Vadász Street 29 in Budapest, owing its name to the unusual combination of its glass windows, roof and door. Artur Weiss, the owner, put the house at the disposal of the Swiss consulate. In October 1944 it became a shelter for Jews protected by the Swiss consulate in Budapest.

Hagana: The Jewish underground army from which the Israeli army was evolved after the establishment of the State of Israel.

Hahshara: Hebrew for training & preparation: The process of and the framework for training members and groups of Zionist youth movements for self-fulfillment in Eretz Israel / the State of Israel.

Hashlama: A term used for groups whose members join existing kibbutzim.

Heder: A traditional Jewish school, part of the Jewish Community, teaching 3 to 13 year old children Hebrew, prayers, Torah and other Jewish teachings.

Histadrut: Hebrew acronym for the General Federation of Labor in Eretz Israel / the State of Israel.

IDF: Israel Defence Forces - the Israeli Army.

Ihud: The name by which Mapai, the centrist labor party of Israel, was known in the Diaspora.

Jewish Agency: Established in 1929 and recognized as the representative organ of the Jews to consult the British government in Eretz Israel on economic, social and other matters.

Jewish Council: A body appointed by the Nazis to administer Jewish affairs under their supervision.

Joint: The American Joint Distribution Committee (AJDC), a Jewish-American philanthropic organization dedicated to helping distressed Jews the world over.

Ken: Hebrew for nest. Both a local entity and meeting place within the Zionist youth movements.

Keren Hayesod - Palestine Construction Fund: A worldwide financial organ, founded in 1921, aimed at the rebuilding of Eretz Israel.

Keren Kayemet LeIsrael - Jewish National Fund (JNF): As of 1901, the major organ of purchasing land for settlement in Eretz Israel.

Kibbutz Artzi: The Hashomer Hatzair kibbutz movement.

Olim (sing.: Oleh): Immigrants and newcomers to Eretz Israel (Palestine) and the State of Israel (Aliya and Olim stem from the same source in the Hebrew language).

Palmah: Acronym for Plugot Mahatz (Striking Force), special military units that functioned within the Hagana as of 1941 until after Israel's War of Independence.

Protected houses: Buildings in Budapest where Jews were protected by neutral foreign countries or the International Red Cross.

Protection documents: Protective passes issued to many Jews in Budapest by legations of neutral countries and by the Nunciature.

Relief and Rescue Committee: Headed by Nathan Komoly, in 1943 the Committee helped Jewish refugees who fled from Austria, Slovakia and Poland into Hungary. In 1944 the Committee concentrated in dealing with the German authorities for the relief and rescue of Jews in Hungary.

Return-tiyul: The smuggling Jews out of Hungary, after the German occupation of the country in March 1944, to Slovakia.

Tiyul: Hebrew for trip, the code name of the Zionist underground which dealt with the smuggling of Jews from Poland and Slovakia into Hungary, and from Hungary to Romania.

Yellow-Star House: One of a series of buildings in Budapest identified by a yellow star in which thousands of Jews were concentrated in 1944.

Yeshiva: A Jewish institution and rabbinical school for studying the teachings of the Torah and the Talmud.

Yishuv: Hebrew for settlement; usually denoting the Jewish community of Eretz Israel (Palestine).

BIBLIOGRAPHY

1. *A Hasomér Hacair a Zsidó Ellenállási Mozgalomban 1942-1944* (Hashomer Hatzair within the Jewish Resistance Movement 1942-1944), Budapest 1948 (Hungarian).

2. Giles Lambert, *Operation Hatzalah*, Translated by Robert Bullen and Rosette , Letellier, The Bobbs-Merril Company, Inc. Indianapolis/New York, 1974. Original French language edition 1972, Librairia Hachette.

3. Rafi Benshalom, *Ne'evaknu Lema'an Hahaim* (We Struggled for Life), Moreshet-Sifriyat Poalim, 1978, 1979, 2001 (Hebrew).

4. Tzvi Goldfarb, *Ad Kav Haketz* (On the Verge of the End), published by Beit Lohamei Hagetaot, 1980 (Hebrew).

5. *Al Tzvi: Parod-Budapest-Warsha* (About Tzvi: Parod-Budapest-Warsaw), Hakibbutz Hameuhad (Hebrew).

6. Sarah Nadivi, *Bagrut Mukdemet* (Early Maturity), Reshafim, 1983 (Hebrew).

7. Asher Cohen, *Hamahteret Hahalutzit BeHungaria* (The Halutz Underground in Hungary), Hakibbutz Hameuhad (Hebrew).

8. Simon Menahem (editor), *Lizkor Vedavar lo lishkoah, 40 Shana Lekibush Hungaria al-yedey HaGermanim* (Remember and Never Forget, 40 Years after the German Occupation of Hungary), memoirs of members of Kibbutz Daliya, 1984 (Hebrew).

9. Shlomo Zamir (editor), *40 Shana Legerush Yehudei Hungaria* (40 Years after the Deportation of Hungarian Jewry) 32 Testimonies of Kibbutz Shomrat Members, Kibbutz Shomrat, 1984 (Hebrew).

10. Joseph Ben-Porat (editor), *Lifnei Bo Hashiheha* (Before Oblivion Prevails), Kibbutz Gaaton Archives, 1985 (Hebrew).

11. Yehudit Rotem, *BeBrit Yahad* (Together in a Covenant), World Zionist Organization, 1985 (Hebrew).

12. Alexander Grossman, *Nur das Gewissen,* Verlag im Waldgut, Schweiz, 1986 (German).

13. Tusia Herzberg, *Hahol Hatzohek* (The Laughing Sand), Ahiassaf, 1986 (Hebrew).

14. Asher Cohen, *The Halutz Resistance in Hungary 1942-1944,* Social Sciences Monographs, Boulder and Institute for Holocaust Studies of the City University of New York, 1986.

15. Arie Haran (editor) *Asher Zaharnu Lesaper* (We Told what We Remembered), twenty four members of Kibbutz Meggido Testify, Moreshet - Sifriyat Poalim, 1988 (Hebrew).

16. Nathan Ben-Haim (editor), *Yad LeBeitar Hungaria 1928-1948* (commemorating Beitar in Hungary, 1928-1948) [no mention of the publisher], Hebrew.

17. Benedek István - Vámos György, *Tépd le a sárga csillagot* (Tear off the Yellow Star), Pallas Lap és Könyvkiadó, Budapest, 1990 (Hungarian).

18. Edei Haim (The Living Testify), *Testimonies of members of Nir Galim*, edited by Moshe Davis, Nir Galim, 1990 (Hebrew).

19. Miriam Akavia, *Hadereh Ha'aheret, Sipura shel Kvutza* (The Other Way, a Story of a Group), Yediot Ahronot, 1992 (Hebrew).

20. Shlomo Schmidt (editor), *Begalui Uvemahteret - Hanoar Hatzioni Hadati Bemercaz Europa miShoah Litkuma* (In the Open and in Underground -Zionist Religious Youth in Central Europe from the Holocaust to Revival), Moreshet, 1992 (Hebrew).

21. Michael Lazar, *Ma'avak Lehaim Vetikva Ligeulah* (Struggle for Life and Hope for Redemption), private publishing, 1992 (Hebrew).

22. Naomi Blank and Haim Genizi, *Mahteret Hatzalah - Bnei Akiva beHungaria Bitkufat Hashoah* (Rescue Underground - Bne Akiva in Hungary during the Holocaust), Bar-Ilan University, 1993 (Hebrew).

23. Lea Gadish (editor), *Ata Hanhel Lebaneha* (Pass your Heritage on to your Children), Testimonies on the Holocaust by members of Kibbutz Parod, 1993 (Hebrew) .

24. Dov Fogel, *Mibeit Avi LeParod* (From my Father's Home to Parod), published by the author, 1993 (Hebrew).

25. Avihu Ronen, *Hakrav al Hahaim* (The Battle for Life), Yad Yaari, 1994 (Hebrew).

26. Moshe Yisrael and Dov Lazar, *Dror, Habonim, Haoved, 1994* (Hebrew).

27. *Yalkut Moreshet - 50 Years After the Destruction of Hungarian Jewry*, No. 57, May 1994 (Hebrew).

28. Until Ildikó Ruth, *A névtelen Smulik* (The nameless Shmulik), Tel Aviv, 1994 (Hungarian).

29. Menahem Tzvi Kadari (editor), *Zeher Mordehai* (Remembrance of Mordehai), in memoriam of Mordehai Rasel, Nir Etzion, 1995 (Hebrew).

30. Eli Netzer, *G'dolim Migoralam* (Above their Fate), Maarechet, Kibbutz Daliya, 1995.

31. Mordechai Ben David, *Parsot Susim* (Horseshoes), Bialik Institute, Jerusalem 1995 (Hebrew).

32. Chava Eichler & Yehuda Talmi, Halom, *Ma'avak, Hatzalah - Toldot Tnuat Hanoar Hatzioni Bishtahim Dovrei Hungarit 1931-1947* (Dreams, Struggles, Rescue by Hanoar Hatzioni in Hungarian Speaking Areas1931 - 1947, Massuah, 1996 (Hebrew).

33. Tusia Herzberg, ***Der lachende Sand***, Alekta Verlag - Klagenfurt 1996 (german-translated from Hebrew, see No.13).

34. Robert Offner, ***Véletlenül életben maradtam***, Budapest 1944 (I survived by Chance, Budapest 1944), published in Israel by the author, 1996 (Hungarian) and 1997 by the author and "Maarechet" Kibbutz Daliya (Hebrew).

35. Baruch Tsachor, ***Lo Haiti Gibor*** (I wasn't a Hero), Maarechet Kibbutz Daliya, 1997 (Hebrew).

36. Menahem, Daniv (editor), ***Halohamim Habonim, Habonim beTransylvania uveHungaria, Dror Habonim in Romania 1932-1949*** (Dreamers and Builders "Habonim" in Transylvania and Hungary, "Dror-Habonim" in Romania 1932-1949, Beit Hatzanhan Kibbutz Ma'agan, 1998.

37. Avihu Ronen, ***Harc az életért***, Belvárosi Kiadó Budapest, 1998 (Hungarian, translated from Hebrew (See No. 25).

38. Eli Netzer, ***Nagyobbak a sorsuknál***, Belvárosi Kiadó Budapest, 1998 (Hungarian, translated from Hebrew (See No. 30).

39. Moshe Israel, ***Mevasrim, Magshimim, Lohamim uMatzilim, Dror Habonim, Hahalutz Hatzair, Haoved: Tnuot Halutziot shel Hakibbutz Hameuhad beHungaria*** (The Hakibbutz Hameuhad Youth Movements in Hungary), Volume I-II, Maarechet Kibbutz Dalia, 1999 (Hebrew).

40. Alexander Barzel, ***Halomot Uma'avakim, Toldot Tnuat Gordonia-Maccabi Hatzair beHungaria 1938-1950*** (Dreams and Struggles, The history of Gordonia-Maccabi Hatzair in Hungary 1938-1950), Maarechet Kibbutz Dalia, 2000 (Hebrew).

41. Győri György, ***Megmeneküléseim, Hosszú levél unokáimnak*** (My Escapes, a Long Letter to my Grandchildren), C.E.T. Belvárosi, 2001 (Hungarian).

42. Peretz Révész, ***Mul Nahsholei Haroa*** (Against the Surge of Evil), Maarechet Kibbutz Dalia, 2001 (Hebrew).

43. Rafi Benshalom, ***We struggled for Life***, Gefen Publishing House, Jerusalem 2001 (translated from Hebrew, see No. 3).

44. Moshe Alpan, ***Be'ein Hasa'ara*** (Weathering the Storm), Moreshet, The Society for Research of the History of the Zionist Youth Movement in Hungary, 2001 (Hebrew).

45. Yehudit Rotem, ***Ish Asher Ruah Bo, Tzvi Goldfarb - Hayav*** (A Man in whom is the Spirit, Tzvi Goldfarb - His Life), The Society for Research of the History of the Zionist Youth Movement in Hungary, 2002 (Hebrew).

46. Asher Arányi, ***Ayin Ahat Boha - Ayin Ahat Tzoheket*** (One Eye Cries While The Other Laughs), The Society for Research of the History of the Zionist Youth Movement in Hungary, 2002 (Hebrew).

47. Asher Cohen, *A haluc ellenállás Magyarországon 1942-1944*, Balassi Kiadó, 2002 (Hungarian, translated from Hebrew, see No. 7).

48. Rafi Benshalom, *Mert élni akartunk, Holocaust Dokumentációs Központ és Emlékgyüjtmény Közalapitvány*, Budapest, 2003 (Hungarian, translated from Hebrew, see No. 3).

49. Alexander Grossmann, *Első a lelkiismeret* (Conscience above All), C.E.T. Belvárosi Könyvkiadó, Budapest 2003 (Hungarian, translated from German, see No. 12).

50. *Be'ein Hasa'ara - Hamahteret shel Tnuot Hanoar Hatzioniot beHungaria be'et Hakibush Hagermani, 1944* (In the Storm Center - The Underground Zionist Youth Movement in Hungary during the German Occupation, 1944), Study Program by Massuah & Yad Vashem, 2004 (Hebrew).

51. *Yalkut Moreshet - 60 Shana leShoat Yehudei Hungaria* (60 Years After the Destruction of Hungarian Jewry), No. 77, Moreshet, April 2004 (Hebrew).

52. Asher Arányi, *One Eye Cries While The Other Laughs*, Maarechet Kibbutz Dalia, 2004 (translated from Hebrew, see No. 46).

53. A vihar közepén. A cionista ifjúsági mozgalmak földalatti ellenállása Magyarországon a német megszállás alatt. Oktatási program. 2004 Budapest, A magyarországi Hasomér Hacair kiadása. 60 oldal. (In the Storm Center, The Underground Zionist Youth Movement in Hungary During the German Occupation 1944. Study program. Edited by the Hashomer Hatzair in Hungary, Budapest, 2004. 60 pages.) (Hungarian. Translated from Hebrew, see No. 50.)

54. Mose Alpan: *A viharban*. Budapest. Makkabea Kiado, 2004. See: No. 44, Moshe Alpan: *Weathering the Storm*. Hungarian, Translated from Hebrew. p. 20.

INDEX OF NAMES